WALTER JOHANNES STEIN

W.J. Stein in about 1950.

W.J. STEIN
A Biography

Johannes Tautz

TEMPLE LODGE

Translated by John M. and Marguerite A. Wood

Temple Lodge Publishing Ltd.
Hillside House, The Square
Forest Row, RH18 5ES

www.templelodge.com

First published in English by Temple Lodge Publishing, 1990
Reprinted 2015

Originally published in German under the title *W.J. Stein, Eine Biographie*
by Verlag am Goetheanum, Dornach, 1989

A CIP catalogue record for this book is available from the British Library

ISBN 978 1 906999 76 6

Cover by Morgan Creative
Typeset by DP Photosetting, Neath, West Glamorgan
Printed by 4Edge Ltd., Essex

O, do not lose the drama of knowledge
in striving after the grammar of knowledge,
nor fear falling into the abyss of individuality;
for we shall climb out of this abyss
in the company of many other spirits
and will experience our kinship with them;
by that we shall be born out of the spirit,
shall have raised up death;
we shall become destroyers of created things,
shall personify these in the spirit
and participate in their destruction.[1]

Rudolf Steiner

[   ] = interpolations by author or translator

Contents

List of Illustrations

Picture 5: privately owned
Picture 6: Photo by Rietmann, Goetheanum Press

Picture 13: Rudolf Steiner Nachlass Co
Picture 15: Photo by Rietmann, Goetheanum Press
Picture 17: Goetheanum Press
Pictures 22 and 24: from the Author's archive
All other pictures from the estate of W.J. Stein in the possession of
Thomas Meyer

Acknowledgements

The author thanks Mr Thomas Meyer, the owner of the copyright of W.J. Stein's estate, for making unpublished letters and documents available to him; also for years of participation and help in advising him and assessing the present biography.

The author thanks Mr Emanuel Zeylmans for letting him see the correspondence between Ita Wegman and W.J. Stein and allowing him to quote therefrom.

The author is indebted to Mr Walter Streffer for his readiness to hand over material from the estate of W.J. Stein.

Further rights still pertaining to Rudolf Steiner rest with the Rudolf Steiner Nachlass Administration in Dornach.

The duplication of letters by and to Rudolf Steiner are published by permission of the Rudolf Steiner Nachlassverwaltung (trustees of Rudolf Steiner's estate), Dornach.

I
SETTING FORTH INTO LIFE

1
Prologue

Walter Johannes Stein is one of the pioneers of Anthroposophy. His life, which was full of inner change, presents us with many difficult riddles. The first sketchy portrait is given us by Herbert Hahn,[2] who calls Stein 'one of the most notable pupils of Rudolf Steiner' and draws our attention to the tragic background of the events and developments within the Anthroposophical Society with which his life was bound up.

The present biography is an attempt to amplify what was given to us in Hahn's sketch. The present author was already personally acquainted with Stein when he was a young teacher in the first Waldorf School in Stuttgart. He considered it necessary to get to know the person who was the first one to be appointed by Rudolf Steiner to teach the same lessons as he in that school. The first meeting with Stein came about in London in August 1951. Our conversation lasted three and a half days. Throughout that time notes were being taken; a whole sheaf of crammed pages still exists in Stein's and my own handwriting. Stein, who used to give about three hundred lectures a year in England, had reserved a few days for the interview and was willing to answer my questions. It was as if the flood gates had been opened and a large head of water had been released. Our conversation still rings in my memory as though issuing from the sphere of timelessness. Stein appeared like a hermit in the world metropolis to the visitor who imagined himself the recipient of the instructions of a Trevrizent.

Further meetings for discussion took place. They awakened in me a desire to follow in the footsteps of the person who had such a clearly stamped individuality. Hidden activity streamed out from it, which did not cease with Stein's death in 1957, but spread out to ever widening circles of people. It animated people and stimulated them to give of themselves. During the sixties a new edition of Stein's main work, *Weltgeschichte im Lichte des Heiligen Gral*[3] appeared. Erich Gabert was able to make use of Stein's diaries and incorporate extracts from them in his new edition of the 'Conferences'[4] which Rudolf Steiner held with the teachers of the Stuttgart Waldorf School. And then a collection of Stein's writings on historical and pedagogical subjects was brought out.[5] Under the title *Der Tod Merlins* Thomas Meyer edited a collection of Stein's studies on spiritual historic subjects and with his *Documentation of an orientative collaboration* between Stein and Rudolf Steiner he produced a commentated edition of Stein's dissertation.[6]

The invitation given by Stein's daughter, Clarissa Johanna Muller, to set in order the belongings of her father gave the final incentive to attempting a presentation of Stein's life and the dramatic course of his search for knowledge. But years passed by before the work could be brought to a conclusion and then only with the pressing demands of persistent reminders.

2

'Grown up in Anthroposophy as by Matter of Course'

A public anthroposophical-scientific lecture course took place in the Hague from 7-12 April 1922. Rudolf Steiner gave a course of lectures introducing the subject of spiritual-scientific research and a number of speakers, mainly teachers from the Free Waldorf School in Stuttgart, showed the results of their work. In his report in the weekly periodical *Das Goetheanum* Rudolf Steiner characterised the qualities of the participants in outline so that Albert Steffen, the minute keeper, could speak of a 'portrait gallery.' Included is the portrait of Stein, who was the first to be mentioned. Rudolf Steiner said:

The first lecture (of the Anthroposophical Science Course at the Hague from 7-12 April 1922)—after the opening words of greeting given by G. Schubert-Knobel, for the heartiness of which we are all grateful—was by W.J. Stein on 'The Importance of Goethe for the Whole of Evolution.' Through an inner talent for the anthroposophical way of thinking and researching Dr Stein has grown up in this as by matter of course. He is a clear thinker and lectures on Anthroposophy in a courageous manner as though it were the revelation of his own innermost being. His comprehensive survey of the results of anthroposophical work presented today enables him to produce proofs, confirmation and explanations from divers angles for whatever subject it is with which he is dealilng. And so his lecture has something about it which, I think, must be stimulating to many of the serious members of his audience. It must give them the conviction that Anthroposophy is something which is founded on a conscientiously acquired knowledge and way of life.

Dr Stein then sat beside me before delivering his next lecture entitled 'The Connection of the Theory of Knowledge to Organic Science.' He felt the need of discussing certain things with me before giving this lecture. I said to him: 'You have grown up in Anthroposophy as by matter of course; as a result of this and just because you know so much and are so mobile in your thinking, you will encounter great personal difficulties with regard to the tasks with which you will be confronted in your search for knowledge. You may succeed in adding to that fulness the most beautiful gift of all; you may be able to give to your audience the whole of yourself.'[7]

. This 'portrait' points to 'the great personal difficulties' of the tasks confronting Stein in his search for knowledge. The search for the 'whole of the self' meant for Stein: the treading of the path of self knowledge. The word of the Delphic Oracle: 'know thyself' became for him a threefold summons: to develop his soul powers, to unfold them in the service of others and to contribute towards the building up of the Anthroposophical Society and movement.

As a seeker of egohood Stein persisted in describing the course of his life as the karmic path to Rudolf Steiner. Immediately after the death of his spiritual leader Stein wrote the essay: 'How I found my guide, Rudolf Steiner.'[8] The description, like a confession, was the first of a series of essays in which colleagues and pupils contributed out of their personal experience to the answering of the question: Who was the man Rudolf Steiner, who created the monumental work of Anthroposophy? And how was he experienced by those who knew him well? Stein already gives his answer in the title. The meaning of his life was to discover in Rudolf Steiner the guide to the spiritual in man and the cosmos. In his discipleship to him he was searching for the path to becoming truly man. He was able to say: 'I owe him everything. Health of wife and child. My calling. My inner strength. The meaning of my life. This life itself. In return for such gifts can the stammering thanks be anything else but love? Love beyond death, love which is so close and intimate that words fail when its nearness is felt?'

His meeting with Anthroposophy and its creator entitled him, so he felt, to write the story of his life; for he wished to bear witness to the spiritual leadership which he had experienced. But only on a single occasion did he succeed in providing a connected account when, at the age of forty-five, he wrote an autobiographical sketch for the readers of his periodical *The Present Age* under the title: 'Reminiscences of Life as an aid to the Understanding of our Time.'[9] All further attempts remained fragmentary.

3
Childhood in Vienna

Vienna, a very European town, metropolis and imperial residential seat of a multi-racial State—this Vienna of yesterday was the home town of Walter Johannes Stein. It was here that his life began on 6 February 1891. The census of that year registered nearly 1.4 million inhabitants. The great boom in Vienna started in the sixties when the inner fortifications of the town were demolished and the pompous state buildings of the Ringstrasse were erected in their place. At the turn of the century the accomplishments of the 'Viennese Moderns'[9a] were produced in poetry and the formative arts, in music and opera, in drama and the arts and crafts. The 'Young Vienna' in the beginnings of which Rudolf Steiner had participated, not only comprises the names of Hofmannsthal and Altenberg, Bahr, Kraus or Schnitzler, but also includes Hugo Wolf and Gustav Mahler and Schoenberg's transition from tonality to atonality. During the same period there arose in this milieu the Zionism of Herzl, the psychoanalysis of Freud and the Viennese Medical School which had such important results for the twentieth century. Vienna at the turn of the century seems like a multiplicity of tensely opposing forces.

'Every Viennese person,' notes Stefan Zweig,[10] 'had a Hungarian, a Pole, a Czech or a Jew for a grandfather or brother-in-law.' In Stein's ancestry, too, various elements come together. The father, Wilhelm Stein, was a Hungarian by birth. He came to Vienna when he was 18 years old and, after studying law, settled down there as a 'qualified lawyer in the imperial and civil courts and as a certified interpreter.' He was widely educated and knowledgeable in foreign affairs, spoke several languages fluently, occupied himself with the theory of languages and studied medical scientific journals. It was in his library that the son found a copy of Lazarus Geiger's book *Human Language and Reason* which led him to the first question he asked Rudolf Steiner. The painstaking education and coaching from a private music teacher and regular educational trips are attributable to the father's influence.

Quite different was the influence of the mother. Hermine Weiss was descended from a large Jewish family. She was Austrian by birth and, as her son recollected, she had in her way of speaking 'a light and pleasant Viennese intonation', whereas the father spoke a correct and educated literary German. The boy listened to Grimm's Fairy Stories and to the Greek and Germanic Sagas of the Gods and Heroes in the Austrian dialect. Hermine Stein made contact with Anthroposophy at the time when Rudolf Steiner was still laying the foundations of modern spiritual science within the framework of the Theosophical Society. In the small circles, the 'Lodges' of that time, the new members, Hermine included, were presented to Rudolf Steiner. It was his mother with her spirit-orientated soul who brought her son onto the pathway leading to Anthrosophy.

Walter Johannes grew up with his brother Friedrich, who was five years older than he. The two brothers were radically different: the older one took after his father and was to have taken over the chancellery; the younger one was so like his mother that Rudolf Steiner recognised him immediately on their first encounter. Whereas the younger one spent a lifetime searching for new forms in which to clothe the knowledge he acquired, the older one attained a level of maturity early in life. He was an eloquent lawyer and advocate for the defence, a witty conversationalist, correct in all aspects of life. He entered the war as an artillery officer. Surrounded by the Russians in the fortress of Przemysl, he sought death by blowing himself up with his guns on the day of surrender rather than become a prisoner in the hands of the enemy. Before doing this he had dispatched his diary to his relatives ending it with the words: 'Thus ends the war for me—the war which others feared and I have loved.' Rudolf Steiner composed the following epitaph for him:

> During his life his thoughts
> Were turned towards the spirit
> So may he find in death
> The life of spirit

> With him are
> The Thoughts of his loved ones.

Rudolf Steiner was able to follow him in his after-death experiences and saw—according to the report of Walter Johannes Stein[9]—how the dead person became aware of the effects of his past life and immersed himself in the thought substance of the book he had last studied: *A Theory of Knowledge Based on Goethe's World Conception.*[11]

In his life together with his father, mother and brother the boy encountered what in later years he would think of as a basic trinitarian experience. Three events stand out in his memory with archetypal importance. Stein recounts how, as a small child, he accompanied his father through a Viennese park. 'It was towards the end of a long and hot summer's day and a cool evening breeze suddenly wafted over our heads. My father came to a standstill and took a deep breath and I imitated him. He lifted his finger as if to warn me and, although he never said a word, a whole lesson lay in his gesture. This is not the first memory I have of my father, but it is the one I most often remember when I think of him. Veneration towards the divine in all living things and in the whole of nature: that was what I inherited from him.' The earliest recollection he had of his mother was connected with a trip in the vicinity of Vienna. She was waiting at the station with her tired child for the arrival of the train which was to take her home. 'It was dark and I had gone to sleep in mother's arms. The train roared into the station and we had to get in. My head lay on mother's breast, so that she was forced to waken me. She did this so gently and tenderly that her loving concern made a much greater impression on me than the fact that I was woken up. It was the picture of the "love-filled woman who woke me" which presented itself to the soul of the little child as "mother" and this has remained with me throughout life as an enduring memory.' From his brother he received his first incentive towards self-education. A childish squabble in which he bit the much stronger one's arm led him to take over responsibility for his actions for the first time. This deed of his gave him such a shock that he vowed then and there 'never to be so heartless towards him again whatever might happen. I believe that was the first promise I ever gave myself and I may say that I kept it faithfully until the time of his death during the war.'[9]

1   His mother Hermine Stein around 1905

The first glimmer of inner certainty that 'I am an I,' of which Jean Paul says that it takes place 'in the veiled Holy of Holies within man' was given by Stein with exact notification of date: '9 October 1893—ego experience—two years, six months, three days.'[12] The details had impressed themselves deeply on his mind.

> In my earliest memory-picture I see myself standing in the middle of a road on a wooded height, a little insecure on my little feet, faced with the task of crossing the road alone and unaided. The women who is looking after me has hidden herself behind the trunk of a tree, and I know for certain that she is there and that she is not my mother. The lady is obviously making an experiment to see how independent the little man has become ... Simple as the incident is, it is of great importance in the totality of my life, for at this moment I first became aware of the fact that I was an *I*. The feeling of having to direct my little body alone and unaided across the road gave me this experience in consciousness. I can remember distinctly how different my experience of space was from that of a grown-up person ... I had the distinct experience of being spread out over the whole surrounding scene. My self included the whole width of the road and, too, the neighbouring trees, including the one behind which my governess was hiding. I still remember the inner feeling of delight it gave me to know that she imagined she was hidden from me, while actually my self was spread out over the space in which she was. She and the tree were within my experience of self, and though the little body down there felt something like fear at being left alone, the true self rejoiced in this fear and in the feeling, 'I am an I,' which went with it. Thenceforward, the dual nature of the Ego-experience stood before my soul... From this time onward, then, I knew that every human being is there twice, once in the sphere he senses all around him, the sphere which he embraces with his spatial feeling, and once again within his body. It was many years before I was able philosophically to understand this dual nature of the lower and the higher self in man.[9]

The accessibility of the childish experience to the sphere of the higher self is the basis in later life for access to spiritual experiences and the views of spiritual science. Herein lie the preconditions for Stein's cognitive-scientific work. He clearly recollects the threshold experience which lies between the world of the senses and the cosmic world of the spirit.

As a child, when I lay between waking and sleeping and remained

2 **W.J. Stein 1894**

conscious while all my inner life was already in the attitude of sleep, I could see myself go out of myself; I felt it enveloping me as if it were a second and much smaller starry firmament . . . Such experiences of my childhood afterwards made it possible for me to penetrate into the ideas of ancient times about the soul. I could understand, for example, in the light of such experiences, the passage in which Plutarch says, 'In addition to the part of the soul which is submerged in the earthly body, the human being has another and purer part, hovering outside him like a star above his head. This is rightly called his Daimon or Genius; it is the Genius which guides him and which he willingly follows through his life!' This star that illumines our path is ever carried and protected by the Angel-being who guards us throughout life. It is a phenomenon known to every occultist. . . The star is the focus of activity towards which the forces of the surrounding sphere are tending, and whence we constantly enspirit our corporeal nature.[9]

Walter Johannes Stein had understanding teachers. They let the child experience in the picture-language of fairy-tale plays, what later became transformed into moral endurance in the trials of life. In his 'Recollections' he depicts the scene in which he once had to play the part of a sleeping youngster threatened by a dangerous dragon. The nursery was spread out with green coloured paper to indicate grass. The dragon, meticulously cut out of cardboard and garishly painted, drew close to the sleeper, but behind him appeared the Guardian Angel with a crown of stars. At that time the boy was about seven years old.

He spent the winter of 1900-1901 with his mother in the Riviera. He was to be cured of a persistent cold in the warm climate of Ospidaletti near San Remo. The stay lasted several months. The southern plant-world, the play of colours of sunrise and sunset, the lapping of the waves on the shore and across the sea, the mountains of Corsica rising up out of the distance, all this was the backdrop for a memorable encounter: the person who became his inspiring soul-guide appeared. The childlike love towards a German-American girl about six years older than he filled the soul of the tenderly adoring boy. While he was accompanying her on her walks a presentiment of the reality of the other person's soul and the gesture-language of natural phenomena started to dawn within him.

'Unimportant as the encounter may appear, it led in my case to that experience of "awakening" by which man learns to know

 W.J. Stein, A Biography

3   W J. Stein 1904

himself as a living soul and nature as a being filled with spirit. Whoever is able to read in the original Italian the wonderful words of Brunetto Latini, the teacher of Dante, describing his meeting with the Goddess Natura, will have a slight inkling of that air of magic which wafted through my childlike soul at that time.'[9]

The soul's opening to the spirit announced itself. At about the ninth year, which is a nodal point in man's development, a change in his life of feeling comes about. The child is released from its world of dreams and enters into a new reality. Whoever takes note of life's inner guidelines becomes aware of the effects this step has on development. Out of the intimations of the nine-year-old follows the longing which guides the adult along the pathway to spiritual knowledge. For Stein it was a certainty born out of experience. 'It is not the science which teaches us about nature, but the perfecting of our own capacity for love which allows us, little by little, to penetrate beyond the veils which hide it from our view. It was Rudolf Steiner who encouraged me to work out such thoughts in more detail and eventually to form them into a theory of spiritual knowledge in order to show that it is not the intellect, but love which is able to penetrate into the cosmic secrets.'[9]

4
At the Schottengymnasium

The fact that Walter Johannes Stein went to school in the 'Schottengymnasium' after four years of Primary School was something unusual. His parents belonged to the Protestant minority in Austria and the sons were given religious instruction by the evangelical pastor. The 'Kaiserlich-Koeniglichen Gymnasium zu den Schotten' [Imperial and Royal Grammar School of Scottish Foundation] was, however, a school where exclusively Benedictine monks taught. The reason for the choice of this school was undoubtedly the tradition it had acquired for the high standard of its teaching and humanistic approach. The name 'Schotten' Gymnasium comes from the Iro-Scottish monks who founded monasteries, mainly in South Germany from the seventh century onwards. The school in Vienna was founded by the monks of the Regensburg foundation.

For 10 years—from 1901 until matriculation in the summer of 1911—Stein encountered the monks in their black habits every schoolday. They were excellent teachers. Their pupil realised that when he was taught by them about Luther and the Reformation. In the religion lessons the Protestant pastor had stressed the part played by the reigning princes, the localising forces, whereas the history teacher emphasised the influence and importance of the Universal Church of Rome. 'The teaching of history in the Schottengymnasium was on broad lines and very stimulating. In spite of their individual differences the men who gave the history lessons had this in common: they tried to give not only a sound description of historical facts, but a sufficiency of detail for truly living pictures to emerge. Emperors, scholars, popes or reformers—we were enabled to see the characters of history as men of flesh and blood before us; we learned to know the way they lived and moved, their spiritual heritage, their characters as individuals.'[9]

When Walter Johannes Stein later had to teach history himself he used the same methods; yes, he even improved upon them. He not only developed a wide ranging panorama of ideas, he also made the persons described come alive by imitating their walk and their manner of speech, such, for instance, as the ornate manners of an absolute monarch receiving his devoted courtiers, or the rhetoric of a rebel leader hammering home his speeches to his audience.

The pupil Stein was a 'late developer,' one of those who never reveal their true talents. When he was set the theme 'Germany—the Greece of modern times' in his matriculation examination he revealed to his astonished teachers a hidden knowledge of history, set down on numberless sheets of paper in only five hours.

The traditions of German idealism and the time of Goethe were still alive in the Schottengymnasium. The classicism of Weimar was looked upon as the Periclean Age of the Germans amidst this cultural oasis, as the pinnacle of achievement which had brought poets and thinkers together in this modern Olympus. This historic certainty of the Hellenism of the Germans had become a conviction in the mind of the Goethe researcher Karl Julius Schröer, whose lectures at the Technical High School in Vienna had filled his pupil Rudolf Steiner with enthusiasm; and the influence of Schröer spread to the lessons in the Schottengymnasium and influenced those who were destined much later to meet Rudolf Steiner.

Already in his youth the circles around Stein began to come into contact with those of Rudolf Steiner. This not only happened through the thought-world of Schröer, but also through the Artistotelian research of the philosopher Vincent Knauer, who had been the librarian at the Schottengymnasium. It was thanks to him that Rudolf Steiner became acquainted with the 'Aristotelian spiritual schooling' which 'demanded training, discipline and exercise of soul.'[13] And from Knauer Stein gained understanding of the two basic definitions of Aristotelian philosophy: Form and Matter, Eidos and Hyle. He was 17 years old when he received this piece of insight. At that time, while in the middle of puberty, he began to have his first doubts about the materialistic explanations of the world. The experimental research of his home tutor concerning the influence of form on the strength of certain materials—e.g. that the bearing capacity of a pane of glass increases with the decrease of its area—served to shake his belief in materialism. It aroused a whole chain of questions regarding the stages of world creation, which he sought to answer on the basis of Aristotle's concept of form and matter. Matter, that indefinite thing which allows itself to be shaped, which is taken hold of by Form, the active ingredient—the whole universe a step by step forming of Matter, an eternal outpouring of life from the inexhaustible foundations of existence to ever more ideal forms: seminal thoughts of a universal world-view rose up in the soul of the 17 year old.

As he arrived at this turning point of development his father died. Just the moment before he had had to fetch a cylinder of oxygen from the chemist's for the sick man. When he arrived back with it out of breath the doctor explained that death had occurred:

My mother was weeping. My brother, in despairing grief, fell on his knees beside the bed and began to address his dead father, asking him why he did not respond, and other exclamations of that kind. I myself, on the other hand, what with bodily exhaustion and being out of breath, was unable to feel anything at all. I stood before my dead father, whom I had loved so deeply, and yet, in spite of the fact that I was fully aware of our loss and of its meaning, I was not only incapable of tears, I could not bring forth any feeling at all. With absolute composure I stood there before my dead father and surveyed the scene.

At this moment it became clear to me that the human being can uplift himself in mind and spirit into a world that abides eternally in silence, far beyond the surging wages of pain and passion. The experience I had had as a little child in the middle of the road in the Wienerwald, where I had recognised 'I am an I' and had taken my first independent step in life, was now repeated and carried further. Once again I knew, 'I am an I', and with this *I* I am rooted in the world of reality wherein my father too is living now, compared to which the events of our daily life are but a medley of dreams, an ebb and flow of surging movement.

I stood for a long time motionless and in silence. The cylinder of oxygen lay on the ground where I had dropped it. At last I said to my brother, 'Pull yourself together now. Why are you so in despair?' The doctor, however, drew me aside, saying, 'Let him be! It is only once that one's father dies!'

After this experience I knew that every human being lives in a threefold way. First, we live on earth in our earthly body. Then we express our life and being in a second way, namely, in all our passions, our pains and joys, our hopes and fears—in the world of the soul. And thirdly, we reach out into a spiritual world, a world beyond all personal emotions, through our membership of which we with our true Being are rooted in the objective Spirit. The three succeeding years, 1909, 1910, 1911, wherein my schooldays came to an end and I had to take leave of the Schottengymnasium, were constantly occupied with thoughts about this threefold nature of man, and in this way I became prepared for my ultimate meeting with Rudolf Steiner and his teaching.[9]

The proximity of death had also been experienced by Stein through a life-endangering illness of his own. The situation was so serious, owing to the fact that the disease could not be diagnosed, that Dr Josef Breuer, one of the most sought after specialists for inner disorders in Vienna was called in. After careful examination he prescribed a meat diet, to which Stein observes: 'I found that an excellent idea and preferred to recover. If it was the ham which cured me, I do not know.'[9]

Rudolf Steiner also knew Breuer and in his autobiography he gives a characterisation of this unusual doctor who published an account of the first psychoanalytical investigations together with Freud, but later separated from him.[14]

The dominant therapeutic theme which was to play a decisive role in the second half of Stein's life was sounded already during his youth. The family doctor reminded him every time he visited: 'Do not forget, you are going to be a doctor some day!'[9] But to begin with the interests and choice of training went in another direction. Already as a grammar school pupil he had taken part in lecture courses in mathematics. They started at 7.00 a.m., one hour earlier than school began. Owing to his regular attendance he even attracted the attention of the Professor, who occasionally called him to the blackboard for the solving of mathematical problems.

Walter Johannes Stein was attracted to the exact sciences, from which he hoped to get the answers to his questions about knowledge. History and literature were set aside for the time being, also violin and piano which he had practised as a child. He seemed to take life seriously at an early age, as did his contemporaries also; for in the class photos all the older pupils look like adults, wearing jackets, waistcoats and collars in the style of their fathers. The bearing of the grown-ups was still impressive and exemplary; the tutors continued to win the confidence of the younger ones and the Schottengymnasium had excellent teachers. 'Vienna has always been the place for famous teaching personalities. They were able to unfold their talents here, because Austria was always receptive to the fructifying forces of the Spirit conveyed to it by many exceptional, even eccentric people.'[9] Stein could count such personalities among his teachers; and they helped him further along the road towards himself.

4   The Staff of the Schottengymnasium 1907

5

Friendship with Eugen Kolisko

Walter Johannes Stein had to repeat the third class at the High School, because his results in mathematics were not good enough. The result of this set-back was that he now developed an especial liking for mathematics, which he later chose as the subject for his studies. But there was still another result of this which was of karmic importance: Stein became a classmate of Eugen Kolisko and sat beside him in the classroom for seven years. Their older brothers, too, Friedrich Stein and Fritz Kolisko were in a class together. Thus began the friendship in 1904 which was to last until Kolisko's death in 1939.

Lili Kolisko, the important anthroposophical researcher in natural science, writes in the biography she published about her husband Eugen Kolisko: ... 'on the one hand there was great friendship between the two (Stein and Kolisko), on the other hand, however, a great difference in their whole make-up. Their character and their views about many things were often diametrically opposed. It was a strange friendship which grew up slowly over the years, which was not founded on mutual understanding and sympathy. Stein was about two years older and looked down upon the younger one with a certain superiority. One could almost say that they fell upon one another like two fighting cocks. The bond which united them was built upon absolute frankness towards one another. One might ask: "How is it that the two could unite so strongly to a real life-long friendship when they could not bear one another?" '[15]

Eugen Kolisko was descended from a well known medical family. His father, Professor for judicial medicine at Vienna University, had to give his verdict on the death of the Archduke Rudolf, as to whether it was an accident or suicide. (The mysterious happenings are known as 'the tragedy of Mayerlng').

Professor Kolisko stood out against the version of it being an accident, as the Viennese Court would have it—one of the 'most courageous Viennese doctors'[16] as Rudolf Steiner observed—and declared that he would not sign something which was not supported by objective facts.

The sensitive mother turned her whole attention towards her son Eugen, who was often ill as a child and had to be accompanied from one spa to the next. Only in his second septennium did his health so far improve that he could take the entrance examination of the Schottengymnasium, after being coached by a private tutor. There, at the age of eleven, he met Walter Johannes Stein.

But the relationship remained dormant for a long time; karmic intervention was needed before the two souls could awaken to each other. In 1908 Walter Johannes Stein lost his father. In the following year Eugen Kolisko lost his admired and much loved brother, who at that time was still studying medicine. 'Now I am all on my own. I have lost my spiritual father' he complains in his diary. Then Friedrich Stein explained to his brother that it was now his task to care for his bereaved school mate. It was a resolve with important results through which their friendship was forged. Stein wrote: 'I actually took my friendship to Eugen consciously in hand from then on.' Their friendship began as they entered the years of their youth.

When Stein self-critically reviewed his life after the death of Kolisko he declared: 'My relationship to Eugen was such that we used to discuss with great thoroughness the interests we had in common, but Eugen was always on the defensive where I was personally concerned. A kind of urge to protect his independence was expressed therein.'[15] The youthful friends discussed with equal intensity both the basic laws of differential calculus and of geometry as also problems of physics. On their walks together they were wont to observe the appearance and behaviour of passers by, attempted to guess their occupations in life, temperament and traits of character and then sought to verify their conjectures. Whether someone walked on the outside of the pavement or the inside, what the difference was between male and female behaviour became a psychological puzzle to them.

When in 1910 Halley's Comet made its appearance, people feared that the earth might intercept the path of its tail and that the air might be contaminated with cyanide from the comet's

5   Eugen Kolisko about 1914

atmosphere. The friends painted in vivid colours the terrible scenes of the possible catastrophe. It was during the final year before leaving school that they fought their way through tormenting doubts to find the meaning of the search for knowledge. The 17 year old Kolisko wrote in a letter: 'Theoretical thinking demands the greatest renunciation—if one is willing to sacrifice all romanticism and the triviliaty of speech which inflames the heart. But were not the monks of the middle Ages also happy in their renunciation, which appeared to them as their highest ideal?'[15] A remark such as this sounds like a memory behind the memory in which the karmic past is coming to expression.*

In spite of the marked contrast between the young friends, the further course of their life showed striking conformity. Kolisko was incited by Stein to become familiar with Anthroposophy. A competition of spirits was engaged in, to see which of them could penetrate more quickly and deeply into the cosmos of spiritual-scientific ideas. Kolisko wrote to Stein from Graz on 11 January 1914: 'I will get a copy of *Occult Science* in Vienna straight away.'[17] Stein had worked through this compendium of spiritual science already in 1912. A fresh intimacy of spirit grew up between the friends: 'When you return we shall be able to cooperate mightily, for in the way we complement one another something very beautiful can grow, as you know.' That is what Kolisko avers in a letter to Stein who had been serving on the [Polish] Galician front since the beginning of the war.[15] The death of Friedrich Stein in 1915 seems to have brought the friend closer together, as did also the early death of Fritz Kolisko. The strands of their lives seem to interweave into a combined pattern of destiny; their friendship becomes a life-long alliance in the search for the spirit, in which the dead also participate.

'Both our brothers, who once brought us together, have passed over into other realms of existence. One of them remained uninfluenced by the spiritual treasures which have been bestowed upon us during the last years, but was not far distant in his way and in his development (Fritz Kolisko); the other underwent a change from the very depths of his being during the latter part of his life (Friedrich Stein).' Kolisko felt the proximity of the dead, whom he would have liked to follow on their soul journey after death.

---

* See Appendix.

After the war both then became teachers at the Stuttgart Waldorf School. Kolisko handed over to Rudolf Steiner in person that letter of Stein's which held so many questions that the writer of the letter was invited to take part in the preparatory teachers' courses, where all his questions would be answered. Half a year later Kolisko decided to give up his university career and started, like Stein, as a substitute teacher, before he was able to build up his new practice as school doctor. Soon there was added to that the mutual work in the leading bodies in the Society. The names Stein and Kolisko were uttered in one breath and to many who saw them in Rudolf Steiner's proximity they appeared as his spiritual sons.

Their way led them finally to London, the last scene of their activity. There the life span of both ended, as in Vienna it had begun.

6
Destiny Calls

'Youth dreams the truth which the old have to recognise' is the saying in Steffen's *Lebensgeschichte eines jungen Menschen* (Biography of a young person). The web of dreams grows more complex when adolescence comes to an end. Then a soul drama begins: the call of destiny, which one has chosen oneself, pushes towards the threshold of consciousness and the feeling that we are standing before the decision of a lifetime takes hold of him who is awakening to independence. This is how Stein experienced it when he came across *Occult Science* by Rudolf Steiner.

This mood had been growing in him since the end of his school days. Gifted with a mobility of thought and a capacity for abstract thinking he sought after knowledge in the relationships of nature. His matriculation certificate from the 'K.K. Obergymnasium zu den Schotten' in Vienna of 11 July 1911 rated his achievements in physics, mathematics, geography, history and the introduction to philosophy as good and very good. This is where his academic abilities lay. An Aristotelian spirit lived within him. He became conscious of the strong affinity of his way of thinking to that of Aristotle when he looked back on his meeting with Rudolf Steiner. He wanted to penetrate to the foundations of mechanical physics, to the realities of time, space and substance, to comprehend the structure and evolution of nature in its entirety. These natural-scientific enquiries and the riddles of human existence which had been with him since the death of his father led the twenty-one-year-old to Anthroposophy.

The time between leaving school and the start of his one-year voluntary military service was used by him in embarking on an 'educational journey'—which his father had always recommended—whilst his fellow matriculation candidate Eugen Kolisko set off for Athens and Dalmatia, Stein set out for Germany.

By way of Salzburg, Munich, Stuttgart and Mainz the journey took him as far as Cologne and then back again to Stuttgart, when he spontaneously decided to turn back for home. His parting from his mother, the release from his habitual relationships, the feeling that a new period in his life was beginning, made his soul receptive to the upsurge of new impressions. He wrote to Kolisko from Munich on 27 August 1911:[15]

Dear Eugen,

The curtain which veiled the wide Hall of Art has been raised very slightly, but just enough for an inquisitive eye to glimpse what it can take for stimulation. The summer was thus of importance to me because, for the first time, I have come into contact with the formative arts, and most unusually—in historic garb. Everything I only *learned* up till now, I have now *seen* and my avid imagination has had plenty of nourishment. The summer was important, too, in other ways, but I will not and may not tell you about that at the moment.

It may be that I have conjectured more in the works I was permitted to see than lies in them, just as I did where human beings were concerned—it may be so. But I would rather enjoy a richer kind of life than one which is all too wretched. Exact reasoning—to be sure, only in one subject—has become something I can handle, and that is a good start. That I am a philosopher and not a mathematician has been known to us both for a long time, but that will not hinder me from studying mathematics. For this is where it starts—even though the end, that is the goal, lies in life itself, in rosy sun-filled life full of the joy of working. Per abstracte ad vitam—through abstract theory to life. Granted, it may be one only arrives at life just before death. Especially in Austria. But, nevertheless, nowhere is it written that Austria is the world. I have become quite many-sided, and that is a good thing. Painting, sculpture, ceramics, anthropology, ethnology, architecture, drama and many other things dance their gay measures in my brain-pan, and it is good to have had experience and to have been personally involved, otherwise one would become a living museum. I have seen at least five hundred old tiled stoves and am now able to live in rooms with no stoves. I make long detours round royal palaces and look straight ahead when passing town halls. In spite of that I have spent three hours today looking at Greek vases. Perhaps I should feel ashamed that it needed Munich to bring me back again to 'faith and homeland'—but—what does that matter? It almost seems that we come closer to one another the further away we go from each other. The world is round—perhaps we may meet somewhere.

Hearty greetings—Yours Walter.

It seems that for the first time he had satisfied the longing for reality, which he had not found through his schooling.

His way led him twice to Stuttgart. Without knowing it he visited the place of his future employment: the restaurant on the Uhlandshöhe which Emil Molt converted after the First World War into the first Waldorf School. This incident was like a promise of the decisive Stuttgart phase of his life.

Stein has fixed this karmically significant moment in his biography:

I remember walking up the hill to the *Uhlandshöhe* from where the beautiful garden city stretches out before one, filling the entire valley and the steep terraces of the surrounding hills, covered with crimson roses and ramblers. A king who loved roses and who used to sign his name in Arabian Characters had once had these roses transplanted from the ramparts of Granada to Stuttgart. To me it was like a city from the Arabian Nights, and I wandered through it as in a dream. There is a little castle there, too, with the surrounding gardens laid out in the Arabian style. The clean and tidy country with the red-tiled cottages to the left and right of the railway line, where even factory workers have their little gardens or plots of land to tend in their spare time, seemed to me like the promised land as it lay there bathed in the red of roses. I went along the road to which Napoleon's artillery had climbed and which is called to this day *Kanonenweg* [today Haussmannstrasse]. Here the great army had passed on its long march, which did not end till it came to Vienna. I reached number 44, a building known at that time as the Restaurant Uhlandshöhe. It was a kind of café, and there was a flight of steps leading up to it. Standing upon those steps, an inexplicable feeling inspired me, but I could not then tell what it was. Yet all of a sudden I knew that my journey was at an end. I must return. So I went down to the railway station and took the next train home to Vienna.[9]

Later he sometimes called Stuttgart New Granada because it was here that spiritual battles were fought, just as once the Christian Scholastics had fought against the Arabian thinkers and interpreters of Aristotle; and Stein, who recognised himself as a Christian Aristotelian, had taken part passionately in such battles.

Then began his year of military training. Stein joined the Artillery. He liked being a soldier and became qualified as a Reserve Officer. There was a combative, downright daredevil streak in his nature.

In October 1912 his name was entered for the study of mathematics, physics and philosophy at the University in Vienna. He signed up for lectures on ethics and the philosophy of Kant, on psychology and the development of modern problems of knowledge, on pure mathematics and experimental physics; a task involving thirty-two lectures a week that was undertaken by the ardent beginner. Among his High School teachers was the well-known philosopher Friedrich Jodl who, following on in the traditions of John Stuart Mill, Auguste Comte and Ludwig Feuerbach, belonged to the positivistic, spirit-denying direction of thought of the nineteenth century.

He aimed at acquiring a methodical training in the mathematical-physical sciences. In that he was helped by the knowledge he had gained in the upper school and by his extensive memory, the items of which he could call to mind at any moment.

Just when knowledge was breaking through an event occurred which changed his whole life. Stein has described what happened many times—in general and in detail. His glance fell upon the book: *Occult Science—an Outline*.[17] He discovered the voluminous work on his mother's writing desk. This outline of anthroposophical spiritual science, which had been written by Rudolf Steiner between 1906 and 1908, had appeared in the Altmann Press in Leipzig in 1910. Its central chapter portrays a spiritual scientific cosmogony, which contains an inexhaustible fund of facts and evolutionary laws. It was through his spiritual research that Rudolf Steiner was able to follow by means of exact clairvoyant investigation the existence and progressive evolution of a self contained cosmos of warmth—called 'Saturn'—to the stage of earth development.

After opening *Occult Science* his searching enquiry into its methods and results gave him no peace. His coming to grips with it was fired by the problem of warmth—the Saturn evolution—in the first chapter of this spiritual scientific cosmogony. The first sentences he read were a challenge to students of physics. Warmth cannot be envisaged as matter, but only as a form of energy—so he had learned. In this book, however, it was maintained that heat was a quality, an element of impulse-giving activity. 'This man must have slept through the whole development of modern physics,' concluded Stein. This contention, however, had been anticipated by Rudolf Steiner, who had explained in the foreword that, on the basis of his studies in natural science, he was able to show 'how the statements of this book were in agreement with all the advances of modern science.'[18]

First meetings are moments of heightened awareness. Stein felt immediately: 'There speaks a world view which is either true, in which case I must embrace it, or it is false and I must oppose it to the utmost. But I felt immediately that I was confronting a decision affecting my whole life.'[9]

The call of destiny stood our clearly before his mind's eye: if the test of truth turned out positively then his way would lead him into the world of anthroposophical ideas. He wanted to become familiar with every line that Rudolf Steiner had written, with every word that he had spoken. He began to work through all available copies of lectures and books with his customary intensity. He set on one side the studies which he had just begun and sat for up to ten hours daily poring over the lecture cycles and books of Rudolf Steiner.

Even at the first reading of *Occult Science* its unusual style had struck him. In the manner of a mathematical text book the contents of supersensible consciousness are developed. By that means the author brings it about that 'the very reading of it is an initial step in spiritual training, inasmuch as the necessary effort of quiet thought and contemplation strengthen the powers of the soul, making them capable of drawing nearer to the spiritual world.'[19] Thus Rudolf Steiner himself characterises the effect that his method of thought and language bring about. It is true that the cultivation of this element of style which leads the alert reader from an intellectual to an observing consciousness (if noticed at all) is something which has been little studied in the development of the German language.

Stein set about the study of Anthroposophy in a systematic way. He describes how his judgement of spiritual-scientific statements developed in three stages and their continued testing led to a first discussion with Rudolf Steiner:

As I read on and on, I went through three distinct stages in my judgement of Rudolf Steiner. The first was when I had read a certain number of books and lecture-cycles. 'All that he says,' I said to myself, 'is in itself consistent, but I am well aware from mathematics that a system of thought need not represent any reality just because it is logical and free of contradictions.'

In the second phase of my investigation, I began to compare Dr Steiner's teaching with other philosophies, religions and mystical systems. I found his work contained the key to all, and that all other systems were to his as parts are to the whole. 'Still it may be,' I said to myself, 'that these spiritual world conceptions do not represent any reality at all. I must, however, admit that the system Dr Steiner puts before us is not only consistent in itself; it contains the key to all the others.'

In the third place I began to study the relation of Dr Steiner's teaching to Natural Science—that is, in all the branches of Science that were accessible to me. Where he diverged from the orthodox teaching I found he did so for good reasons. He was indeed further advanced than the official Science and his system did, in fact, represent a reality, namely, the reality of Nature.

When I had got thus far a lecture was announced to be given by Rudolf Steiner in Vienna, and I resolved to attend it.[9]

It concerns the lectures 'Die Übersinnlichen Welten und das Wesen der Menschenseele' (The super-sensible worlds and the being of man's soul) and 'Geisteswissenschaft und Naturwissenschaft in ihrem Verhaltnis zu den Lebensträtseln' (Spiritual Science and Natural Science in their relationship to the Riddles of Life) on 20 January 1913 of which there are no notes.

Rudolf Steiner gave a magnificant lecture on the trichotomy or three-fold being of man. He explained how Thinking, Feeling, and Willing can be developed by an inner training of the soul into spiritual powers of cognition. Thinking is then transformed from being shadowlike and abstract into a living picture-thought, to Imagination, to Spiritual Vision. Out of our Feeling, when Feeling is made selfless, grows the faculty of receiving divine Inspiration. Willing, finally, when we direct it to the transformation of our own character and being, gives birth to what may truly be described as Intuition; that is the form of knowledge wherein we become at one with the universe and out of this 'at oneness' we form and guide our own 'I' or Ego, until the harmony of inner life and outer universe produces insight which is no longer subject to error. I said to myself as I listened to this lecture: 'This man called Rudolf Steiner is actually giving instructions for the development of a threefold faculty of clairvoyance. Now in his books he tells us that he teaches nothing he has not himself discovered. Therefore he must himself possess these faculties; he must be clairvoyant. If that is so, he will also be able to read my thoughts; he will be able to read what I am now thinking. I can therefore ask him questions by merely thinking them and he will be able to answer me in the course of his lecture.' This I now did. I asked again and again, and every time he answered. Being however, brought up in a critical and scientific school, I said to myself: 'Why should it be any more than an illusion? The questions I am asking are ones that arise in a logical way from the content of his lecture. He, on the other hand, is developing his subject logically. He is not answering me at all; there is no need to conclude that he is aware of my questions. I am but imagining that it is so because that is what I really wish.'

However, after the lecture there was an opportunity to send up written questions. I wrote on a sheet of paper, 'Which came first, human language or human reason?' Rudolf Steiner read my question in its turn and answered, but he did not do so from the point of view I had had in mind. My question was inspired by a book I had been reading, Lazarus Geiger's *Human Language and Reason*. I wanted to know in what way and in what mutual relation language and reason had developed in the long history of mankind on earth; he, however, was answering from the point of view not of the history of mankind, but of the individual child's development. I was bitterly disappointed; he evidently had not understood my question. Rudolf Steiner put down my paper and was silent for a few moments. Thereupon he picked it up once more and said: 'What I have been saying is only one point of view; there is another aspect which the writer of the question had in mind.' And he went on to tell how in the evolution of mankind language and reason had evolved by means of one another.

When question-time was over, I went up to him and said: 'I am aware of who you are and I would like to become your pupil.' Rudolf Steiner said, 'I take it you know English?' 'No,' I said. Nevertheless, he continued: 'Read the philosophical works of Berkeley, who denied the existence of matter, and of Locke, who based everything upon the senses. Then write a theory of cognition of spiritual knowledge, avoiding both of these one-sided points of view. Do it as I have done: learn to know the fullness of the world through Aristotle, and the act of cognition itself through the philosophy of Fichte.'

So I became Rudolf Steiner's pupil, and the remainder of my life has been lived in the sign of this discipleship.[9]

The encounter is in every way unusual: the whole way in which Stein expresses himself and Rudolf Steiner answers him. To be

6   Rudolf Steiner 1908

sure, later records suggest that in the biography from *The Present Age* the contents of two conversations have been condensed into one. In the later account, after the reference to Locke and Berkeley, he says: 'You must find the balance between these two. I shall speak to you further about it.'[20]

A series of conversations and meetings now took place, which continued until Rudolf Steiner's death. The next opportunity presented itself at the time when Stein, in August 1913 in Munich, was anxious to be present at the performance of the Mystery Plays.

But first there was an obstacle to be overcome. The performances at that time were only for members of the Anthroposophical Society and Stein had not yet become a member. How it was that he was nevertheless still allowed to attend he describes thus:

> With the determination to bridge the gap between natural science and Anthroposophy, I came to Munich to attend the performances of the Mystery Plays. But I was not yet a member and was not allowed to enter. Countess Kalkreuth informed me of this and said: 'The bridge to natural science has already been built, you come much too late.' I was, however, in no mind to leave Munich without having seen the plays and appealed to Dr Steiner. He appeared out of his consulting room with unending kindness and said: 'Yes, Herr Stein, the performances are only for members. But you can become a member and immediately after the performance you can leave the Society again.' To that I gave my consent. And in that way I was able to take part in those wonderful plays and live in that atmosphere of delicate and intimate warmth of soul which pervaded everything at that time. After the performance Dr Steiner came to me and asked me: 'Now, Herr Stein, did you enjoy it?' I answered 'I am not now such an ass as I was before and I will also never leave the Society any more.' It was thus that I became a member.[21]

It was the last time that the Mystery Plays could be performed in Munich. In 1910 Rudolf Steiner took a new step towards the realisation of Anthroposophy. In the style of a modern Mystery poem he created a series of four dramas. Stein saw the repetition of the third Mystery Play, *The Guardian of the Threshold* and the original first performance of the fourth play, *The Soul's Awakening*. The path of development of very different, but karmically connected people is shown in scenic pictures depicting their ups and downs in life, the miracle of their transformation, the drama of initiation in their search for the spirit. With growing amazement Stein experienced the action on the stage as a foretaste of the drama of his own search for knowledge.

'This festival in Munich was the most beautiful time of the year,' reported Marie Steiner, who took a main part in the Mystery Plays as Maria, a pupil of the spirit. 'During the day we rehearsed; during the night Rudolf Steiner wrote the plays which were already complete in his mind. In between whiles he directed and supervised the various workshops in which the carpentry, joinery, painting and modelling, stitching and embroidery were being carried out according to his instructions. For everything he had new ideas; everywhere he could lend a hand.'[22] The actors, who were almost without exception amateurs, were able to surpass themselves because of the faith he had in them. Thus the enterprise which was to portray supersensible occurrences on the stage was able to succeed. All reports speak of the power of conviction and soul-stirring effect of these events which allowed the participants to experience spiritual reality.

To the superabundance of unaccustomed novelty was added a further 'first performance': the first demonstration of eurythmy, on Goethe's birthday, 28 August. Rudolf Steiner had started to develop this new art of movement, which he called 'visible speech' and 'visible song,' from 1912 onwards. Already by the following year introductory courses had been arranged, which attracted many visitors. A delicate shimmer surrounded this new undertaking and merged with the artistic impressions of the Mystery Plays.

As a third element there followed the cognitive activity which started with the lecture cycle: *The Secrets of the Threshold*. Rudolf Steiner had to give the lectures in two sittings—at 11.00 a.m. and at 8.00 p.m.—because so many members had arrived—also from abroad. He spoke about the change of consciousness in the twentieth century which introduces unenlightened humanity to the realm of spiritual experience and gives it the task of adding spirituality to its already acquired intellectuality, so that it will be able to withstand the onslaught of spiritual forces. The audience was surprised to hear already in the first lecture about the 'Filioque' dispute. This contention was the precursor of the separation of the Eastern Orthodox Church from the Catholic

Church, because the Western Church asserted that the Holy Ghost proceeds 'from the Son' (Filioque), as well as from the Father, a fact which was not accepted by the Eastern Church. Only western Christianity acknowledged—since the Christ event—that the Spirit had taken on a new form and has become active in the spirit of man. 'When the sword of Charlemagne enforced, on behalf of the West against the East, the confession of faith that the Holy Spirit proceeds from the Father and the Son,—for it was not the Papal Church, but the sword of Charlemagne that enforced this,—it was then that the foundation was laid for what is breaking forth today again in powerful and convulsing wave-beats.'[23] Thus, one year before the outbreak of the First World War, Rudolf Steiner points to a karmic connection between the ninth and the twentieth centuries: how the East-West relationships of the ninth century have prepared the ground for the East-West conflicts of the present day. The theme is introduced which Stein was to incorporate later in his main work: 'World History in the Light of the Holy Grail—the Ninth Century.'*

Christian Morgenstern looked upon the Munich happenings, the Plays and the lectures, as the culmination of European spiritual life.[24]

But the time of the Festival at Munich also marked the culmination of Rudolf Steiner's co-operation with the first generation of anthroposophists, those 'homeless' souls who were looking for guidance for their spiritual life and discovered it in Anthroposophy. So Stein could meet the leading members of the Society, with whom he had joined his destiny: Emil Molt, through their mutual activity in the founding of the Waldorf School, and Carl Unger, the important researcher of knowledge, through their discussions during the time of crisis in the Anthroposophical Society.

Stein returned to Vienna, transformed and with fresh impetus. In retrospect he summed it up: 'I gradually grew into history and found my place in the current of historical events.'[21] Next he divided his time between his academic and his anthroposophical studies. He worked his way through Rudolf Steiner's introduction to *Goethe's Natural History Writings* and sought to build a bridge for his understanding of Anthroposophy and modern physics. In

---

* *The Ninth Century and the Holy Grail* (London, Temple Lodge Press, 1988).

this connection he was helped by an exchange of ideas with his anthroposophical friends, especially with the mathematician Ernst Bluemel, who later became his colleague at the Stuttgart Waldorf School. At that time, he also got to know Karl Schubert, the future Waldorf teacher.

Stein longed for a further meeting with Rudolf Steiner. In the meantime decisive events had taken place. The laying of the foundation stone of the First Goetheanum had taken place in Dornach near Basle on 20 September 1913. This building which was primarily intended to have been built in Munich, was designed by Rudolf Steiner with double cupolas in the Jurassic landscape of Switzerland. The members wanted to have a building of their own for the Mystery Play performances and for the establishment of a Free High School for Spiritual Science. After the laying of the foundation stone Rudolf Steiner began with a series of lectures on *The Fifth Gospel*. It was 'the crowning achievement of his revelations about Christ,' wrote the Russian poet Andrey Belyj, who had been present during the first lecture course in Christiania, the present day Oslo.[25] In these lectures Rudolf Steiner developed the historical aspect of the Christ event, portraying the life of Jesus of Nazareth as a historical personality in biographical detail. 1914 arrived, the year that the Goetheanum was to have been completed. The topping out ceremony was held on 1 April. Following that Rudolf Steiner arrived in Vienna to hold the lecture cycle: *The Inner Nature of Man and the Life between Death and a New Birth*. Whole parties of members travelled to such lecture courses; as members of a 'mobile university' they followed the 'Doctor's' courses from one town to the next. Michael Bauer, the friend of Christian Morgenstern who died on 31 March 1914, was there too.

The lecture cycle had been constructed like a work of art. The lectures concluded with the parts of the trinitarian formula: Ex Deo nascimur, In Christo morimur, Per Spiritum Sanctum reviviscimus. As spiritual nourishment for times of future need, Rudolf Steiner had bestowed this old wise saying upon his hearers. In the last of his lectures he spoke about 'the terrible tendency to social ulcers'—as the result of over-burgeoning production and competitive markets—and concluded with the call to awake in order to develop the consciousness needed at the present day to penetrate to the upbuilding spiritual forces.

The phenomenon of Rudolf Steiner as lecturer has been vividly described by several members of his audiences, including Walter Johannes Stein. The lectures of Rudolf Steiner were not verbal essays. Their content was formed spontaneously out of the immediate presence of the spirit. Whoever would experience this creative force must needs unfold a meditative alertness. Then it might happen that, oscillating in harmony with the etheric rhythm, he would be lifted out of his body and attain to a visionary experience. That is how Stein experienced it when listening to a lecture for the first time:

> One could experience Rudolf Steiner as a 'coming to oneself', not to a self as one was formerly, but to a self to which one would aspire, perhaps only in a far distant future, perhaps at the end of all evolution, but he brought one back to oneself. One was tempted to think: 'You are what I ought to be; but I am not you, because I have neither the love nor the knowledge which you already possess.' Such feelings as these are hard to describe. But in dimly sensing him one had the feeling that he was Christian. For he was not only himself, but every *other* person who was present, too. He went out from his body as he spoke, became one with every single objective intention and spoke from that. And this coalescence with all things—and just by that expressing his truly loving and understanding individuality—was what was so Christ-permeated about him. For did not Christ say: 'Inasmuch as ye have done it unto one of the least of these my brethren, ye have done it unto me?' Thus my meeting with Rudolf Steiner became for me a real meeting with the Christ principle. There he was, the true announcer of Christ, who had made the sacrifice of incarnating into the age of natural science, so that even those who lived in the world of mathematics and physics could find the Christ.[26]

At last the time for the long awaited interview had come. It was at Easter, during the Viennese lecture cycle. Stein gave a report of his studies, whereupon Rudolf Steiner, referring to their first conversation, declared:

> You must do as I did. I balanced Aristotle with Johann Gottlich Fichte. Aristotle has a knowledge of nature and receives his thoughts by way of perception. He says that there is no content to thought except what has entered by way of the senses. Fichte, however, deals actively. He has got spiritual activity. That was impossible for Aristotle, it came

only later with the progressive development of personality. The 'Nous Poietikos' of Aristotle is, after all, not the same as Fichte's thought activity. For Aristotle did *not* actually experience the fact that he produced his own thoughts. His 'Nous Poietikos' is only the production of the light which illuminates the thoughts. He experienced the light as the product of his own activity, but not the thoughts themselves. If then, you extend the thoughts of Aristotle by those of Fichte, you will arrived at Anthroposophy. Anthroposophy rests on the creative ego-conscious thinking which in the human spirit which creates it, can no longer be experienced today merely as the old divine revelation. For your doctor's examination you must write a thesis about the theory of knowledge of this spiritual view and compare it with natural science which has not yet discovered what is spiritual.[12]

This piece of advice was decisive for Stein's development. Rudolf Steiner indicated what his own method of work had been: to unlock the secret of 'becoming' through a living reconciliation of polarities and to establish a view of reality which explains how the spirit is revealed in matter, how the cosmic is manifested in the earthly. With that Stein had arrived at the starting point for his studies which embrace both natural science and spiritual science. With persistent energy he set about his tasks.

But Rudolf Steiner's presence in Vienna had still another karmic consequence. Before the last lecture he gave an address about the Dornach building which was in the course of construction. Through the language of its artistic forms this building was intended to signify the spirit of Anthroposophy. Built, as it were, at the 'boundary of the visible world,' its walls were so constructed as to dissolve and become 'communicators, which lay the life of the spirit open to the illimitable cosmic distances.'[27] Under the impression of these words Hermine Stein decided to take part in the building of the Goetheanum. There was a kind of 'Architect's Lodge' in Dornach. Hundreds of members, professional artists and amateurs, streamed together from all quarters of the globe and assisted as painters, wood carvers and glass engravers under Rudolf Steiner's direction, contributing to 'the whole great work of art.'

Walter Johannes Stein joined his mother, too—as he had done for the Mystery Plays—and visited her there at the end of July. Just at that time the cupolas were being roofed with the slate which Rudolf Steiner had himself chosen in Norway. One hundred and

7   W.J Stein and his mother 1914

fifty wood carvers were at work on the capitals and architraves. Among the artists were Hanns Strauss and Max Wolfhügel, whom Rudolf Steiner later called to the Waldorf School. Stein was allowed to carve on one of the architraves. Equipped with gouge and mallet he was given the advice: 'Feeling in your left hand— feel the form with the gouge; strength in your right. The co-operation of these two is the most important thing.'[28]

In summer it was still hoped that the building would be completed by the end of the year and that a fifth Mystery Play could be performed there.

But since the assassination at Sarajevo political tension had been growing from day to day. In Austria mobilisation against Serbia was already under way. On 26 July Rudolf Steiner, just returned from Scandinavia, gave his last lecture before the outbreak of war. Stein was also in the audience which was gathered together among the machinery and stacks of timber in the joiner's shop. After the call to awaken which concluded the Vienna lectures, Stein now had the feeling that the Dornach lecture was a farewell speech. 'Truly, even in these days of sadness, in these hours which seem so full of foreboding, we may well—nay, not only *may* but *must*—speak of the sacred affairs of our spiritual movement, for we can have faith that, small as it appears today, this sun that is spiritual science will grow ever brighter—this peace-giving sun of love and harmony among humanity.'[29] Then came the news that the Austrian frontier had been closed. A call-up order could no longer reach him. His brother Friedrich had already been called up. In this situation he asked the advice of Rudolf Steiner. 'Follow the inner voice of your heart' was the reply. And his heart told him that he should depart. At the station in Basle he realised that this departure into the unknown might be a departure with no return. During the last quarter of an hour before the train left he wrote the following letter to Rudolf Steiner in the waiting room of the station (see facsimile reproduction on previous page):

Buffet of the Swiss Railways,
Basel.

Greatly revered Herr Doctor!
News has been received that the telegraphic and telephonic

Buffet S.B.B.
Basel.
—
Ch. Pfau Prop.

Basel, den   191

Hochverehrter Herr Doktor!

Es liegt die Nachricht vor, daß Telegraph und Telephon nach Österreich abgeschnitten sind, und dies veranlaßt mich, auch ohne Einberufungs-Karte nach Wien zu fahren, da es meine militärische Pflicht ist erreichbar zu sein. Ich habe nicht mehr die Möglichkeit mit Ihnen, hochverehrter Herr Doktor, zu sprechen. Es sind nur wenige Worte des Dankes, die ich darum an Sie niederschreibe, die ein äußeres Zeichen eines tief innerlich Erlebten sein mögen. Die Schlußworte Ihres Vortrages waren so recht Abschiedsworte – eine Ermahnung und eine Anfeuerung des Wollens. Als solche hat ich sie empfunden und genommen. Daß ich jetzt einer Zukunft wie sie sich mir nun darstellt, fest und sicher entgegen sehen darf, das ist es, was ich restlos Ihnen, hochverehrter Herr Doktor, verdanke. An welchen Platz ich nun gestellt werde, weiß ich nicht – daß ich aber alle Ideale, alles schöne und große, das Geisteswissenschaft mir geben konnte an diesem Platz ausleben will, das weiß ich. Und ich fühle mich, wenn Dankbarkeit mir Kraft des Wollens leiht, Ihnen verbunden, in einem Gefühle das einer Persönlichkeit, einer Idee und eine vollen lebendigen Weltinhalt zugleich gilt.

In Dankbarkeit und Verehrung

Ihr

Sehr ergebener

Walter Stein

8   Letter by W.J. Stein to Rudolf Steiner

communication with Austria has been cut and this induces me to travel to Vienna, even without call-up papers, because it is my military duty to make myself available. There is no longer an opportunity of speaking with you, greatly revered Herr Doktor. I can only write a few words of thanks to you, as an outward sign of something which I experience very deeply. The concluding words of your lecture were so rightly words of farewell—a caution and an incitement to the will. I experienced and understood it in that sense. That I am able to face the future, as it now presents itself, with firmness and confidence, I owe entirely to you, greatly revered Herr Doktor. Where I am to be stationed is not known to me—all I know is that I will carry into my life into that place all the ideals, all that is beautiful and great which I have received from spiritual science.

And if gratitude lends me strength of will, I shall feel faithfully bound to you with a feeling due to a personality, an idea and the contents of a whole universe.

In gratitude and esteem
Your very devoted
Walter Stein.

This letter was mentioned twice by Rudolf Steiner as an example of the frame of mind which Anthroposophy engenders: faith in the 'triumph of the spirit.'

7
Study of the Theory of Cognition continued throughout the First World War

On 28 July Austro-Hungary declared war on Serbia. The proclamation which the 84 year old Emperor Franz Joseph delivered to his people concluded with the words: 'I trust in Austro-Hungary's brave and devoted armed forces. And I trust in the Almighty, that He may send my troops the victory.' The nervous tension which had built up to the utmost after the assassination at Sarajevo quickly turned into a frivolous belief in victory. But the Austrian declaration of war was immediately followed by the Russian mobilisation. The automatic reaction of the treaties functioned and within a week a European war had broken out, which spread to a World War, which in retrospect seems to be the greatest catastrophe of the century. Once again a nationalistic feeling flared up in the peoples of Europe so that those who were affected by the force of the historic occasion were welded into a unanimous collective ego. Many volunteered for military service and almost all obeyed the mobilisation order willingly. They set out with flower-wreathed helmets and climbed into the military trains, taking them to the battlefields—and to the sobering reality of war. Among the volunteers was also the philosopher Ludwig Wittgenstein, who wrote his now famous treatise during the war; among those who went willingly was the poet Georg Trakl, who was unable to bear the indescribable horror of the battle of Grodek and took his own life.

There is no evidence to show that Walter Johannes Stein was seized by the general euphoria. He was led by his sense of duty and a feeling for his karmic connection to the land of his birth. In his biography he gives an account of the action at the Front during the first two years of the war:

It was at Jaroslaw in Galicia that we left the train, and from there we marched. Eighteen months in rain and snow and swamp, without roof, without protection, without hope that it would ever again be otherwise. Eighteen months of the world war; yet lovely months in spite of cold and snow and rain, swamp fever, cholera and dysentery, typhoid and war. A year and a half of Nature! Should I without the war ever have had the patience to lie entrenched in the ground, watching how the plants grow before me on a level with my very eyes? Or to watch how the hares were burrowing in the sand? Throughout all the seasons, through all the hours of day and night, sunrise and sunset, we were there in the immense forests of Russia. What did it matter that we also fired, that there were days of battle, that many of us were killed or taken ill, and so we ourselves might be tomorrow or the day after? What did it matter? We had Nature about us as never before in life, the greatest imaginable subject for meditation. While I lay there in slime or sand I read Locke and Berkeley—in translation only at that time. I occupied myself intensively with the thoughts of these two English philosophers, seeking the middle way between the two extremes of thought. I noted the words from the original: 'Notion' for *Begriff*, 'idea' for *Vorstellung*. So I plodded through. And between riding, fighting and bouts of fever, I wrote continuously the notes for my Dissertation.

On all hands my comrades were laughing at me. I was the one who would not touch a single drop of alcohol. That was the only condition Rudolf Steiner had made: not a drop of alcohol any more, nor have I ever taken any since. My captain wanted to force me; I declined to obey him. He poured alcohol into my coffee; the water was infected with cholera. I was resolved to die if need be, but I would not drink any alcohol. Was it really a matter of such importance? Probably not, but it was the exercise I had undertaken and I was determined to carry it through to the end. So then I read and wrote. My copy of Rudolf Steiner's *Theosophy* twice went up and down the front. Everyone who had read it wrote his name inside. Twice it came back into my hands. Hundreds had read it: the chapters on the life after death and the eternal being of the human soul. On the third occasion the book did not return into my hands; it was buried with one of our comrades who was killed soon after he had read it. Somewhere on the eastern front it may be unearthed one day—the book which worked so powerfully in the souls of all who read it. Rudolf Steiner had once said to me: 'Whoever writes an occult book takes on himself the obligation to help everyone who reads even a single line of it, throughout his future lives.' If this were so, he would have much to do! The last words of one of my comrades who had read it were about this book; a few hours later we buried him beneath the snow. What a power war is!

9   W J Stein 1917

Meanwhile I read and read; riding across country, in the midst of battle, in the long days of waiting, I read and wrote—mountains full of paper.

One day the order came through the telephone from Headquarters: 'All officers who have been in the firing line continuously for the past eighteen months are to retire at once!' It was like a dream. Two hours later I was on the way in a farmcart through woods of oak and birch and across the marshes. I had not realised how far away we were. While the cart swayed and rattled and the thunder of the cannon could still be heard in the distance I had time to think of the past months. We passed by the place where I had been left behind with two of the guns to cover our retreat. The brigadier had said, 'Hold this position until six o'clock tomorrow morning. We are not reckoning on your return.' Here again was the place where we had been in battle all night long. Machine gun bullets came on us like hailstones, while we could do nothing with our big guns in the forest. Here was the place where we had been so hungry—three days without bread, water or sleep—and where a mule from the Russian army strayed into our lines, rice soup still warm in the field-kitchen it was dragging. All these and other recollections went through my mind. And then the march into Przemýsl, the watch-fires burning at the entrance gates, and every one of us—officers and men alike—having a hot potato thrown into his cap as we rode into the fortress. And how we ate them! That was the great retreat. Here were the crosses we had erected over the graves of our dead comrades. It was like a journey back through one's own life, as in a dream. And then at last came Vienna. Yes, this was Vienna, the city where I had been born, which I had thought never to see again.[9]

Stein soon landed in the thick of the battles where many were killed. In Galicia the Austro-Hungarian troops suffered annihilatory defeats right at the beginning of the war as a result of the numerical and tactical superiority of the Russians. In the end, the attack which was aimed at Vienna could be halted and during the winter of 1914-15 the fronts dug in in the Carpathians. As artillery observer in the front line he experienced the gruesomeness of war at first hand. But he was also aware of the inner aspect of the conflict. He had studied Anthroposophy; now he tested its sustaining power under fear of perishing and in proximity to death, when his bodily frame was loosening and his soul becoming free. At such moments he felt the protective nearness of his teacher.

When the war started Stein was at a decisive phase of self-discovery. He now wished to get to grips with the motives of his life provided by destiny, by means of his ego. In his fourth septennium, the classic years of apprenticeship and of travel, the demands of destiny and the fulfilment of that destiny are in balance with one another. It is now a matter of putting to the test all that he had gained from life up till then. The characterisation of this phase of life which Rudolf Steiner gave—in answer to a question by Herbert Hahn—is fairly representative of Stein's inner state. During his twenties a man should ask himself: 'How do my experiences measure up in every detai to the active impulse of Christ? How does my present state of knowledge measure up to Him? And now one should not merely remain at the stage of memory but, with great inner activity, should again work through all that one has achieved up to that point and link it up in every detail with the all-pervading living power of Christ.'[30]

In the fourth septennium one is given the task of working consciously upon one's self-development, and Stein took up this task with energy, for how else could be attain his self-appointed goal? In page-long letters which conveyed his questions to Rudolf Steiner and to Marie Steiner, who passed his questions on, he reported unreservedly and with complete trust the difficulty of his project. Through his study of Locke and Berkeley he became aware of the fundamental conflict of consciousness which is fired by the question of the origin of knowledge. Does knowledge spring primarily from without, out of that which I observe and about which I make my thoughts; or mainly from within, out of that which I create out of myself? How is thinking placed between sense experience and non-sensual experience of one's own being? Thinking does not come about unless I exercise it. Thus, behind the original question about the origin of knowledge, there looms the riddle of the ego, that secret real power which to Fichte, as spiritual activity, becomes the essence of all reality. And, as though by matter of course, the riddle of the ego leads to the third basic question about the being of man who is of individual as much as of universal nature, for man does not only speak the idiom of his mother tongue, but also the universal human language of thought. But the being of man can only be understood—and through that the circle is completed—if the central question about the achievements of thinking and the origin of knowledge can be convincingly answered. From that, as Stein knew, depends the scientific nature of Anthroposophy.

Such questions as these were passing through the mind of the young artillery officer when, on duty at the observation post or during a lull in the fighting, he pondered over the opinions and experiences he had acquired. While in the dugout he read the main works of Berkeley and Locke. With difficulty he acquired a knowledge of English to the extent that, with the help of a dictionary, he could understand the original. In November 1915 he was given a three weeks' leave which he spent with his mother in Vienna. Back at the Front—in a 'misty landscape of snow and ice'—he wrote a long letter to Rudolf Steiner on 12 November 1915: 'A silent night, which I am spending as artillery watchman in a very snug dugout where a fire is crackling cheerfully, provides me with the quiet which I need for this letter.' Thus he introduces what he has to say about the results of his self-knowledge.

My thinking has grown less productive, the pleasure I had in producing thoughts has grown cold. My endeavour is more the putting of two thoughts side by side and observing, as selflessly as possible, what happens when they react upon one another—and less the moving from one thought to the next. The thought is not so lineal—more like a triad in which two thoughts are joined by a third. That is partly due to reading the *Principles* of Berkeley, who writes in such difficult language that it becomes a training in unselfishness and which is so impossible to translate that my respect for the strange thoughts inspires me with a feeling of reverence. My feelings have become more lively and small insignificant occurrences can awaken strong reactions. My self-examination has revealed many defects of my character which often worry me, but not too seriously. My study of the English language seems to work beneficially upon these deficiencies. The low esteem in which I hold the thoughts which gave me pleasure and pride when they were conceived—in the reflexion of my own being—makes itself felt and produces in me a strong self-criticism which kills off many things in embroyo and drives me to destroy other things after I have written them down. It seems that I am learning to let what I have received rest quietly. A feeling of my own moral inadequacy is becoming ever more pronounced—a heavy con-science—regret—of what I have spoken and written. There is something untrue in nearly everything which is spoken and is not to be eradicated in spite of all my efforts. Often it is only a phrase; for instance, I say: 'I have *often* experienced...' although I have only experienced the said thing *once*. Something or other, which I cannot control, makes me say *often*—and then my conscience says clearly: '*once*—only *once*.' But I also experience defects in my feelings— especially in cases where I should feel something and do not do so— it is as though I carried about with me something dead, which I stumble against and ask: 'What is the matter with you?—why do you not react?' My willing is such that I can far more readily say 'I' to it than to my feelings and thinking. Only when I feel that I must will something of which I am afraid is it any different.

Stein experienced the moral dimension of recognising that three steps are needed in moral development before one step can be made in spiritual knowledge. The way of knowledge became for him the way of development. Whoever desires to penetrate in thought to the basis of reality must first create the organ for knowledge free of the senses. He makes the first steps on the path to 'sense-free thinking' by progressing from thinking to the experience of the thinking. This requires a change of the direction of one's will, which is no longer turned outward, but is deflected inwards, it no longer flows into outward activity but is transformed into the forces of devotion and receptivity. The fruits of this exercise of soul is a new state of consciousness which grows out of the transformation of ordinary thinking into a fine and delicate activity of the will illumined by the light of thought. The tender but powerful weaving of the newly won quality of consciousness is the reality of thought in which thinking takes hold of the will. Along such paths as these Stein searches for the 'transition from the theory of knowledge to occultism,' for his goal is the synthesis of these two. But he knows: 'I must become much more unselfish before I will be able to write my dissertation.'

He was not spared the outward and inner difficulties which Rudolf Steiner predicted for him. Amid the dangers of war he experienced the intense drama of the search for reality—the intoxication of flying up to the heights when the sought for solution seemed to be within his grasp, and the plunge into despair when what he had thought to have achieved sank into oblivion; but, when the weakness had passed, the moments of consolidation in which the thinking became will-force which gripped the whole human being.

After one and a half years of mortal danger and exhausting hardship Stein returned to his homeland. He had passed through the stages of an initiation imposed by life, which familiarised him with the realities of life's hidden background and he had participated in the experiences which Rudolf Steiner calls 'the threshold event of mankind.' In the continual catastrophes and crises of the twentieth century a change of consciousness is being announced: humanity is entering unknowingly, by means of modern events, into an experience of spiritual reality which the individual must attain by the exertion of his consciousness.

In his letter of 21 March 1916 Stein squares up the account. He had been in his homeland for four weeks but was obliged to go into the military hospital in Wiener Neustadt because of suspected typhoid. After the suspicion had been proved groundless he was given convalescent leave, which he made use of for his investigation. Now he was able to use his own library, too, and continue with his study of Locke and Berkeley. In so doing it occurred to him that these philosophers unconsciously shy away from the step leading to the knowledge of the essential being, a step which he had to make consciously. He writes: 'I have to experience in fear and trembling what lies at the heart of the philosophy of Locke and Berkeley. And my strength fails me—so often I lack the strong force which leads me from the concept to the reality. I am only able to think it, but not experience it.' And he concludes with the plea: 'That is where I need the help for which I earnestly beseech. For all that I am able to do is not sufficient to reach into the spiritual reality.'

Stein demands a lot of himself. He seeks to take up the whole of Anthroposophy into his will and to place his will entirely in the service of Anthroposophy. That was his self-imposed duty which he had bound himself to fulfil after having survived the battles intact.

After 1916 the circumstances became more bearable. Stein now gave lessons as an instructions officer in the officers' training schools where he had to lecture on 'the elements of artillery instruction and the rules of drill.' The testimonials confirm that his influence on the 18 year old recruits was 'a lasting and good one, also from a moral point of view.' He was in command of 'a specially developed pedagogical ability' which was distinguished by 'an understanding response to the abilities of the individual candidate.' The novelty of style and content of his lectures was attested to by Paul Regenstreif, who became well known after the Second World War as an anthroposophical lecturer and author. He owed his first introduction to Anthroposophy to Stein and recalls the amazement of the 200 one-year volunteers when:

> a mild, rather roundish lieutenant with kindly eyes appeared for the ballistics lessons, speaking with a perfectly quiet voice, in contrast to the other officers who were inclined to speak more loudly and somewhat roughly. In his classes, however, it was as still as a mouse in the daily lessons, the rapt attention of the 200 pupils was directed entirely to him. He by no means lectured on the subject of artillery, but merely stated at the beginning of the lesson: 'It would be best for you to study the contents of the textbook from page so-and-so to page so-and-so; I cannot anyway tell you any more than what is given there'—and then, after a pause, he asked us questions, such as: 'student so-and-so, how do you envisage the evolution of the world? I mean the Creation?' Whereupon we answered according to our Secondary School knowledge and lieutenant Walter Johannes Stein took over and gave a lecture on some such subject as *Occult Science* or the like. Only once did he actually say anything about artillery instruction and that was not so good, it was more like reading from the textbook, that was on the occasion of an inspection by a General.

For most of them such lessons were not of much significance, they were only a welcome change from the monotonous drill of the training. It was different for Regenstreif, who had no peace after what he had heard. He looked up the home of Stein, put on his uniform, and discovered the instructor in his study filled with books. Abruptly he asked him, who was now in civvies and looked even less military than before: 'Herr Lieutenant, may I know whence you have your conception of the world?' Without hesitation the answer came back: 'My teacher is Rudolf Steiner, he is at present in Berlin.' Regenstreif now had the wish, not so much to learn about world conceptions, but to hear about the man Rudolf Steiner, to which Stein readily acquiesced. The account impressed him so deeply that he decided there and then to become a pupil of Rudolf Steiner.

The important mathematician and Waldorf teacher Hermann von Baravalle was also led to Anthroposophy through the instruction of Stein in the Officers' Training School.

Even before his educational work started Stein had met the girl-friend of his brother who had died in the war, Nora von Baditz, at his mother's house. She was the daughter of a Hungarian father and an Austrian mother. The riddle of Friedrich Stein's early self-chosen death occupied them both. They spoke about their connection to the dead person and about the active presence of Christ. And Stein, who had first become interested in anthroposophical cosmology, decided—as he writes in his memoirs—'to concentrate his studies on the Being of Christ.' Nora von Baditz played a decisive part in that. In his encounter with her he had an experience as though his higher self was illumined—as though directing him towards a search for Christ. He confessed to her in a letter from 2 October 1916: 'One has to experience the duality within and then begins the pilgrimage, entirely out of the force of this antithesis. One makes a pilgrimage to oneself.' They decided on a journey through life together. Their betrothal was on Christmas Day 1916, the wedding on 11 August 1918 in Vienna. Nora von Baditz had a supersensible presentiment that they would not find it easy together on the material basis of their marriage—which Stein related to outer circumstances. For that reason he started to prepare himself to become a teacher alongside his further work on the dissertation.

But this further work came to a deadlock. He tried to write down what he had worked out, but the repeated attempts failed. At last he found a fresh starting point. He had become aware through Rudolf Steiner that life and knowledge are inseparable and identical in character. By taking human encounters seriously and through devoted study Stein became conscious that 'there must be a point at which knowledge turns into love.' He informed Rudolf Steiner of this newly acquired piece of insight on 14 March 1917. Love has stages; and when the one who loves experiences the being of the loved one directly within himself, his devotion becomes perception of the other person's being, it acquires the quality of knowledge, which Stein describes as 'direct, intuitive, consolidating into matter, ego-like. One must therefore create a theory of spiritual knowledge based on compassion, on love; otherwise one does not emerge from the ego. One must investigate how the ego experiences the world within itself.' And because the experiencing of the world begins with perception, Stein adds to this an investigation of the inner activity of the ego;

compassion and love are already active in perception and can be enhanced to a limitless receptivity. When this development takes place an awakening to spiritual reality begins; at the same time perception becomes transparent for spiritual realities. Stein draws the conclusion: 'Love (through perception) transforms the objective utilitarian world into a world of revelation for the beings of the hierarchies.' The question he now asked Rudolf Steiner is whether he should steer his work in this direction or 'modestly work out the details, merely comparing historical aspects.'

It was a crisis in the work process. Stein did not know how to continue. Letters piled up in which he searched for a solution to his task and he asked Rudolf Steiner for advice. He had begun the work three years earlier when he began to compare the positions of Locke and Berekely. But he still found himself at the forefront of the attempt to solve the problem. Then followed, after deep contemplation, the confessional letter of 2 June 1917. Once again he described the starting point and the experiences upon which the dissertation was based and how it had progressed up to the time of the breakthrough in knowledge in which he gained insight into the formulation of the theme:

And while I wrestled and struggled, it was all of a sudden clear to me: 'You have to write about Dr Steiner's world conception.' As the idea shone forth all the love flowed up in me. I have never forgotten your glance as it glowed during the lectures and inspired me with new impulses, filling-in a pause for breath or a meaningful gap in the dialogue. The impulse this glance conveyed accompanied me in battles and skirmishes. When the sounds of battle were ringing and metal was whirring—the shrapnel—then there was deep peace within me. And from this peace in the midst of battle there arose my deep love for that which this glance had conveyed to me. I wanted to grasp with my will what sprang up within it so that it might serve this impulse.

What Stein experienced in his innermost soul is echoed in the concluding words of his letter. He wishes to co-operate creatively in discovering for himself the realms of the soul which the Spirit-Investigator had made accessible to him. 'I have been with you in my thoughts lately and with the thoughts which you represent.

10   Nora von Baditz 1917

Let me stand beside you in all modesty with forces which are but weak, but with strong determination. Let me create with you together. The current of living will-forces worked *through* me— I, however, would only engender love and gratitude to all with whom I am so deeply connected—let me be your pupil and your fighting comrade.'

The direction for the work is now clear. The dissertation shall bear the title: 'The Concepts of Modern Natural Science and Goethe's View of the World as represented by Rudolf Steiner.' But the inner regulating factor for the material which had been amassed had not yet been discovered. 'The basic idea which creates unity out of the many details is still lacking. For that I need your help.' Rudolf Steiner responds to this cry for help. The dramatic circumstances are described in the autobiography.

There was a telegram from Rudolf Steiner: 'Am in Berlin for three days longer; can discuss dissertation with you if you can come.' How I hastened to the Ministry of War! I wonder if they will hang me after the event if I now relate what happened. I asked for a few days' leave of absence. 'Leave of absence, and to go abroad, in the middle of the war! Are you mad?' 'Yes' I admitted it, 'I am, but I must see Rudolf Steiner.' 'No, impossible!' So there I stood. There was no higher authority to which I might appeal. At that moment a little private on orderly duty passed by, carrying a mountain-load of papers. He stopped before me, seeing my look of despair. 'What's up?' said he. I showed him my form of application which had been refused. 'I absolutely must go on this journey but the General . . .' 'Put it here,' said the little soldier. And he laid my application on the very top of his pile of papers. A few minutes later he came out again. My application form was signed, signed by the very officer who had only just refused me. I do not know to this day what exactly happened, but a few hours later I was on my way to Berlin.[9]

When Stein arrived in Berlin in the second half of July Rudolf Steiner was already engaged in intense activity. Nevertheless, he was able to spare the time for full length conversations, the main gist of which Stein has preserved for us.[30a] In the centre of the discussion there was, of course, the subject of the dissertation. To the question of its inner intention Rudolf Steiner replied: 'Your dissertation must provide a justification of the supersensible. That is the spiritual aim which you must set yourself.' And then he continued: 'Take exact account in everything you write in your dissertation of the occult realities, but make it so that, while avoiding the occult details, you present the whole occult reality. You will be able to do that if you transform every bit of occult fact into concepts. You will then succeed in remaining in the realm of the theory of knowledge.' Then he handed him the print of the unpublished book: *Anthroposophy*:[31] 'Look, here I have written a book which I have had printed as far as page 64, but I am unable to finish writing it.' Noticing Stein's speechless astonishment he continued: 'Yes, I really cannot. I cannot succeed in forming it in such a way that it can be understood. The book will remain a fragment. But I would like you to read this book tonight, insofar as I have written it, and come again to me early tomorrow. You may not, however, make a word for word copy of it, you may only take notes from it.'

The printing of the book *Anthroposophy* was announced by Rudolf Steiner in December 1910. At that time he set about describing physical man by means of spiritual science, beginning with an extension of the study of the senses. He had first made known the results of his research in the autumn of 1909, seven years after the first introduction of Anthroposophy. But in adapting what had been delivered orally into a written account, insurmountable difficulties arose. The limitations of the language were too great—as he later explained—to hold fast to the imaginations and to put them into words that would give them sharp contours.[32] The almost completed book was laid aside, until in 1951 it was published under the title *Anthroposophy—a Fragment*.

During the years 1916-17—seven years after the lectures on 'Anthroposophy' and the fragmentary written version of the same—Rudolf Steiner took the step of openly challenging the conceptions of natural science. In his book: *Vom Menschenrätsel* (Riddles of Man) 1916, in the final chapter 'Further Prospects,' he says: 'Natural Science forms its views of the world from observation, which cannot be observed by means of its own nature.' It only yields hypotheses and models, because it excludes a knowledge of the essence of things and claims the subjectivity of all qualities such as warmth, colour, sound, scent, etc. In the book which followed—*Riddles of the Soul*[32a], 1917—which contains the now almost completed Study of the Senses and seems to be a metamorphosis of the fragment: *Anthroposophy*, Rudolf Steiner delineates the boundary between natural science, which founds its views on sense observation, and spiritual science, which is based on supersensible experience. Where natural science ends Anthroposophy begins; they correspond to one another as the positive and negative of a photograph.

Rudolf Steiner was engaged upon these fundamental studies, a rounding off of the early writings on the theory of knowledge, when he received the visit of Stein. The impetuous questioner appears to have been a welcome guest; desiring as he did, through his work, to justify the anthroposophical path of knowledge in the eyes of natural science, which was Rudolf Steiner's own declared aim in the book *Riddles of the Soul*.

The result of the visit was that Stein's appetite for asking questions was still further whetted. He decided to inform Marie Steiner about his work and the questions which arose from it, hoping that she might forward to him the answers of Rudolf Steiner. Thus he enquired about what happens when we perceive the colour yellow and he received an answer from Rudolf Steiner which described the occult aspect of this phenomenon at great length.[33] Stein was enraptured. The answer arrived, namely, just at the time when he was preparing to write down his dissertation. In September 1917 he had been given a fortnight's leave which he was spending in the Hungarian home village of his bride in order to be able to find the necessary concentration in the seclusion of the country. And in actual fact he was able to unburden himself of the whole of this inwardly experienced train of thought during this short space of time and set it down in writing in such a form that he only needed to check the quotations when he was at home. In his letters to Rudolf Steiner and Marie Steiner he tells the secret of his treatise's composition. 'Following a definite impulse, I have set out the chapters of my work according to the twelve scenes of Goethe's Fairy Story as one lets these pass before one's mind's eye. There is certainly nothing of this to be found in the work itself, but in the impulse of my soul the Beautiful Lily was giving me help. I owe her a great debt of gratitude.' This is what he wrote to Rudolf Steiner on 24 September—and, almost ecstatically to Marie Steiner on 16 October: 'I feel so little that I am its author, that, without being immodest, I can confidently say that it is a valuable piece of work.'

He was still being carried along on the crest of the wave while writing his neat copy. He read from his work every week at the Vienna Group Meetings. At Christmas 1917 he concluded his readings with a rousing appeal to the will:

Into the cold universal night of a materialistic civilisation the spirit investigator has placed his Anthroposophy to be a fire to which men of today can come to enjoy its light and warmth. I was able to procure this fire for them. Many a log of wood I was able to provide so that it could burn up brightly and supply them with light and warmth. Oh, do not merely warm yourselves at this glowing fire until the flames die down. Let each one take a brand from the fire and bear it like a torch far afield into the materialistic culture of the present day, which is the culture of universal winter's night.

Fire of will and fearlessness in standing up for the truth which he experienced; that is the stamp which characterised Walter Johannes Stein's speaking and writing. But he needed Rudolf Steiner to make corrections and these are what he asked for when he sent him the typed copy of his dissertation on 28 January 1918. Rudolf Steiner read this copy through and added notes. Afterwards a discussion evidently took place in Dornach, for there exists a rough draft of an entry permit for Stein in Rudolf Stiner's handwriting ('because Dr Rudolf Steiner, one of those employed at the Goetheanum, has to hold a discussion with him about his dissertation, which is of importance for his livelihood'), to which was added the explanation: 'After previously held discussions with Walter Stein about the subject of his dissertation, I can attest to the correctness of his assertion that further consultation with me is now necessary, since his revision of the text. Dr Rudolf Steiner, scientific-artistic director of the Goetheanum, Dornach.'

The consultation was with reference to the contents and form of the work, which had to conform to the usual academic requirements. Stein followed all Rudolf Steiner's advice, supplemented and clarified, but deleted a whole chapter. The final draft then bore the title: *Historical critical contribution concerning the development of modern philosophy*.

What was intended by the author can be read in the last paragraph: 'These considerations show that the higher kinds of consciousness are germinally present in human consciousness;

and just as ordinary consciousness finds *its* reality when it pays regard to perceptions by means of concepts and ideas, so do the three stages of higher consciousness find *their* reality in other ways. That these three stages of supersensible knowledge have their sciences, too, it is the purpose of this study of their theory of knowledge to confirm.' The higher kinds of consciousness present in embryo are the imaginative, inspirational and intuitive faculties. These capacities come about as a result of the enhancement and transformation of the human soul forces of thinking, feeling and willing. They embrace the higher spheres of reality which are not accessible to the everyday consciousness. In the language of academic science Stein presented what Rudolf Steiner had put forward in the forms of expression of clairvoyant consciousness concerning the fields of the perception and activity of the hierarchies. The 'theory of knowledge' of these beings was developed by him in the lecture cycle: *The Spiritual Beings in the Heavenly Bodies and in the Kingdoms of Nature*[34] about which Stein says that it was the basis for his doctor's dissertation. 'If one compares these two (lecture cycle and dissertation), one can understand the connection.'[35]

In Stein's experience the sequence of the chapters of his treatise corresponded with the sequence of the scenes in Goethe's Fairy Tale of the Green Snake and the Beautiful Lily. In the background of his last chapter about the different kinds of consciousness there stands the final scene of the Fairy Story: the new Temple beside the river—the confused happenings of our time—and, on the Bridge, striving towards it, the seekers of the Spirit who long to awaken to a higher form of consciousness.

It was a bold undertaking which Stein, the wisdom-seeker, had dared with his dissertation. The first thing he tackled, with Rudolf Steiner's encouragement, was to demonstrate, by scientific means, the appropriateness to our time of the anthroposophical methods of spiritual research. His work establishes the true concept of anthroposophically directed spiritual science, producing clarity about the nature of thinking and discernment. This forms the basis for a science of essential cognition, wherein lies the historical value of Stein's dissertation. But the work remained practically unacknowledged and the relevance and importance of the theme was not noticed owing to the academic language in which it was couched.

Stein also planned a 'habilitation,[*] treatise on the rationalistic philosopher Tetens, to whom can be attributed the view of the threefoldness of the soul functions of thinking, feeling and willing. This subject, too, had been suggested to him by Rudolf Steiner in case the elaboration of the theme of the theory of knowledge should come up against insurmountable difficulties. But Stein succeeded in getting hold of the philosopher Adolf Stöhr to be the mentor for his doctorate. How this came about is related in his memoirs:

The difficulty was to find the professor who would accept it and let it pass as given to me by himself. It was Professor Arthur Stöhr of Vienna who eventually declared himself prepared to do so. I met him on the staircase when I called. What did I want? A subject for a Doctor's Dissertation. He had no time at the moment. 'I must go and get a shave,' he said. 'The barber's shop is round the corner in the adjoining street. If you have time to suggest a subject on the way there, good and well.' 'That will be easy,' said I. 'The difficulty only is, when I have worked out the subject, will Herr Professor recognise it as the one that he agreed to?' 'Write what you like,' he replied, 'only please do not let it be such nonsense as I have had to read this morning. What is it you want to write about?' 'I want to compare the ideas of Nature and the theories of knowledge of Goethe and of Rudolf Steiner,' said I. 'I want to show that human consciousness is only a special kind of consciousness, that there are other forms of consciousness to which we are able to evolve. I want to classify the possible forms of consciousness and examine their relation to what science teaches us about the real world. I want to show the middle way between Locke's one-sided sensualism and Berkeley's denial of all matter.' By this time, however, we had reached the barber's shop. The professor stopped, looked at me keenly, and said: 'I shall remember all right. But one thing more. You are taking the Psychology Examination too, I suppose?' 'Yes, Herr Professor.' 'Well now, there are two possibilities. Either I shall be examining you, or else my colleague Höfler.[†] But if you come to me and tell me Höfler's things, you will probably be ploughed. On the other hand, if you go to Höfler and tell him my things, you will be ploughed before you get there. What will you do?' And at that he disappeared into the shop.[9]

---

[*] A habilitation treatise is what is submitted when one wishes to qualify as a teacher in a German University (Translator's note).

[†] In Austria as in several other European countries, most examinations are oral—note by W.J. Stein.

Stöhr belongs, as does Höfler, to the forgotten ones of Austria's cultural life.[36] He was the pupil of Ernst Mach, a philosopher of Natural Science and a precursor of Russian Marxism, whereas Höfler belonged to the School of Brentano, the psychologist whom Rudolf Steiner appraised so highly.[37]

The final completion of the dissertation dragged on until the summer of 1918. Stein was spared any further service at the Front. He was able to continue his work in Vienna—amidst the disintegration of the multi-national state, of which the military force was long since spent. After the collapse he devoted himself to bringing about the new regulating of society, which Rudolf Steiner described as the 'Threefold Social Order'. Simultaneously he prepared himself for the oral examination by studying Rudolf Steiner's *Riddles of Philosophy* and the lecture cycles connected therewith. He quoted from this during the examinations, giving unreserved acknowledgement to the anthroposophical point of view. When one examiner asked him how it was that he himself could not understand the books of Rudolf Steiner, Stein did not mince matters, but told him outright: 'You have trained your thinking too one-sidedly in the School of Kant. Kant looks for the reality of things behind the phenomena, instead of in the relative connections.' The sureness and strength of Stein's argument resulted in him passing both the philosophical and mathematical examinations with fourfold first class honours. He telegraphed the results to Rudolf Steiner in Dornach; and it was through him that Nora Stein, who was studying eurythmy there, heard about it. Thus, the adventure in knowledge which began with the memorable conversation with Rudolf Steiner about Locke and Berkeley, came to a provisional conclusion.

II
TURNING-POINT OF CONSCIOUSNESS

1
A Historical Year of Decision

Through his work on the theory of knowledge Walter Johannes Stein had experienced the immediacy of the ego at first hand. By perceiving such personal independence he became aware of the spiritual dignity of the individual. At this juncture of his life he was a witness to a historical event which was to be of importance for his own actions two decades later.

At the height of the war Rudolf Steiner had worked out an 'outline of facts' for the Powers of Middle Europe as a response to the historical situation. It was contained in two diplomatic communications which were to be conveyed to the German and Austrian Governments. Through such an initiative it was hoped to prepare the way for a peaceful negotiation to take place. That was the state of affiars in July 1917 when Stein arrived in Berlin. As things turned out Stein was informed about events and was given an important task as courier. He speaks about this in his autobiography:

So I saw Rudolf Steiner again, and it turned out to be an important meeting. Count Ludwig Polzer-Hoditz was hurrying away as I came up to Dr Steiner's door. I had known him for a long time, and we were close friends. At this moment he was deathly pale. I asked him what was the matter. 'I am to get an important document across the frontier', was his reply, 'a letter to the Emperor Karl of Austria'. 'Give it to me', said I. 'No, no; at least I must first ask the Doctor'. So I came into the room. It was in July 1917.

The said document was the memorandum, which was to be conveyed to the Austrian Emperor through the mediacy of his Cabinet Minister Count Arthur Polzer, the brother of Ludwig. Stein continues.

I was prepared to act as messenger. Dr Steiner, however, insisted that I should know what I was carrying, and read the memorandum out to me before handing it over. In Vienna I was simply to post it in a letter-box. Through this event I heard for the first time Dr Steiner's ideas of what should be done in Middle Europe.

I wondered how I should dispose of the paper on my way across the frontier. 'Put it in your suit-case on the very top', said Dr Steiner. So there it lay when I reached the customs. The custom's officer picked it up, put it on one side, and proceeded to rummage through all my other things; thereupon he carefully put the paper on the top again, closed the suit-case and marked it as passed in the customary way.[37]

Polzer adds to this a characteristic detail in his memoirs: 'Walter Johannes Stein said at the time in fun—but in this fun lay the greatest amount of devotion and willingness to help—"in case of emergency I will swallow it." '[38]

Rudolf Steiner's deed stands in relation to a dramatic historical occasion. In the year 1917 the events pressed upon one another. The Tzar was forced to abdicate in March. In April America entered the war. Also in the same month Lenin returned to Russia from exile in Switzerland with the permission of the highest officials of the war cabinet and prepared the revolution with the support of the German Government. The concentration of forces in the West, the vacuum in the East and, added to that, the growing helplessness in the political and military command in the leadership of Middle Europe: this situation moved Count Otto Lerchenfeld to implore Rudolf Steiner for advice. Lerchenfeld was a member of the Anthroposophical Society and, being a cabinet minister of the first Chamber in Bavaria, he was thoroughly familiar with the political situation. His appeal gave Rudolf Steiner the impulse to explain his spiritual scientific views about the constitution of the State and Society to leading politicians. Before that, however, he had elaborated the basic facts of the polito-social reality in a study with Count Lerchenfeld which lasted over three weeks.[39] From this first introductory social-knowledge course Lerchenfeld formed the opinion that politics is an art and that political dealings demand an adequate artistic imagination in line with the processes of life.

Towards the end of this work Rudolf Steiner called on Count Ludwig Polzer-Hoditz, too, a man who was just as familiar with

Austrian conditions as Lerchenfeld was with those of Germany. Polzer, grounded in Anthroposophy and in the German cultural heritage, was wrestling with the question as to what form of positive political policy in agreement with the spirit of Central Europe must take, for he saw in advance that the materialistic attitude of its official representatives would lead to the self-destruction of the Central Powers.[38] In actual fact, a nodal-point of historical development had been attained, the beginning of a new epoch was breaking, which was being announced through flashes and lapses of consciousness, through the world-war catastrophe and in social crises. In the forefront of events were the social and governmental reorganisations, as the Tzarist government fell and the Habsburg monarchy disintegrated and German defeat was foreseeable. Should the rehabilitation take place under the sign of Communism or under that of the 'sovereign rights of the people' which the American President Wilson advocated? What had Germany to offer in this 'age of ideology' which began in 1917? The historian Karl Dietrich Bracher speaks of three world historic answers which became operative as a reaction to the challenge of the industrial revolution, of nationalism and imperialism: liberal democracy represented by America, communistic dictatorship as it was built up by Lenin in Russia, and radical nationalistic authoritarianism which found its most extreme expression in fascism and national socialism.[40]

All three answers are present today in the first, second, and third worlds. These three answers embody great misunderstandings, however: the autonomous misunderstanding which hopes for satisfaction through the sovereign rights of the people; the collectivistic misconception which relies upon the attainment of world socialism; the nationalistic misconception which looks for the revival of the autarchic communal State. The misunderstandings were followed very soon by disappointments and wrong decisions—until the outbreak of the second world war; for this trinity of answers lies in a 'misunderstanding of the realities and truths of the first world war.' Such are the conclusions of Bracher.

These misunderstood realities will be recognised by a deeper knowledge of the development of human relationships. Not only the great drive of the industrial epoch, nationalism and imperialism have to be taken into account, but also the new, very real factor which has shown up since the beginning of the modern age: the power of the individual, which, along with the newly acquired intellectuality, has conquered the sense world and discovered the 'ego' at the centre of man's consciousness and stands up in defence of human rights.

The one who gets a hold over himself comes up more and more against State institutions, against their power politics and universal authority. For that which we call the State is a relic of a far distant past, at a time when the King was the State and the State still claimed to be a human being. The glory which surrounded such a person was handed down from the age of the divinity of kings, as when the Pharaoh ruled over his people as their divinely inspired leader. In the twentieth century the development has progressed so far that the principle of centralising power in the State can give way to a free agreement between mature citizens, which would eliminate the domination of one person over another. The dramatic development of events at the outbreak of the First World War revealed the due historical date when this should have been aknowledged. The hour had struck in which the political structures could have been so altered as to conform to the stage of maturity actually attained by modern mankind. This human historical challenge was answered by Rudolf Steiner by evolving a method of social awareness and upbuilding, which would have allowed a realistic political action to have been put into practice. A way of dealing which would not have failed to take account of the realities, as did the provocative ideologies of East and West, which appeared simultaneously in 1917—those exaggerated power-claims serving either a communistic world revolution or a universal democratisation. Rudolf Steiner called his answer: 'the threefold social order.'

This answer stems from the spiritual perception of the laws of evolution, from the knowledge that a historic turning point has been reached and that an advance in consciousness is due. The crossing of the threshold to spiritual reality is being unconsciously experienced; and this threshold-experience is expressed in the becoming aware of one's own inner autonomy. Rudolf Steiner described this metamorphosis of consciousness in the twentieth century as 'humanity's threshold event.' A sense organ is being developed for what is to happen in future, a sense for what is in the process of becoming, what is asleep at present and has to be awakened into present day existence. An awakening to the reality of the formative and creative powers, for the etheric world, has begun.

For such a form of consciousness as this arrives at its views about a social order by investigating the different spheres of human relationship through their various qualities. The basic conditions vary according to whether a person achieves the results owing to his own ability, whether he is seeking to satisfy his material or spiritual needs, or whether he is engaged in making treaties or drawing up contracts with his fellow men. These three basic activities belong to the functional bodies of culture, commerce and the legal system. Rudolf Steiner was the first to connect their inherent laws with the ideals of the French Revolution and to show that Freedom, as a condition of creative activity, is the basic principle of spiritual life; Equality is a constituent part of the democratic state, and Fraternity the basis of division of labour in commerce in which everyone is dependent on the goods produced by all others.

What Stein conceived just then of 'the threefold economy' came to him in a flash. It was no utopian idea, it was the expression of the new type of thought which he himself had been trying for years to acquire. In this way peace could be established in the world and work could be undertaken towards the creating of a threefold society demanded of the time. For that his eager soul, thirsting for action, was all aflame.

Stein then carefully studied the sequence of events which had led Rudolf Steiner to intervene in the course of historical happenings. He was struck ever more forcibly by the appropriateness of this attempted solution, which was to have safeguarded the living rights of Middle Europe and prevented a split of the world into two sections. The antagonism between Washington and Moscow, out of which the Russo-American military polarity has grown, first became apparent in 1917. The danger of a bipolar world-order, threatening the social structure of humanity, appeared above the horizon; for when the principle of duality becomes accepted, according to which the existence of the enemy creates the possibility of achieving one's own ambitions of domination, a state of tension is created, but no state of peace.

In such a dangerous situation as this a third factor must come into play, which will mediate as a bridge. This historically necessary task was conceived by Rudolf Steiner as belonging to Central Europe, but to a spiritually productive Central Europe which, instead of being militarily on the offensive, would engage in a foreign policy that wages battle with ideas. It should begin with the memorandum of July 1917,[40a] the leading sentence which reads: 'When human beings become free, so will the nations become free *through them*.' Rudolf Steiner wanted to show the contrast between the free choice of mankind within a threefold society and the free choice which Wilson was offering the people as the basis of his territorial new deal.

In the light of the end of the century the endeavours of Rudolf Steiner become ever more significant. His anthroposophical friends with whom he conversed at that time were already impressed by the unusual approach. Friedrich Rittelmeyer, the first leader of the Christian Community, writes: 'In those early months of the year 1917, when Rudolf Steiner came upon the scene, the historical picture was remarkable in the extreme. Out of unknown obscurity appears a man. He goes to the statesmen of Middle Europe and shows them the way to salvation.

Today it can be clearly seen that this indeed would have been the only way to salvation. The statesmen listened to him with interest and partial agreement, but not one of them had the strength and courage to act.'[41] Lerchenfeld related in 1932 that Rudolf Steiner had explained to him during the study they did together from June 1917: 'Work on it, but never work with the idea of success!' When Lerchenfeld expressed the opinion that what Rudolf Steiner proposed to do was impracticable, he received the reply: 'That is so. But just consider that world evolution progresses.'[42]

Polzer remarked in his *Political Observations* that the lack of understanding among the politicians to whom Rudolf Steiner had spoken stemmed from a weakness of comprehension, from an inability to grasp the change of consciousness which was taking place in the twentieth century. 'Those who had been approached with the first outline of the statement about the threefold social order were actually being asked to recognise and to sense a little of what is meant by the catastrophe of the world war in connection with this turning-point of humanity's progress.'[39]

In the year 1916 peace negotiations appeared to be possible, when the war had reached the stage of military stalemate. In

December Germany declared its willingness to make peace. Shortly afterwards there followed Wilson's call for peace. The answer from the side of the Allies, who spoke about the wish to attack, and the desire for domination on the part of the Central Powers, made it obvious that there was no longer any chance of peace through understanding. The perception of Novalis was confirmed: 'It is impossible for temporal powers to come into balance by their own exertions, only a third power, which is both temporal and celestial at the same time, is able to achieve this.'[42a]

Rudolf Steiner, who held lectures on contemporary history in December 1916 and January 1917 and commented therein on current affairs, explained the meaning of this answer which the Allies gave to Wilson's appeal: 'It is a challenge to truth and reality. That is taking things too far. They hoped, that by challenging the spiritual world, the spiritual world itself would of necessity put the matter right, even though it is human beings who have to provide it with the tools to do so.'[43]

It was Rudolf Steiner who answered the challenge. And his answer was the idea of a social structure compatible with the being of man, created out of insight into the laws of evolution and uttered at the time of a turning-point in evolution.

At a time when the whole of mankind is growing together into a unity, into a world-fellowship, a global ordering of life is needed in order to ensure man's survival. Only when the power principle is replaced by the will to understand one's neighbours, will the nations live under equal rights side by side with one another; economic exploitation will be overcome and the production of goods suited to the actual needs of every branch of mankind will set free the spiritually productive powers in their cultural diversity. The example for this social order demanded of our age is to be given by the peoples of Central Europe, who are able to see themselves as at the centre of the East-West-Polarity. Such a centre as this, striving after a build-up of consciousness and not of power, is of vital importance to the whole body of mankind. And when the existence of this centre was put in jeopardy during the World War, Rudolf Steiner wanted to prove its right of existence through a deed which served the progress of mankind and made peace among nations possible.

Stein perceived directly the importance and necessity of such a mode of action.

2
Fighters for the Threefold Social Order

'After having discarded my lieutenant's uniform I decided to hold lectures on the social question.' This was the contribution which Stein wished to make towards the problems of the day, when, in late 1918, the great Habsburg regime collapsed and a political change began to take place in the small Austrian State. The world was changed after the breakdown of the authoritarian regimes in Russia, Austro-Hungary and Germany. People were gripped by a feeling that they were standing at an important moment in history, an almost messianic expectation and the hope of more just conditions prevailed. Was the breakthrough to a new social order possible at this historic moment—or did a retrogression to the old forms of consciousness and behaviour threaten?

Since the second half of December of that year Stein was living in Dornach, where his wife was studying eurythmy, the art of movement developed by Rudolf Steiner. He listened to the members' lectures which took place regularly in the workshop, and took part in a tour of the Goetheanum building led by Rudolf Steiner. The painting of the inside of the cupolas was still in progress. Rudolf Steiner himself painted the central motive—the figure of Christ—and the southern half of the small cupola. The visitors climbed the scaffolding-steps to get a closer look at the painting technique, which was not a colouring in of contoured lines but a form which arose out of the colour itself. What Stein experienced had such a lasting effect on him that he soon decided to write something, which he then sent to Rudolf Steiner. His composition closed with a reference to the forthcoming social activity of the spiritual investigator: 'Whoever gets to know Dr Rudolf Steiner in his manifold capacities as painter, sculptor, architect, philosopher, poet and full and complete human being, will also grasp why it is that this unique personality is at present searching for ways to co-operate actively in a new kind of institution for a proper social structure for mankind.'[44]

The practical application of Anthroposophy was being prepared since the end of the First World War. Rudolf Steiner at first conveyed his spiritual knowledge through the language of scientific concepts and ideas, then he embodied it in the element of artistic forms; next there followed a third step: his intervention in the process of history through social acts. Rudolf Steiner says of the latter phase of the anthroposophical movement that it had been initiated by the 'aspirations' of Stuttgart friends.[45]

The case is this. There was a group of active anthroposophists in Stuttgart, among whom were several business people who wished to prepare the ground for the three-fold social work by means of an industrial trust company. On the instruction of this group advice was sought from Rudolf Steiner in Dornach by Emil Molt, the wealthy director of the Waldorf-Astoria Cigarette factory, the sociologist Roman Boos and Hans Kühn, who had volunteered for work on the Threefold Commonwealth Scheme. At the end of January 1919 the two-day conference took place, out of which actions of great consequence evolved. Rudolf Steiner wrote his proclamation 'To the German People and the Civilised World,'[45a] which gave a sketch of the new methods for social understanding and construction. The way of the Threefold Social Order was to lead the German nation out of the catastrophe which was the result of having succumbed to the thoughtless power-drive of the Bismarck Empire. Rudolf Steiner next gave the impulse for the founding of free schools 'in order to teach people what they needed to know.' Thirdly, came the plan to publish the memoirs of the late Helmuth von Moltke, who died in 1916, who had been the Chief of the General Staff of the German army up to the time of the Battle of the Marne. This document, which contained a detailed account of the Berlin incidents at the outbreak of war, was intended to provide the German Delegation at the forthcoming Peace Conference in Versailles with a counter argument to the contention that it was Germany which was solely to blame for the war.

2 February, the day when Rudolf Steiner handed his 'proclamation' to the visitors from Stuttgart, is the true date of the birth of the Threefold Commonwealth Movement, according to Molt.[46] In order to prepare the ground for the Movement for Social

Renewal, which had emanated from Stuttgart, the text was published in German, Austrian and Swiss newspapers with the names of the signatories, among which were many prominent personalities. As the threefold movement developed, Stein, who had played the part of messenger from the very first beginning of the idea, now gradually inherited the task of making the ideas familiar to the public.

It seemed as if a pattern of destiny would be repeated. At first, aloof from the proceedings, Stein was called in, this time by Molt, to whom Rudolf Steiner, during the two-day conference, had declared: 'There the young Stein from Vienna is hanging about in Dornach wanting to speak to me about an occupation.' Upon this Molt interviewed the workless young man, who was prepared at a moment's notice to gather signatures for the proclamation in Austria. The picture of the ill-clad Stein, with his rucksack and a hundred francs in his pocket, on his way to Vienna, made an impression on Molt.

The journey first went by way of Berne, where Stein sought an extension of his residence permit at the central office of the Aliens' Police. On 5 February he was in Zürich, where Rudolf Steiner had just started his public activity on behalf of the Threefold Social Movement. In the four basic lectures under the heading *The Social Question*[47] he presented to an international audience the results of his research, which he then later summarised in the four chapters of his book: *Towards Social Renewal*.[48] In Zürich Stein had the opportunity of a conversation, the result of which he noted down with a mention of the exact time and place it occurred: 'Twelve o'clock Hotel Bauer, Paradeplatz, conversation with Rudolf Steiner. Then, with him and Frau Dr Steiner in the Vegetarian Restaurant in Fusslistrasse. The Doctor said to Herrn Strakosch:[48a] 1. Body 2. Plane 3. Line 4. Point 5. Inner Space 6. Energy-Space 7. Space without. To me: Evolve towards initiation. If one says "A" then one also says "B".' It was the day before his twenty-eighth birthday; he stood at the threshold of the fifth septennial of his life, which became for him also a cross-roads in his life.

'"Evolve towards initiation", lead the "spirit-pupil" along the path of development,' that was regarded by Rudolf Steiner as his 'deed of inauguration.'[49] Evidently this 'spirit-pupil' was also to be set on the path of development and engage in the pursuit of a methodical spiritual training. At any rate, this word from the mouth of Rudolf Steiner which Stein received at a turning-point in his career, became for him his life's programme.

Next day he travelled on to Vienna where he became actively engaged in the collecting of signatures. The action in which, apart from Count Polzer, Kolisko was also involved, was brought to a conclusion already on the 12 February. At his lecture on 15 February Rudolf Steiner read out the telegram he had received from Vienna: 'Total result: 93 signatures.' Among these were the signatures of well known authors, such as Hermann Bahr, Marie Eugenie della Grazie and Jakob Wassermann. Count Arthur Polzer-Hoditz, the former cabinet minister of Emperor Karl, had also signed, as well as the well-known art-critic Joseph Strzÿgowski.

As to what concerned Stein's prospects in life, he had felt since the end of the war as though he were standing 'before an empty void'. He was challenged by the meaning of life and the need to earn a livelihood: what tasks must he undertake in order to fulfil his destiny? He was without fixed abode, always depending on his friends and acquaintances for provisional accommodation, without financial means. It was similar for his wife, who was undergoing further training. Living together was not to be contemplated at the moment. He wrote a letter of consolation to her in Dornach: 'Serve the work; wait until destiny brings us together.' The general economic situation was oppressive after four and a half years of war. Whoever wished to move house had to have an immigration permit which was not to be obtained without a warrant. Then the weary business of searching for a house began, queuing for rations, the worry about fuel supplies. But the determination 'to serve the work' carried him over all difficulties.

Stein moved to Stuttgart where Rudolf Steiner was eagerly awaited. The 'proclamation' appeared in the papers at the beginning of March and was distributed as a leaflet. A preparatory committee had been formed in Stuttgart composed of the Attorney-at-law Wilhelm von Blume from Tübingen, the creator of the Württemberg constitution (not a member of the Anthroposophical Society), Carl Unger and Emil Molt. The first exploratory gathering was held at the end of March.

During this unquiet spring the second act of the revolution

took place, starting in November 1918 with the fall of the Monarchy. When, to begin with, only the façade of the German Empire had been democratised, a revolutionary stream began to be active, which, supported by the workers, sought to do away completely with what was old. Conditions similar to civil war began to show themselves and the power struggle in Munich, which degenerated into terrorism, threatened Stuttgart, too; but, in well-nigh provincial settings, things passed without incident, although, as a result of the general strike and of the exceptional circumstances, real street battles raged. That was the contemporary background facing the speakers who were telling about the Threefold State. They found an audience, especially among the workers, who became attentive because the descriptions—as distinct from party political speeches—appealed to a deeper understanding.

On 8 March, after a two-day journey, Stein arrived in Stuttgart, which he remembered from his 'educational tour,' as a delightful 'garden city.' He met Hans Kühn in the train, who later became the business manager of the committee for the German Threefold Commonwealth Movement. Soon afterwards he himself had to arrange the business premises in Vienna. In Stuttgart he soon got to know the leading anthroposophists and borrowed from them the lecture-cycles of Rudolf Steiner, which at that time were not available in bookshops. The latest members' lectures were circulating in handwritten notes, of which he made copies. In addition to that he was engaged in the publishing of his dissertation and preparing himself for the oral examination for his doctor's degree. Later, it was said, Stein only read lecture-cycles at that time instead of doing any work.

Finally Rudolf Steiner, accompanied by Marie Steiner, arrived in Stuttgart. His arrival had been delayed on account of the publication of his book: *Towards Social Renewal*. From the end of April until the end of July Stuttgart became the centre of the Threefold Commonwealth Movement. In the space of a quarter of a year the proceedings crowded together, which were aimed at a change in society to bring it in line with the Threefold Social Order: historical actions which did not become a part of history. That it would have been possible at that time to arrive at a breakthrough was noted by the English historian Barraclough. He established the fact that towards the end of the nineteenth century a new world was developing in the shadow of the old; 'after 1918 it acquired an identity and a life of its own . . . but it is remarkable how quickly the danger of a radical social upheaval was suppressed after 1919.'[50]

Stein participated intensely in the stormy events connected with the Threefold Social Movement. No day now passed without being fully occupied with the various enterprises. There were lectures for members of the Anthroposophical Society, for the workers of the Waldorf-Astoria Cigarette factory, for the employees of the Bosch and the Daimler works, discussions in the Trade Union Headquarters, as well as committee meetings and inner council advisory meetings and private discussions with individuals. All that was reflected in the meagre notes from Stein's diary. He notes for 25 April: '5 o'clock Daimler lecture. After lecture address by Dr Riebensam, Manager of Daimler Works . . . Dr (Steiner) is very hoarse.' The description by Herbert Hahn, Stein's later colleague in the Waldorf School, illustrates the situation. Regular discussions took place after the lectures: the members of the audience sat at tables where alcohol was served.

It was never perfectly quiet, because one could always hear the clinking of beer mugs, amongst which the admittedly very subdued, but nevertheless perceptible buzzing sound of voices was intermingled. People were smoking away like chimneys . . . There was a chairman of the meeting with a tinkling bell, there were verbal contributions dealt with in turn, there were calls to order which interrupted everything. The whole proceedings were not at all prim and proper but were geared to straight talk where rough blows were exchanged.[51]

The Waldorf teacher E.A.K. Stockmeyer experienced a lecture given to metal workers which was like the rumblings of a thunderstorm. Rudolf Steiner called upon his audience to recognise the root cause of social distress in the fact that human gifts were not able to be freely developed, because the centralised State prevented people developing spiritual life and those who were financially badly off were precluded from places of learning. After the lecture a unanimous resolution was passed which was to be sent to the Württemberg Government to ask that Rudolf Steiner be called immediately to put into practice 'the threefold

11   W.J Stein about 1920

commonwealth, which appears to be the only solution to the threatened destruction.'

But amidst the rush of events during 'the Stuttgart weeks' there were still opportunities for talks with Rudolf Steiner. In reply to a written enquiry of Stein as to what he should do, the following discussion ensued: ' "Would you be willing to go to Berlin?" asked Doctor Rudolf Steiner. "I am completely uprooted. I will accept any job" I answered. "Well, we will talk about it further on Sunday." ' Rudolf Steiner considered a moment whether he should ask Stein to become secretary to him and Marie Steiner in Berlin, then, however, he posted him to Vienna as a lecturer. He received concrete advice concerning this task. He had Rudolf Steiner's example before him and realised that it was necessary first to introduce a touch of spirituality by presenting the basic principles; after that the best way would be to observe the effects and then to begin work with those who were willing. He had learned that the Threefold State is not a programme of instruction, but opens the way to practical social understanding, which, according to circumstances, can be applied to a variety of measures. Rudolf Steiner then thought it fit that, when resolutions were passed, Count Ludwig Polzer should be put forward for a seat in parliament. And, as for his oral examination, that should be speedily despatched. Stein noted in his diary: 'Learn *Riddles of Philosophy* by heart.'

He left Stuttgart on 12 May. He had to start with a disbursement in Vienna, too, because he was completely without means. 'I had enough capital,' he writes in his memoirs, 'to hire a hall but not enough to put up posters. I could not therefore afford to make any break in my lectures, for I always had to announce the next lecture during the one I was giving. I earned just enough to keep me from starvation.'[9]

The stay in Vienna lasted three months. The entries in the diary, which were now pretty regular, show the variety of his activities. What he experienced in Stuttgart was informative for him, especially the first of Rudolf Steiner's lectures to the workmen of the Waldorf-Astoria Cigarette factory.

Its title 'Proletarian demands and their future practical application' was used by Stein when he made his first public appearance on 25 July. In preparing this he brought to mind the contents and artistic technique of Rudolf Steiner's lecture. The images of this 'unique and historic lecturing event' stood out in his mind's eye.[52] An audience of 800, mainly female workers, had gathered in the tobacco store and had arranged themselves informally in picturesque groups, the youngest on the piled up bales of tobacco. Rudolf Steiner showed that the social question is a spiritual question: the proletarian has been cheated of his birthright through being deprived of further education and thereby suffers a 'curtailment of culture.' He could be relieved of distress of body and soul if a social order were to be instituted which would allow every person a free education until his eighteenth year. No doubt Stein reiterated this statement and varied it.

Stein's closest collaborators were Count Ludwig Polzer and the Dutch wholesale merchant Josef van Leer, who owned an international timber firm in Vienna. The first problem was to acquire the means for various enterprises. For this he sought— but to no avail—to get in touch with Ludwig Wittgenstein who had put a hundred thousand kroner, from his fortune of millions, at the disposal of Austrian artists and had already made provisions for Rilke and Trakl. The 'proclamation' was printed with 5,000 copies, the book, *Towards Social Renewal*, was displayed in bookshops, three copies of it were sent to Moscow—where the painter Margarita Woloschin and the author Andrej Belyj tried to work out of Anthroposophy. Discussions were held with party representatives and parliamentary delegates, talks were had with the state education authorities responsible for the cultural needs of the army and the arranging of study groups in military bases. The course of such a *Social Renewal* study group in the great barrack rooms and dormitories was described by the engineer Alexander Strakosch, the first teacher of technology at the Waldorf School, in his memoirs.

The work-group leader sat on a many times folded army blanket with a table behind him upon which there burned a candle in the neck of an empty beer bottle, because the current had failed once again. In front of him sat those who wished to learn, whilst the others played cards in the background. Most of them were very young cadets, already recruited at 18, who were now looking for a direction in life, since the political collapse, and were enquiring about conditions required for a society worthy of human beings.

But, regardless of outer difficulties and the press of work, Stein managed to pass his oral examination with flying colours.

However, hard on the heels of Stein's brilliant achievement and coinciding with the climax of his activity on behalf of the Threefold Commonwealth, critical situations developed. He was confronted with self-knowledge, reflected as by a mirror held out to him by someone unknown to him and by Viennese friends. He seemed to hear a summons 'to guard against conforming to convention or being led astray by fanatical impulses.' (30 July) 'It is clear to me how much my capacity for love has been taken away from me owing to the fact that I can penetrate beyond the senses. An important soul experience.' (31 July) It is like getting to know those soul powers of the depths which appear to imaginative perception in the form of 'the double.'

A chapter of his life had come to an end, work on the Threefold Commonwealth had reached a kind of conclusion. In the political and economic sphere nothing had come of the enterprise, on all hands the persistent forces had gained the upper hand. There was still a faint chance that new developments could be achieved in the cultural sphere. Stein held a lecture on 1 August on the subject of 'Knowledge of man's being as the basis of future education and of schools.' Three weeks later Rudolf Steiner started his first course for teachers: 'Study of Man.'

In a situation which demanded inner and outer decisions, Stein sent a letter to Rudolf Steiner containing no less than sixty questions. The answer came back immediately—that is, through a telephone call from Emil Molt: 'Rudolf Steiner,' he said, 'has had your letter, containing sixty questions. He cannot possibly answer in writing, but he invites you to attend the course of lectures he is just about to give to the teachers in the school which is being opened for the children of my employees. He asks me to tell you that all your sixty questions will find an answer in this lecture-course.'[9]

After this message Stein travelled by the next train to Stuttgart.[53]

3
'A Festive Deed in Earthly Life'

By June 1919 it was already obvious that the Threefold Social Movement was not going to succeed. The influence of the Trades Unions and the political parties, which opposed the new and turned back to the old policies and strategy, was growing ever stronger. Certainly, the number of those participating was too small and a comprehension of the extent and depth of the social change could only come about slowly. So it was that the will for renewal which had been excluded from the political field, now concentrated on the founding of a free school, which could become the source of free spiritual life independently of all outside influences. It is historically due to the efforts of Emil Molt that the first free school, the first Waldorf School, could come into existence.

The Swabian businessman had already known Rudolf Steiner in pre-war days. He had found the answers to his questions about life through his study of Anthroposophy, deepened through his membership of the 'Esoteric School.' Since that time he had endeavoured to put into practice what he had learned from spiritual science. He provided examplary social conditions for the workers in his factory and founded the school which bears the name of his firm for the children of his employees. This founding of the school presented a risk which demanded enterprising courage, the capacity for moral intuition and willingness to make financial sacrifices. Molt remained faithful to his self-appointed task and gave his support for the school's continuance till the end of his life.

23 April is reckoned as the school's actual 'birthday',[54] for it was on this day that the decision was made. In the meeting of the shop-committee after Rudolf Steiner's first lecture to the workers of the Waldorf-Astoria cigarette factory, Molt expressed his intention of

founding a school for the children of his co-workers; he asked Rudolf Steiner to establish and run the school—and he received an acceptance. Already four and a half months later the inauguration ceremony was able to take place with 256 children in 8 classes. The festive deed which was carried out in Stuttgart's largest hall with the strong participation of the public was regarded by Molt as the culmination of his life's work. But this event was only the conclusion of a sequence of acts which can arouse profound admiration. Molt recalls: 'After that initial discussion (on 23 April) the realisation of the plans was taken up with burning enthusiasm. Apart from the idea and our spiritual leader there was nothing tangible at our disposal, with the exception of the initial sum (100,000 Marks net profit from 1918) and the 200 children to be educated. Next we had to negotiate with the Education Authorities, teachers had to be sought and trained, a building was to be found with corresponding facilities, in short—one was faced in every respect with a completely new beginning!' Out of private funds Molt bought the 'Uhlandshöhe Restaurant', a favourite haunt of holiday makers around Stuttgart, and had it altered according to Rudolf Steiner's instructions for use as a school building. Later he acquired the surrounding property and bequeathed it to the school. He was the school's 'Daddy', just as Bertha Molt was the school's 'Mummy', always ready with practical help and suggestions. Then he engaged in preparatory talks with E.A.K. Stockmeyer and Herbert Hahn, who offered their help as colleagues: Stockmeyer, an anthroposophist of long standing and a trained teacher from Mannheim not yet employed, who had approached the question of education through pamphlets after the war, and the Baltic-German teacher Hahn who had started a workers' study course in the Waldorf-Astoria cigarette factory. The President of the Board of Education agreed to the plan of a standardised primary school [one in which all children were accepted]. The prospective techers needed no State-Certificate at that time, according to the law governing private schools which originated in 1836 (!), and this eased the already difficult problem of finding teachers. By the end of June it had reached the stage where Rudolf Steiner could ask Stockmeyer to provide the addresses of teachers who were known to be Anthroposophists and to 'set out on a journey, like a theatre manager looking for his cast ... As soon as he had an

overall pictire, then he would give a course. During the course
and at the end of it it would then be decided who would take part
in the running of the school.'[55] And that is how it came about.
Stockmeyer set out on a longish journey, visited the prospective
teachers, gave them information about the intended enterprise
and met with readiness to co-operate. Thus a circle of people was
formed which was joined by others who wished to found schools
in their own districts. In addition a doctor, a scientist, a lady artist
and an engineer were invited—and, of course, Emil and Bertha
Molt, so that finally the circle comprised more than 20 people
(see appendix).

Stein was on a lecture tour in Heilbronn and Göppingen before
the start of the course, so that he was unable to be present when
Rudolf Steiner greeted those who were there on the evening
before it started.

On the following morning at 9.00 a.m.—it was Thursday 21
August—the whole circle met together in the so-called 'blue
room' of the house of the Stuttgart-Group. It was a large
conference room of which not only the walls were blue but in
which all the furniture had also been painted blue. The participants sat round a long table, at the head of which Rudolf Steiner
and Marie Steiner took their places.

Stein felt himself in an unusual position in this circle. Rudolf
Steiner had named him on the previous evening as one of the
guests. He was taking part here as a temporary guest, hoping for
an answer to his questions. He felt very grateful for the favour
shown him by his destiny at this hour and awaited what was to
come with great excitement. Since his meeting with Rudolf
Steiner in Vienna his soul had become more receptive to the
intimations of his destiny.

With a solemn opening speech Rudolf Steiner inaugurated the
founding of the new education out of the spirit. The basis for the
new educational work was laid down during two and a half weeks
of work. The impression which it made was so overwhelming that
Stein could only talk about it in restrained words: 'In my life at any
rate, it was a turning point. There opened out before our eyes a
Science of Man beyond our highest expectations. The human
being in his development arose most wonderfully before our
inner vision through Rudolf Steiner's lectures.'[9]

Three courses running parallel to one another awakened the

consciousness of the future teachers to the tasks of the art of teaching.[56] Knowledge of Man and a sense for education were stimulated, inner decisions and resolutions were brought about. Stein experienced it all as an inner re-forming process, as a call to his developing self to integrate it consciously into the spiritual world, which is akin to the higher self. To strive towards the spirit! That was the call he perceived. That was the way for the teacher to become an artist in his work and to acquire a sensitive organ for what was in process of developing and to help the child further along the stages of its development towards its human goal.

The intensity and reverence with which Stein took everything in was noted by Herbert Hahn who sat beside him. The silence which had been imposed upon the visiting guest increased the power of his concentration. 'But *how* this man listened! The way that Rudolf Steiner's train of thought was reflected in the expression of his face, in his eyes—yes, even in the movement of his shoulders—was more eloquent than the detailed discourses of many another. Stein gave his attention a further emphasis. The whole of this time he was holding a little yellowish-grey bone square in his left hand, the sort that is used for geometrical drawings. Every few minutes he applied it to his page and one could truly hear with what ardour he underlined his notes.'[57]

The solemn opening speech of the course was concluded by Rudolf Steiner with the words: 'We should all regard ourselves as human beings placed by karma on a place where something is about to happen of no ordinary importance, but something which will strike those who are participating as a "festive world moment".' The etheric forces which drew the first colleagues together he called 'fulfilled karma'; and he explained during the first teachers' conference on 20 Setpember 1919: 'We come together in this way because we have sought one another.'

Rudolf Steiner called the founding of the school 'a festive deed in earthly life', the start of 'a new pedagogical order of things'.[58] That expresses the spiritual dimension of the founding of the school. Now it can be made possible for the 'good spirit which leads mankind to a higher stage of development in lessons and learning', to enter into its historic task: For that there were two pre-requisites: the outer foundation through Emil Molt, who guaranteed its economic and legal side, and the inner foundation through Rudolf Steiner who, on the strength of his spiritual authority, was able to recognise the aims of those 'good spirits' and carry out their intentions. The future teachers foresaw with divining insight the target-setting significance of the school founding. And Stein noted in his diary on the evening that the course began: 'The gods will work further on the results of our labours'.

The forming of the founder-collegium was only completed on the day of the school opening. As Stein was about to leave on his return to Vienna, Rudolf Steiner asked him to stay, as he 'would be needed to help here in many ways.'[59] Three days later he was engaged by Molt with a monthly salary of 400 Marks and a 14-day term-of-notice as a spare teacher and librarian. Thus Stein was the last of the founder-colleagues to be engaged and was the twelfth member of the original group.

The five lady teachers and seven male teachers composing the original collegium came from all directions in space; from the Baltic, from Austria, from Switzerland and from the various parts of Germany. Even a German-American and a Swabian were among them. But already by the third school year four of them had left either on health grounds or for personal reasons. Others took their places, such as the Austrians Eugen Kolisko, Karl Schubert and Hermann von Baravalle with whom Stein was already acquainted. At the end of November 1919 Stein's wife was called to the school as a second eurythmy teacher alongside Elisabeth Baumann. Now for the first time Stein and his wife were able to live together when accommodation had at last been found. In 1920 was the birth of their daugher Clarissa Johanna, who was named and christened by Rudolf Steiner.

In the drama of events in Stuttgart Stein had encountered something totally unexpected: that he was put in a position of vocational responsibility just at a time of crisis in his own development. The years of his work together with Rudolf Steiner in the Waldorf School, which gave him a direction in life began in the autumn of 1919. Simultaneously he became active, with characteristic energy, in the Anthroposophical Society. The individualities get their corners rubbed off in these fields of experience. Their strong and weak points are revealed in their struggles to gain knowledge. 'Negative infatuation,' as Rudolf Steiner says,[60] can be the result of working together, and tolerance in one's feelings must be the goal towards which one strives. For a fighting nature like Stein's difficulties could not be avoided. He needed and sought the clear correction of others on his path of development. When Molt reproached him, during the course of conversation, with his showering of heaped-up knowledge on those present at the study evenings, instead of responding to questions which had been asked, Stein wrote down for his own guidance:

> I must cease to put side by side things that are spread out in different places. I must not schematise. Learn to be silent. Talk out of practical experience, not from what I have read. I must not ram things down other people's throats in a dogmatic, self-assertive way, without paying heed to what effect it has on them. I knock people flat. They lose courage because they fear that they will never acquire knowledge.—I give everything out in undigested form. I am like the Will-o'-the Wisps in the Fairy Story. I must become like the Green Snake. I must acquire wisdom of life.—Now, for the first time, I shall have a vocation, a career. I must not fragment myself. (2 October, 1919).

In the light of this unsparing self-criticism the 28-year old began his teaching activity, guided by the will to strive towards the spirit!

4
The Waldorf Teacher

The first day of school was on 16 September 1919. The start of lessons had been delayed because the reconstruction of the 'Uhlandshöhe' had taken longer than expected. As Rudolf Steiner was away lecturing, Molt greeted the members of the School with a short address, after which teachers and pupils withdrew to their classes. Stein had to step in as a substitute teacher straight away and take the main-lesson in a second class. Because benches and tables were still lacking, the children had to sit on chairs from the restaurant, which possessed the quality of inviting children to slide about on them in the classroom. The new teacher had first of all to get to know the children, to gain their trust and to give a two-hour main-lesson. Unworried and with confidence he trod the new ground of Waldorf education, the basic elements of which had been outlined by Rudolf Steiner only a few weeks previously.

Three days later Stein had to step in for a first class, and on 20 October work started in the seventh class. From now onwards he taught subjects dealing with cultural matters in the seventh and eighth classes, alternating with Stockmeyer who taught the natural sciences. It needed a considerable amount of energy to control the pupils of the upper classes who had come from primary and secondary schools and varied very much in their abilities. It was only when the abilities of each one could be recognised for what they were and co-ordinated into a class as a whole that a working basis could be established.

For Stein it was a period of intense pedagogical learning. He was inspired by what Rudolf Steiner expected of a Waldorf School: that it—as the first of the cultural establishments conceived out of the modern spirit—should not teach out of the heritage of the past, but should take its lessons from life and make the pupils familiar with conditions of life as it is today and inspire a regeneration of society. Even before the school was started Stein had written to his acquaintance, the timber-merchant Josef van Leer: 'Something is taught here which is the "science of life". Already before they are 14 years old the children must become generally acquainted with all the crafts and industries, factories, shops, etc: To this end we need short surveys relative to all branches of industry written by experts.' If, for instance, the teacher can learn in this way about the historical and geographical requirements of the timber trade, then he would be able to give the pupils in one of his lessons a survey of timber production and processing. Through that, at the same time, the germ of a science of industry could be planted in the children. Further to that, the teachers would need to have specialised works written in the spirit of Goetheanism, e.g. a new Chemistry to be worked out by Kolisko. 'It is a spiritual world conquest which is envisaged and, if our friends do not let us down, we shall soon have got so far that from this unified school the whole of spiritual life right up to University will become established.' For this reason 'the Waldorf School will have to become a focal point for the spiritual work of Anthroposophy.' Such expectations as these were attached by Stein to the newly-founded school. During Rudolf Steiner's lifetime the Waldorf School did actually represent such a focal point through the activity of the teachers he appointed, whom he regarded as 'the intelligence of Central Europe.'[61]

Stein was not a little surprised when he, the mathematician and physicist, was called to teach history and literature. But he interpreted this ploy of Rudolf Steiner's as an invitation to teach in a subject which he had to discover and master for himself. He tackled his new task, for which Rudolf Steiner provided him with enlightening viewpoints, with his customary enthusiasm, determination and thoughtful self consciousness. He laid the way for future followers and was the first to work out the contents of the lessons in an exemplary way: the description of the pre-Christian civilisations in Class ten, the Parzival epoch in Class eleven, the historical and literary surveys in Class twelve. He possessed the faculty of presenting the subject matter in a way which was penetrated by leading thoughts and was easily comprehensible, so that the pupils who co-operated experienced the years spent in the upper school as a step by step pathway to self-recognition.

12   A class of the Waldorf School in Stuttgart, W.J Stein second from right back row [next to him Max Wolfhugel left; Stockmeyer right, Graf Bothmer seated front right], Teachers' House in the background

Twenty years after Stein's departure from the Waldorf School he still spoke with enthusiasm and exactitude about the construction and details of the curriculum.

The years spent with Rudolf Steiner in the Waldorf School were the never to be repeated moments of a 'primordial beginning' to which Stein was called in order to take part in the building up of this young school movement. From this favour bestowed on him by destiny he was able to draw the lively enthusiasm which set free the will forces of his pupils. He showed them that the Waldorf School was placed in a world historic context and was carrying out a task of humanity which they could continue if they wished. 'Our school is itself a part of world history', is how Stein puts it in his contribution on 'World History in the Waldorf School' to the first self-portrayal of the school (1926).

Freedom rays forth from this school, freedom which is acquired through a proper experience of authority in childhood. *This* kind of freedom leads to an exercising of spiritual powers in the widest sense of the word. Spirit, however, wants to enter into the world and the task of our school is to prepare the way for it. What was still cultivated during the eighth and ninth centuries, that *Spirit* which lives on in the legend of the Holy Grail, which the world started to deny and which was eradicated from history by the Council of 869—that spirit is seeking out the hearts of all who would search for it *today*, the spirit which heals, the spirit which restores to health because it is the unifying spirit of universal humanity.[62]

The germs of ideas of the spirit-pupil ripened under the eyes of his spiritual guide. Again and again opportunities for private discussion arose, the results of which Stein noted down in a special notebook: the advice and suggestions of Rudolf Steiner regarding his lessons and educational problems; information regarding the karmic background of whole classes or of single pupils; suggestions for the developing of organs of the soul. Thus Stein's powers grew, for he felt himself strengthened in his innermost being. Looking back over the first years of the Stuttgart school Stein's friend Hahn once said: 'When Rudolf Steiner was still with us, each one of us was raised above himself and could do things which originated from higher powers than those of the present ego.' Something of the lustre of that super-personal element which surrounded many of Rudolf Steiner's pupils still clung to Stein and, during heightened moments of conversation, a shimmer of it would gleam forth occasionally. And yet, to be called to work alongside Rudolf Steiner was not just a great distinction, it was also a strict schooling; and Stein left no doubt about the fact that he had undergone some severe correction—especially after he had made use of what he had heard in a lecture the previous night for his next day's lesson. He had to learn that inner work of the soul can only be acquired step by step and that a teacher must allow to mature within himself whatever is to work creatively.

A picture of Stein's activity during the years when Rudolf Steiner was in charge of the school is given by Rudolf Grosse, the long-serving President of the Anthroposophical Society, in his autobiography:[63]

Walter Johannes Stein was a charming, fascinating teacher of history. His friendly, hearty manner was irradiated during his history lessons by the thrust of the historical investigator, who with impressive sureness could reveal the spiritual connections of the course of history: In spite of his outwardly unpretentious quiet appearance, which needed no disciplinary measure to preserve complete calm during his lessons, he acted as the undisputed authority through his spiritual power. His lessons, delivered in a quiet composed voice, were, however, enormously dramatic and ingenious, his discussions with the pupils were unsurpassed in ready wit and quickness of repartee. It was as though the Golden Age of Scholasticism had been revived. The most convincing and inimitably living quality of his lessons consisted in a technique which represented and described events as though he himself had been present. He was able to do that because he pursued such an immense study of the sources which provided him with detailed knowledge of the environment and personalities, of circumstances and motives of historical events such as was to be found in no history book. In every pocket of his misshapen suit he carried rare books from which he could verify particular occurrences. He himself had the privilege of having discussed the background and details of history with Rudolf Steiner and worked from his instructions. The masterpieces of his art of description were, for instance, the development and significance of the Seven Liberal Arts of the Middle Ages, the history of the Councils of Nicaea and Constantinople with the Filioque Dispute and the Dogma of the abolition of the human spirit as an independent part of his being, the

Grail-stream and the ninth Century, Arabism, the background to the Age of Discovery—real pearls of spiritual history. He expected much from his pupils in the way of spiritual understanding, but he also set himself a very high standard of teaching.

Without doubt Stein was 'one of the most prominent teachers of the Free Waldorf School' and 'one of the most successful lecturers of the movement,' as Friedrich Hiebel writes in his memoirs: *Entscheidungszeit mit Rudolf Steiner,*[64] (*A time of decision with Rudolf Steiner*). But he attracted opposition to himself, in which his anthroposophical lecturing and his teaching came under fire. This criticism increased to attacks, which reached their climax at the Members' Meeting of the Anthroposophical Society in Dornach in 1932. Stein, who was in Holland at the time, and found himself judged in his absence, explained that he was not prepared to allow himself to be restricted in the free exercise of his activities. He drew the consequences of that, gave in his notice and left the school. (See appendix.)

This rapid decision, along with a report from shorthand notes taken at the general meeting in Dornach and circulated in Stuttgart, aroused violent protests from parents, former pupils and members of the Anthroposophical Society. Errors and misunderstandings aggravated the situation. Letters and enquiries, also to members of the Vorstand in Dornach, demanded that the teachers should express their attitude. A meeting was called which certainly manifested more sympathy for Stein than understanding of what the teachers said.

These events appear hard to understand at the present day. It seems that cause and effect had got mixed up. The cause of Stein's departure from Stuttgart does not rest with the votes of the Dornach assembly; far rather these votes are the result of Stein's critically appraised position in the Anthroposophical Society. But this position was associated with the difficulties which had arisen in the leadership of the Anthroposophical Society after Rudolf Steiner's death. Stein, as a member of the Society feeling responsibility in this crisis, had taken sides in it. The determination with which he held his views about it had finally placed him in such a position that the only answer he could see was to give up his work in the Waldorf School and in the Society. In spite of the pleas of his friends he held fast to his decision, which seemed to him to be a leap into freedom and which became for him a turning-point in his life. In the Spring of 1932—after 13 years of united labour—he made his departure from the Waldorf School. His family followed after him. After 1933 he never returned to Germany.

5

The Midpoint of Life

Soon after his thirty-third birthday the event took place which Walter Johannes Stein experienced as a break-through in his inner life. The course it took was dramatic and of great consequence. Unexpected inner experiences of consciousness convulsed his whole being. When the tempestuous experiences had passed, he reached the conclusion that he had reached the zenith of his life: he had lived through 33 years of life, he hoped that life would bestow on him another 33 years. This expectation was founded on the belief that the span of a man's life is to be thought of as an organism in time, built up around a central and hidden axis of symmetry. A well-intentioned guardian-spirit brought his expectation to fulfilment and granted him the exact number of 66 years and five months. He thought he had discovered the same pattern in the biography of Rudolf Steiner who, at the midpoint of his life—in 1893 at the age of 32— finished writing his *Philosophy of Spiritual Activity* which, as he told Stein contains the whole content of Anthroposophy for those who can bring to realisation the act of freedom described therein.[64a]

Every Sunday morning the religion teachers of the Waldorf School held the services connected with the Free Religious Instruction which Rudolf Steiner had entrusted to their observance and care: the Children's Service for the children of Classes one to eight; the Youth Service (Festival of Youth) for the 14-16 year-olds of the ninth and tenth classes; the Offering Service for the oldest pupils. The simple festive service took place in a room which was in part subterranean, which almost gave the impression of a catacomb; this impression was heightened when the walls were covered by red curtains for the duration of the service and the candles spread a dim light from the altar. Stein, who was one of the regular attenders, immersed himself in the cultic part of Rudolf Steiner's activities with the same reverence in which he held everything which came from Rudolf Steiner. While participating in the Sunday Service Stein experienced what he has indicated in a memoir written for his friend Karl Schubert, who died in 1949:

While he (Schubert) was holding the Sunday Service in the School on 9 March 1924, I was as deeply moved as were the people who once listened to the words of Johannes Tauler, that speaker who, after ten years of silence, gave utterance to words which freed one from the body, so that many who heard him fell to the ground in a swoon. Schubert was capable of that, too. His religious zeal freed from the body, brought the soul before the Countenance of God and into contact with Christ. Rudolf Steiner even confirmed the reality of this experience in a letter which he wrote me.[65]

The participation in the service had so overwhelmed Stein that he lost consciousness and had to receive medical attention. Rudolf Steiner was, of course, informed about it immediately. At first he gave Stein written advice and later explanatory indications verbally. His undated letter, which bears testimony to the freedom with which he guided the souls of his pupils reads as follows:

My dear Doctor Stein! Experiences such as yours must be taken inwardly in a purely objective way without any excitement and, as it were, just accepted for what they are. You should have the feeling that what is to come out of it will take place if I observe the events in complete calm. These experiences will not affect the body, but will weave in the spirit. That is necessary. That you have arrived at this experience is a good result of the living way you have devoted yourself to concrete ideas out of the spiritual world. Now accept with complete serenity the fact that the soul-spirit part of you will be carried by your ideas into the experience of the spirit.
 Observe the following:

1. Calm spreads out over the whole realm of my soul.
2. I gratefully receive what the spirit wishes to reveal to me.
3. I wish to remain calm, so that my destiny can give shape to what is to come about through me out of the experiences I have observed.

There must be no inner tumult, nor any tumult of thoughts in your soul. Emotions darken the spirit and sap the powers of the physical.

With warm thoughts
Rudolf Steiner.

The Sunday Service which so shook Stein that he thought he was at the brink of death was the Youth Service. This service, comparable to the Confirmation Service, is for the developing youngsters seeking the spiritual direction to aid them in their future trials in life. It commences and ends with the call to 'remember the importance of this moment in life' in which the Spirit who overcame death sends them His creative strength, for, as they rise from childhood to youth the Creative Spirit of the Logos, hidden in each human soul, will bestow His gifts upon them. Stein experienced what was happening at the altar as an image of his own destiny: a preliminary epoch, lived by virtue of those forces he had brought with him into life, provided by nature, was now coming to an end; a second epoch, to be formed by newly entering forces bestowing freedom, was being proclaimed from afar. He stood at the 'abyss of the individuality,' but at the other side of this abyss towered the spiritual realities with which he hoped to unite himself in his dramatic struggle for knowledge.

Rudolf Steiner once explained in a private connection, that the bodily-upbuilding natural forces are dominant until the thirty-third year; for this length of time a human being lives his life according to the necessities of his karmic past. From then on the forces of disintegration, out of which the life of soul and spirit awake, gradually gain the ascendancy. Thus, only after this time, that is, in the second half of life, there begins to emerge what will form the basis of destiny in a next life.[65a] This piece of spiritual-scientific knowledge became for Stein at the mid-point of his life a certainty gained out of his own experience. The breakthrough in consciousness which announced itself so stormily had long been prepared. Rudolf Steiner called it 'the good result of the living way' in which Stein had devoted himself to 'concrete ideas out of the spiritual world.' Since working upon his dissertation Stein had been learning to deal in such 'concrete ideas.' For Rudolf Steiner's instructions to him to create 'a theory of

Mein lieber Doctor Stein!

Erlebnisse wie die Ihrigen müssen in rein objectiver Art innerlich ohne alle Erregung, gewissermaßen bloss anschauend hingenommen werden. Sie sollen das Gefühl treiben, was daraus werden soll, wird schon, wenn ich die Erlebnisse nur in voller Ruhe anschaue. Diese Erlebnisse ergreifen dann das Körperliche nicht, sondern weben in dem Geistigen. Das ist notwendig. Dass Sie dazu gekommen sind, ist eine Folge der lebendigen Art, mit der Sie sich unseren Ideen aus der geistigen Welt hingegeben haben. Jetzt nehmen Sie in absoluter Gelassenheit, dass die Ideen ihr Geistig-Seelisches in das Erleben des Geistigen tragen. Beobachten Sie:

1) Ruhe breite sich aus in meinem ganzen Seelenbereiche.

2.) Dankbar nehme ich auf, was der Geist mir offenbaren will.

3.) Gelassen möge ich sein können, auf dass Karma aus dem anschauend-Erlebten gestaltet, was durch mich werden soll.

Es darf kein innerer Tumult, auch kein Gedankentumult in Ihrer Seele sein. Emotionen verdunkeln das Geistige und entziehen dem Physischen Kräfte.

Herzlichste Gedanken

Rudolf Steiner

13   Letter from Rudolf Steiner to W.J. Stein

knowledge out of spiritual cognition' was neither more nor less than to ask him to develop a theory of knowledge of spiritual individualities—the hierarchies. Starting from the theory of sense knowledge he had to answer the question: how is knowledge modified when it passes over into the world of the supersensible? A knowledge such as this means that one must learn to understand the kinds of knowledge possessed by spiritual beings who stand above mankind and who are described in Christian tradition as the nine-fold 'heavenly hierarchies.' To approach this world presupposes that one has developed supersensible faculties of consciousness, which can be attained along the path of the systematic training of the soul powers. A person can have made the first steps along the road to supersensible perception when he is active in production of thoughts.

A further step can be made when one begins to wake up and become aware of the supersensible reality of the etheric. Stein had made the first steps along the path leading to this kind of experience. He was now seeking for certainty of knowledge in the realm of experience founded on meditative devotion, and he worked his way through explanations which Rudolf Steiner had given about 'true intuition.' The results of his efforts are to be found in the essay 'von der intuitiven Erkenntnis' (concerning intuitive knowledge). This study, from the eventful year 1924, appears to resemble a critical self-examination of his previous experiences in the realm of consciousness. From their substance he conceived his insight into the essence of intuitive knowledge, which he described as an experience of the consciousness 'of other beings or one's own being in former lives on earth.'[66]

After years of striving after knowledge, which were accompanied by his spiritual teacher, the first fruits of the pupil's endeavours now began to ripen. His first concern was to get clear about the experience of 9 March. His consultation about it with Rudolf Steiner came on 27 April when the latter came to visit Stuttgart for the Education Conference. He made clear to Stein the meaning of what his soul had experienced in cosmic heights while free from the body and summarised the results in a meditative verse:

> My head bears the being
> of the resting Stars.

> My Breast harbours the life
> of the wandering Stars.
> My Body lives and moves
> amid the Elements
> This am I.

The amenable spirit-pupil now learned, on the advice of his teacher, to acquire a consciousness free of the body. First and foremost stood his experiences of that Sunday in March: the merging with his surroundings, the submersion into the sphere of the World-Ego, the Cosmic Communion. This experience can be understood as a real initiation, as it is encountered on the pathway of knowledge when the consciousness centred on the ego is transformed into a consciousness belonging to the cosmic periphery. Through that, knowledge becomes devotion, a festive act of knowledge, and the Mystery of Golgotha enters into the experience.

Step by step Stein penetrated further into this new realm of experience and simultaneously deepened his outlook by studying occult literature. During this process he came across the *Chemical Writings* of Basil Valentine, an alchemist and Benedictine monk who lived during the fifteenth century. Rudolf Steiner called these writings a 'compendium of higher knowledge' and recommended them to Stein as a book for meditating. These works describe in the pictorial style of the alchemists the four stages of inner development, in which Stein recognised his own stages of progress. The black Raven representing the pupil striving for spiritual light by means of study; the many-coloured Peacock, when imaginitive experience dawns; the Swan, when the pupil dies to what is earthly, gives voice to his 'Swan-Song' and perceives the spirit-word of inspiration; the Pelican, when the stage of initiation is reached through self-sacrifice in devotion.[67] Thus what he himself had experienced was confirmed by a spiritual tradition, and Stein knew from Rudolf Steiner that he had passed the first two stages through the study of Anthroposophy.

A growing cognitive dynamism led Stein to new experiences of himself. The question was bound to occur to him: 'How can one *experience* repeated earthly lives?' And the answer he gave himself was: 'they cannot enter man's consciousness before he has learned to develop a consciousness outside the body and independently of the physical organism.'[68]

On 27 June [1924] he noted in his diary: 'Retrospect of past life.' He notified Rudolf Steiner of the fact in a comprehensive letter and in a talk he had with him on 16 July he received the explanation: 'You have experienced your last death.' Rudolf Steiner made clear by means of a sketch how the present life is a result of the earlier one and gave him the advice: 'Do not merely re-live your experience again and again, occupy yourself with it, clarify and deepen it in meditation, but bring into connection with it everything with which life presents you. Do not interpret, but observe. Live with what you observe.' Stein now proceeded to test the reliability of his observations on life itself. And two months later, on 28 August, he succeeded in historically identifying the contents of his retrospective vision. On 14 September he draws a preliminary conclusion: 'One must verify supersensible experiences against life. Through that one guards against fantasising. What one has seen is recognised again in life. But things have become metamorphosed.'

At this time—September 1924—the lecturing activity of Rudolf Steiner culminated in an abundance of teaching-courses and a legacy of information from his investigations into karma. Since the turn of the year 1923/1924, when the Anthroposophical Society had been newly founded at the Christmas Conference at the Goetheanum, he had begun to systematically develop the results of his knowledge of karma and to illustrate it with examples from history. Stein could immediately familiarise himself with the contents of these lectures and could occasionally get leave from the School in order to hear and speak with Rudolf Steiner in Dornach. So—according to the testimony of Friedrich Hiebel— he was present at the last karma lecture, in which Rudolf Steiner showed the greatness and tragedy of the karma of the Goethe-scholar Karl Julius Schroer, his teacher and friend from Vienna days, in its effect upon his own life's work.[69] Whoever took part in these lecture-courses perceived the uniqueness of the situation. Here spoke a human being with the authority of clairvoyance. The force of his knowledge illuminated the spiritual background of history with the 'luminous, fiery truth' of re-incarnation and destiny. 'We carry the fruits of past incarnations into our present earthly life.' 'If one takes karma seriously history resolves itself into human deeds, into human life-currents from the remote past, working into the present and on into the future.'[70]

In these far-reaching statements history becomes a mirror of knowledge in which the beholder meets his own destiny and awakens to an enhanced feeling of responsibility.

Thus the midpoint of Stein's life became a second birthday for him. He regarded Rudolf Steiner as the Godfather of the second half of his life. But, already one year later, his Pater Spiritualis died—too early, thought Stein, for the new beginning in 1924.

6
The Grail-Book

From the changes which took place at the midpoint of Stein's life grew the germs of the plan for his most comprehensive work, the Grail-book. The occasion of his Grail research came about in the fourth year of the Waldorf School when the eleventh class was inaugurated. Rudolf Steiner had worked out the time-table for this class in the teachers' conference on 20 June 1922: In the middle of adolescence, when questions about the meaning of life crop up, the young people should learn about the Parzival poem of Wolfram von Eschenbach and become acquainted with the background of the Grail events. Four weeks before the start of the first Parzival main-lesson, in the conference of 9 December 1922 Rudolf Steiner added in an amendment: 'the esoteric aspect of the Grail and Arthurian sagas' are to be elaborated: these indications, particularly the latter, brought Stein into a flurry of activity. A multitude of unanswered questions crowded in upon him. What had an 'esoteric' quality to do with the Grail and Arthurian currents? Did it mean that there was a reality performed in the eyes of the world, but accessible only to those who had been inwardly prepared to receive it? And was what he himself had prepared adequate? Certainly, ten years previously, when first studying *Occult Science*, he had read about the 'Science of the Grail' where it was said, that for a deeper understanding, 'the knowledge of the new initiation centred on the Christ Mystery' was symbolically depicted in the Grail legend. 'The modern initiates could therefore also be called the "initiates of the Grail". From the "science of the Grail" there is a way leading into the supersensible worlds, the first steps of which are described in that book.'[71]

Modern spiritual science is the 'science of the Grail'. That was the accepted basis for Stein's work. But now the task in hand was to enquire about the historical background of the Grail current, for in the ensuing main-lesson period the quest for the Grail by Parzival and its historical connections were to be depicted. In January 1923, two weeks after the catastrophe of the fire on New Year's Eve which destroyed the Goetheanum building with its two cupolas, the first Parzival main-lesson took place. On 16 January Rudolf Steiner visited the Waldorf School, as was his wont when staying in Stuttgart. This time he came into the lesson of the eleventh class. There are two reports of this visit: one from the diary of the teacher concerned and the other from the pupil, present at that time, Rudolf Grosse, in his memoirs *Erlebte Padagogik* (*Education as I Experienced it*)[72] The exactitude with which Stein recorded the event is not his usual style and this could be explained as the result of the importance which Rudolf Steiner's statements had for his Grail studies:

16 January 1923 Dr Steiner was in class eleven today. He said many wonderful things about the Grail and Parzival. I will write it down just as I heard it. He said: Grail comes from *Gradalis* = gradual. Parzival rises gradually by stages from stupidity, through doubt to blessedness (*Saelde*). *Saelde* is related to soul, blissfulness of soul. In the description of Parzival's experiences the conditions in the eighth and ninth centuries are portrayed. Those were times of much bloodshed. People of that time used to live in the forces of the blood. On every hand there were wild forests. Battles were waged there. Blood-sacrifices were offered on every hand. When worldly knights came people put their heads together and did not go out fighting. The knights kept order. The Arthurian knights formed the centre of these universally dispersed knights. There were not only the Arthurian knights, knights of the sword, there were other knights, too. Dr Steiner let the children guess what kind of knights those others were. He brought them to see that they were not knights of the sword but knights of the word. The word, he said, is the Grail-sword. That is no ordinary sword, but it is the sword which issues from man's mouth. Dr Steiner entered the classroom just as we were reading the following passage:

> The sword will withstand the first blow,
>   at the next it will break in twain.
> An' thou to these waters bring it,
>   from their flow 'twill be whole again.
> Yet where at its source the streamlet flows

forth from its rocky bed,
Shalt thou seek those healing waters
ere the sun stand high o'erhead.

(*Parzival*, Book V, line 477)[73]

The Grail-sword, the sword of the spirit, shatters when it grows old; then one has to take that of which only fragments remain, to the source again. What is old has to be renewed at the living source. There, at the Spiritual source, the Grail-sword becomes whole again. The dragon, which sits over the well whence the spring bubbles forth, shows the wildness of the people of that time. It is this wildness, the wildness of the forces of the blood, which Parzival has to conquer. I now asked: 'Dr Steiner, we were unable to explain why the same pictures often occur twice over in the Parzival poem, but the second time better, in a cleaner more noble way?' Dr Steiner gave the following answer: 'The reason why the pictures of the Parzival story always occur twice is that they always appear in their old form first; one finds that this is of no use; then they are experienced in a new form, renewed from the spiritual source, then they are of use. All Grail pictures have a historical as well as a universally human meaning. One must, for instance, always return to the source, just as Parzival did, who was able to maintain a connection with his spiritual source by repeatedly sending the knights he had conquered to the lady who guarded the spring (Kuneware) after every deed which he performed'.

Stein elaborated this information and included it in his book. It forms the content of the first chapter with the title: 'Rudolf Steiner's visit to the eleventh class of the Waldorf school' and it forms the starting point of his Grail-research. Two pieces of information by Rudolf Steiner were his guides: the eighth and ninth centuries are to be regarded as the time of Parzival; and, as regards the method of setting to work; 'The way to the source must be found'.

This visit to his lesson had karmic repercussions in the life of Stein. He set to work immediately on his project and searched in two directions; firstly, for the historical events and people hidden behind the veil of poetry; secondly, for the source of inspiration out of which Wolfram created his Parzival epic. He now used every conversation with Rudolf Steiner to get enlightenment about the methods of historical interpretation and presentation.

Through that he became aware of the fact that the historian very often arrives at his result not by means of systematic search, but rather through karmic circumstances. When Stein worked in a spiritual-scientific manner he could even learn, through finding certain pieces of evidence, that he was on the right track. Rudolf Steiner told him the following: 'You can have a good control over the truth of an inner experience if, at the same time as you meet it in inner experience, it confronts you outwardly in the form of karma'. From this Stein concluded that 'for an anthroposophical methodology of historical research what is most important is what belongs to the realm of destiny.'[74] As far as the portrayal of history during the lessons was concerned, Rudolf Steiner gave him the advice to reproduce inwardly with exact and productive powers of conception what often was only an incomplete fragment, and then to allow what had been gained in this way to ripen, until it could present a more complete picture. 'Try to think all historic things in their completeness, even those which are only preserved in fragmentary form. Complete it in your thoughts: Make all your concepts concrete with the help of imagination, but of course after first having taken all historical information into account. Then carry what you have thus acquired into your sleep and see how it becomes changed; what has been gained in this way can safely be presented to the children.' He countered my suggestion that by using one's imagination one might become inexact: He said: "You take account of all that has been handed down and you take with you into your sleep what you have pictorially imagined. It will really undergo a change, for the spiritual world sees to it that the truth becomes known. You will be able to observe, if you continue in this way with the same material, perhaps saying the same thing for several years running, that it undergoes a change. And it changes in such a way that it comes ever nearer to the truth. It will be much truer than the "convenient fable" which one calls history.'

Along paths such as these, pointed out by Rudolf Steiner, Stein succeeded in obtaining historical confirmation for traces of the Grail legend in the eighth and ninth centuries. What method he used he has described both orally and in writing: in lectures, including those given to the national assembly of the Anthroposophical Society in Germany and in a detailed exposition which he sent to experts and interested friends. He accounted for his action by saying that after Rudolf Steiner's death the advice of the initiate was to be replaced by 'self-advice': through the advice of friends who corrected or supplemented what was wrong or one-sided in the rough copy he set before them. Stein found many helpers in his work, to whom he was indebted for suggestions and material. One of those with whom he communicated over the subtle questions of soul development was Maria Röschl—a personal pupil of Rudolf Steiner—who was the first to be appointed leader of the Youth Section at the Free High School. His friend Wilhelm Rath discovered 'by accident' in a second-hand bookshop a periodical which contained a Grail legend going back to the year 799. A second equally ancient legend he discovered himself in a nunnery on Mount St Odilie after Dr Ita Wegman, a member of the original Vorstand in Dornach, had drawn his attention to the importance of St Odilie. It was through these discoveries that the first historic connections came to light. The Grail legends told the story of precious relics in which the Blood shed by Christ on Golgotha is preserved. The main characters of the stories were portrayed as the recipients of a blood relic and as advisors to Charlemagne. They are connected with Mount St Odilie and the Monastery of Reichenau in the far-flung East-West relationship and they are representatives of an esoteric, anti-Catholic Christiantiy. Thus it was confirmed that the story of the Grail began in the eighth and ninth centuries. When Stein lectured in Berlin in 1926 about the results of his Odilie research, an immediate intensive working relationship was established with Eliza von Moltke, the widow of the top-ranking General Helmuth von Moltke. Impressed by his account she allowed him to see private notes from Rudolf Steiner concerning the historical Odilie and her connection with the Grail-stream, about Pope Nicholas I and the effects of his term of office. Four of these documents she put at his disposal for use in his Grail-book.[75] The working relationship which continued until her death was of karma-revealing importance for Stein, because they showed him the world historic connection between the Grail century and the present day.*

Now the question arises as to whether the historical personage whom Wolfram describes in the figure of Parzival can be more

---

* See appendix and also Chapter 16, 'After Rudolf Steiner's death'.

closely envisaged. Wolfram's poem is about the destiny of an individual who treads the 'Perceval-path'. That signifies a particular method of arriving at knowledge and of moral development. Clues in his search for sources were given by Rudolf Steiner, who spoke about Lohengrin, the son, and Herzeloyde, the mother of Parzival, as historical personalities.[76] In addition to that he explained, in answer to a question by Stein, that Klingsor was a 'real person', who lived as the Duke of Capua at the time of Parzival.[77] Eugen Kolisko furnished the proof that Landulf II, who became the sole Duke of Capua after his brother's death in 862, is to be regarded as the bearer of the anti-Grail Klingsor power. From that the conclusion can be drawn that Parzival had lived as a contemporary of Klingsor during the middle of the ninth century and that 'the time around 869 provides the background for what appears in Wolfram von Eschenbach's Parzival transformed in a poetic way'.[78]

In 869 the eighth ecumenical council of Constantinople took place, which, according to the assertion of the historian of philosophy Otto Willman, who was much esteemed by Rudolf Steiner, decreed the 'express rejection of the trichotomy'.[79] The Council Fathers denied that man is a threefold being consisting of body, soul and spirit. In the eleventh canon they condemned the 'twin-soul doctrine' and asserted 'that man has a *single* thinking and spiritual soul'.[80] Rudolf Steiner recognised the world-historical importance of the Council's decision, which he characterised as the 'abolition of the spirit'; and he countered this with a deed; with the bringing into being of his *Philosophy of Spiritual Activity* which makes the renounced spirit once more available to mankind as a fact testifying to the reality of life and freedom.

At the historical moment of the Spirit's denial through the Council of 869 the Grail-current reached its zenith. It works in the background of history. The participants of the Grail Community, the 'quiet ones of the land', experience in their gatherings the healing power of Christ which descends to earth in order to renew life. They receive the ray of cosmic life through the Grail-Mystery, which becomes active in their hearts and enspirits their blood. They are preparing for the time when love will become knowledge which grasps the essence of what is hidden behind the outward appearance. The healing essence of the Grail leads to the interpenetration of love and knowledge; and Parzival is the human being who attains to knowledge through compassion, who heals the ailing Amfortas and succeeds him as the Grail King.

Stein describes in the main chapter of his book his approach to the Grail-Mystery, the wellspring of life. He gives there the interpretation of the Parzival story 'as the way of man's inner development, as the direction for the development of an organ for the perception of the sway of karma and the portrayal of events of the ninth century'. Wolfram's poem appears in his eyes as an inspired document, which does not merely set *down* Parzival's search for the spirit, but sets *up* the organ for a recognition of destiny in the sensitive listener. This courtly epic poem is a fascinating picture-book and, at the same time, 'it creates a delicate and subtle organ of knowledge in the human being which, through its own conformity to rule, demands a conformity in the architectural design of the poem itself'.[81] With that a reference has been made to the language of form, to the artistic occult composition of the work as a whole, which is divided into 16 'adventures'. As an image of this structure of the poem is the town Patelamunt with its 16 gates, which is described by the poet in the first 'adventure'. A black and a white army each lay siege to eight of the gates of the town: a metaphor for a higher reality which was known to the 'thoroughly well initiated' Wolfram (Rudolf Steiner's characterisation)[81a] as the spiritual sense-organ of the 16-petalled lotus-flower. Its petals are formed out of soul functions; eight belong to the past and work in a state of dulled consciousness whereas the other eight must still come into play in clear consciousness in the future. Only the great Masters are in command of the language of form, in expressing themselves they conceal the Mystery which can only be revealed to the true 'lovers' of their art.

At the heart of the poem lies the teaching about the Grail in which Parzival is instructed by the hermit Trevrizent. He tells him about the origin and effect of the Grail, about the enmity of Klingsor who dealt Amfortas, the Grail King, a wound which was incurable, about the Mystery of Destiny. The way of trial leads through the abyss of the crisis of the human ego into that Kingdom where human spirit confronts the Spirit of Humanity. Wolfram speaks about this 'secret inward path' in the language of imagination. It is this activity of the Grail, a 'stone from heaven' that burns the phoenix. But then it rises renewed out of the ashes and gleams forth brighter than before. The same power which the phoenix possesses is contained in the Grail for the human beings. The picture of the phoenix shows how the soul leaves the body and enters into the world of the spirit, the mystic death and rebirth: it is a process which Stein describes out of first hand knowledge.[82] But this experience of the falling asleep of the senses and the awakening to the spirit, led him to further experiences in his consciousness, from which he gained certainty about the past life of his ego. Stein became conscious of his karmic connection to the century of the Holy Grail and discovered his spiritual home in the landscape of the Grail. He believed he had recognised his innermost being in the person of Trevrizent. Sigune mentions the name of the hermit when she tells about the Grail family to the simpleton who had been expelled from the Grail Castle. At this point of the fifth 'adventure' Stein inserts a characterisation of Trevrizent:

> The poet Albrecht von Scharfenberg supplies us with the nickname of Treverikunt (Trevrizent) in his 'Titurel'. He calls him the 'deed-hasty'. He is a man of action who manifests his activity wherever there is a need in the universe to redress the balance. Thus he often appears to overshoot the mark because others fail to keep the balance. If one were to consider him on his own one would do him an injustice and would fail to understand him. What he does only has meaning and importance because he holds in balance the deeds of others. When he discovered that his brother Amfortas had transgressed against the Grail percepts through his love of a lady, Trevrizent wished to redress this and perform the opposite deed. He renounced all renown, renounced proud knighthood and delight in life and became a hermit. It was not in keeping with his nature to be an ascetic. He persisted in this one-sidedness, fed upon roots and herbs, slept on a bed of moss under an overhanging cliff in a wretched hut, which gave him meagre protection from the rain, because he was creating the counterbalance to the deeds of Amfortas. And so much of what he did was connected with what was happening at the Grail Castle. He performs an outer service.[83]

In the course of the work Stein clarifies and enlarges the picture of the ninth century. Two history-making events can be discerned: the revelation of the Grail and the denial of the Grail through the Council of 869. The Grail-current worked in the background of history at that time. In the twentieth century it steps into the foreground in order to work as a cultural element through Anthroposophy. Through its coming a renewal of the controversy with the opponents of the Grail comes about, which Stein experienced as the world-historic consequence of the ninth century. These two centuries appeared to him like the counterpart of one another: the ninth century as the karmic ground out of which the destinies of the twentieth century grow. Thus the present became for him a decisive battle between the powers of the Grail and the powers of Klingsor.

The courageous intention of Stein to write the 'World-history in the Light of the Holy Grail,' remains a fragment. A monumental work had been intended, which was to have shown the hidden stream of Christ's deeds with their historic effect. The first volume about the ninth century appeared in the year 1928. The author stresses the fact that he was only able to present a collection of material, for such a difficult task as this is only possible through the co-operation of many. Nevertheless, this collection contains much valuable and hard-to-come-by source-material, quite apart from the orally given and written information from Rudolf Steiner which is of basic importance for a knowledge of history; however, what gives to the whole undertaking its special character is why it was undertaken in the first place, its spiritual basis of experience and, likewise, the competence of the author in dealing with the Grail, which he had acquired as Rudolf Steiner's pupil.

7

The Goetheanum Lecturer

After the war Stuttgart became the centre of anthroposophical activities. People of the most diverse spiritual convictions met under the auspices of the Anthroposophical Society and were confronted with the task of 'co-operating with opposites'. Three generations could be distinguished: older anthroposophists who had belonged to the Society before the war and had attended Rudolf Steiner's lecture courses in the 'Lodges', those meetings of intimate pupils; then the younger academic students who undertook tasks in concrete situations in educational and medical institutions; thirdly those who were represented by people born at the turn of the century who were searching for a leader to guide them in a 'Mystery cult'.

Their meeting came about at a time of world-historic change. Deeply incisive events happened behind the scenes of history at the end of the nineteenth century which are described by spiritual science as the coincidence of the threshold of two epochs.

The first event is part of the lesser cycle of history and ushers in the renewed activity of the Archai-spirit whom Rudolf Steiner referred to as the Being of Michael. This Being helps man to come of age so that he can draw the impulses of his thinking and actions out of his own inner being independently of tradition. Anthroposophically-directed spiritual science is the outcome of Michaelic inspiration leading to a knowledge of supersensible being, just as natural science is the result of the previous Gabriel-inspired epoch which led mankind to the limits of sense impressions and intellectual comprehension.

Stein commenced his activity in Stuttgart from an understanding such as this of the history of the times. Rudolf Steiner wanted to have his participation in the Anthroposophical Society and made sure that he was given leave of absence from his work in the school. Stein attacked his self-chosen task with burning enthusiasm: the task of defending Anthroposophy, both orally and in writing, and opposing its enemies. He was one of those onward-pressing, enthusiastic activists and characterised himself as 'quick of action'. There was something volcanic in his nature, and the way he rode out to attack his enemies and dispense his wordy blows reminded some people of a medieval knight forcing his foes to surrender by his bold sword strokes.

When Anthroposophy made its first steps towards publicity it came up against a growing libellous and spiteful antagonism. It was in a situation such as this, prior to his first lecture-cycle on 'The Mission of Michael', that Rudolf Steiner found himself obliged to characterise the thought-forms which hindered the progress of knowledge. He took for his example an article by a theological opponent, Friedrich Traub.[83a] At the time Stein was working on a counter-attack which went into a second edition.[84] He also entered into discussion with Traub at the end of one of the latter's lectures and mercilessly routed the speaker when he called him: 'an enemy of human spiritual life'.[85] The vehemence of this attack can be gauged from the report which Stein sent to his wife in Dornach, which Rudolf Steiner quoted in a lecture of the 14 December 1919:[86]

I was in Reutlingen yesterday where Professor Traub spoke against Rudolf Steiner. I asked to be allowed to say something. It was a fight to the death. I portrayed Traub as a man without scruple who was completely ignorant in the subject with which he was dealing. He was only able to stammer out his final words. He was a broken man. The town priest who introduced the speakers was so cornered by me with Bible texts that, in conjunction with the passage where Christ speaks of reincarnation, he said: 'That is where Christ was *wrong*'.—The town parson of Reutlingen! Then I stood up and called out: 'Listen to that! That is present day religion; a God who errs!'—The audience went wild. They tried to interrupt me at first, prevent me from speaking; they called out: 'Stick to the point!' They shuffled and stamped. But I went on speaking quietly, pointing at Professor Traub and said: 'There is your authority!' I was acclaimed and was victorious. The man is finished. I am still half dead.

The scene is of historic cultural importance. Rudolf Steiner—and

Stein, too—were not intent on polemics, but on 'justifying the anthroposophical path of knowledge', in the eyes of the 'authorities' who attacked Anthroposophy as scientists. They did not notice how unscientific was their own train of thought by comparison with the scientific thinking upon which Anthroposophy was built. Rudolf Steiner's chapter: 'Max Dessoir on Anthroposophy' from his book *Riddles of the Soul* provided Stein with an example of the method which he himself adopted:[87] not merely to take into account the errors of the opponent, but to demonstrate the fact that what is promulgated by the Universities is an unscrupulous science leading to untruthfulness. Thus is manifested the downfall of a civilisation which, with its narrow view of reality, denies the effectiveness of the supersensible. Stein was a fiery spirit who fought in full consciousness of the fact that a dragon-like power has to be overcome, a power which seeks to destroy the Michaelically-inspired spiritual science which contains the germ of the future within it. The war of spirits which broke out in the twentieth century seemed to him to be a reflection of the cosmic battle between Michael and Ahriman, between the bestower of freedom and the Lord of Imperatives who would stifle human freedom through the authority of science.

Stein also demonstrated his intrepidity in Göttingen, a citadel of opposition. Alongside Eugen Kolisko he waged war against the attacks of a High School teacher and faced 'two thousand students with trumpets and drums'.[88] Something similar happened to Rudolf Steiner when, at the invitation of a group of socialist students, he held a lecture in Tübingen on 2 June 1919 on the 'Threefold Social Order'.[89] Those participating in these activities thought for a time in those days that the new forces, manifesting especially in the anthroposophical social impulse, would be able to succeed. They experienced the decisive character of the historic moment and stood up firmly in the way demanded by such a spiritual controversy.

During this phase of its development those engaged in the scientific work asked that their particular subjects be imbued with Anthroposophy. Rudolf Steiner thereupon started to give lectures and courses in the various branches of science, such as medicine, physics, astronomy. A proof was to be furnished to show that Anthroposophy 'can satisfy every scientific demand for a factual basis and is able to work strictly in accordance with scientific principles'.[90] Following in the spirit of these words High School courses were then arranged in which Stein regularly took part. They were inaugurated by the Goetheanum, the Free High School of Spiritual Science. The first course given by the Anthroposophical High School took place from 26 Setpember to 16 October 1920 in the Main Hall of the yet unfinished Goetheanum building. It was an important moment when Rudolf Steiner—seven years after the solemn laying of the foundation stone—opened the work of the High School during the Michaelmas season. The music of organ and orchestra filled the room spanned by the painted cupola and surrounded by the mighty pillars. The light flooded in through the tripartite windows with their hollowed-out designs and produced a many-graded profusion of colour. Then Rudolf Steiner directed his first words to the expectant audience. He spoke of the threefoldness of the cultural elements of Art, Science and Religion which, in spite of their different natures, can be reconciled to one another in a civilisation renewed by Anthroposophy; for they grip the whole human being when they become creative out of the well-spring of the spirit—expressed through an artistic, wise and religious human nature. Reference is hereby made to a new Mystery-teaching which is able to fructify the sciences and work upon the social surroundings. The speaker concluded: 'The kind of spirit which is cultivated here at the Goetheanum harbours the conviction that it is not the old spirit of the lecture-hall which is to be put before the public, but a new stream of wisdom springing from spiritual knowledge. Whatever flows from such knowledge will form the spiritual life which will also be the true education of the people and the power to shape the social order'.[91]

Apart from Rudolf Steiner, who gave a scientific and an artistic course there were about thirty lecturers, among whom were a whole group of Waldorf teachers who presented the results of their work. The variety of their themes is impressive, but in some of the contributions the academic way of thinking had not been overcome. On looking back on this course Rudolf Steiner remarked that the form of the Goetheanum was the test which would show whether a lecturer was speaking out of the living completeness of Anthroposophy or out of a narrow specialised knowledge; for the forms of this work of art in its entirey did not harmonise with specialised training at a University, but only with what was spoken out of an anthroposophical context.

Stein held three lectures on '"concept", "idea" and "judgement" in the teaching of Rudolf Steiner'.[92] What could have induced him to deal with such a seemingly out-of-the-way subject as this on this particular occasion? It was seven years since his first conversation with Rudolf Steiner which had set him on the track of his information-seeking and exploratory work; and three years since he had talked with Rudolf Steiner about his dissertation which had resulted therefrom. Since that time certainty had grown in him that true knowing consists in having faith in one's own ability of comprehension.

This path of research demanded a renunciatory energy and a strong devotion to what is abstract. Through continual exerting of one's thinking changes are brought about in one's spiritual make-up which spiritual science describes as a freeing and making independent of the etheric from the physical body. Thinking is enhanced until it becomes experience which includes feeling and willing. In this way an ability of the perception of spiritual beings and events is attained, an active perception of the spirit which is an intuitive thought experience. 'In intuitively experienced thinking man is carried into the spiritual world also as perceiver' is how Rudolf Steiner expresses it in his *Philosophy of Freedom*.[93]

Here lies the transition from the experiencing of thoughts to the higher stages of knowledge, from philosophical intuition to that kind of intuition which is an enactment of 'spiritual communion', from an idealised union with a known being to an actual submergence into the spiritual beings themselves. Here begins what could be called 'a dramatic initiation experience', a 'process of initiation', a 'drama of acquiring knowledge'. Destiny becomes knowledge—and knowledge becomes a drama of destiny. Here begins the awakening to spiritual reality.

While Stein was holding lectures in the Goetheanum his soul was undergoing dramatic experiences such as this along his inner pathway of development. His lectures were the best and strongest he could produce at that time from his inner strivings after knowledge. He spoke about man, who, through the trinity of 'concept', 'idea' and 'judgment' in his inner life knows himself to be connected with the trinity of Art, Science and Religion in the spiritual life of man. As Art rests on the appreciation or portrayal of what is beautiful, and what is beautiful lives as concept in the soul; as Science sees itself as the co-ordinated comprehension or portrayal of truth and truth is revealed as the many-sided harmonisation of ideas; as Religion consists of the recognition of Spirit as the 'Divinely Good' expressed in the utterance 'Thou art'—namely, the Ground of Existence of all that is: that is what Stein expounded in this three lectures.

To conclude, Stein cited the Christ-initiated Christian Rosenkreutz, who selected his pupils by rescuing them from mortal danger. Through being chosen in this way the awareness was implanted into them that a new lease of life had been bestowed upon them which they were henceforth to use in the service of humanity as a whole. Stein was imbued with a similar awareness, since he had experienced the wonder of his life having been protected during the fierce battles on the Gallician front. He now knew that, as a pupil of the spirit, it was his task to help found the new Mystery-culture. A note of spirit-certainty is sounded in the final sentence: 'It seems to me that out of the fountain-head which flows from the Goetheanum in Dornach an ideal is formed which must be carried out into *life*, not, however, as legend reports of Christian Rosenkreutz, for the chosen *few*, but for the *whole of mankind* . . . It is an ideal which must find fulfilment in each one of us!'[94]

With this High School course in Dornach the work of the High School begins, but it was also pursued further in Germany, Holland and Austria. Already during the winter term of 1920 the teachers from the Stuttgart Waldorf School arranged courses of lectures for the Goetheanum and for the High School with the co-operation of some anthroposophical speakers. Stein took part in these until the time he left Germany. The Anthroposophical Society organised public conferences in a big way. This attempt to fructify the various branches of science with Anthroposophy took place mainly during the years 1920 to 1922. The climax came with the Vienna Congress at Whitsuntide 1922, its name 'West-East' being suggested by Stein[95] and the Congress as a whole being entitled 'West-East—towards an understanding of western and eastern world contrast'. Stein participated in all the High School activities. His name was not missing from a single programme. Rudolf Steiner had once remarked—as has been recorded by his medical co-worker Ita Wegman—'I keep Stein for my great effects'.[96] When it was a case of presenting Anthroposophy to the general public and substantiating its scientific basis, it was Stein who was called upon to do this. He took on the task of presenting documentary evidence, providing systematic surveys of whole fields of anthroposophical work and he carried on critical arguments with opponents. He was often asked to make the opening speech at lecture courses or conferences. His comprehensive knowledge of anthroposophical literature, his eloquence and his practical experience in the following up of thoughts qualified him for such tasks. Those written lectures which have survived testify to a wide-ranging knowledge of Anthroposophy. Many of these lectures were worked up by him into essays which appeared in anthroposophical periodicals; some of them were published in printed form and were included in collected editions.[97] He dealt with motives relating to philosophy and the theory of knowledge, themes from his lesson material in literature and history, questions concerning social-science, science of man, cosmology and Christology. When the political horizon became more gloomy during the early thirties he turned to the contemporary social and economic problems and published three of these lectures in 1932: 'Gold in History and at the Present Day—a discourse on the World Economic Crisis', 'What does the West Owe to the East?' and 'The Labour question in History and at the Present Day'.[98]

When Rudolf Steiner made suggestions at a teachers' meeting for the programme of the Stuttgart High School course in the summer of 1924 and incited those present to take such subjects as aesthetics and literature, history, theory of knowledge, mathematics, geodesy (surveying) and present them in the light of the newest discoveries, from the point of view of what one can gain from these fields of knowledge for one's view of life, Stein immediately responded. (Teachers' meeting 30.4.24.) The periodical 'Die Drei' 1924/25 brought out a full report of this course in nine instalments, in which Stein gave a survey of the years 1870 to 1914, under the heading: 'What does the learning of History contribute to our view of the World?' He summarised what Rudolf Steiner had said about this period and characterised the symptomatic events by means of illustrative examples which he drew from his detailed study of the sources. He had at his disposal the experience of being a history teacher, who was practised in the art of describing historical scenes and filling out the characters with living images. The things which stand out in our minds are the events at the Vatican Council of 1869/1870, which led to the dogmatisation of the statement of the Pope's infallibility, or the psychological background revealed by the proceedings taken against the murderers of Sarajewo. Equally impressive was the conclusion of his lecture, filled with wistful pathos:

> History teaches us that world-events are significant, but that it is necessary for further progress that man on earth, who is a free being, also makes use of his freedom. When man exerts this freedom then the sun-forces of Christ dawn in him. Christ, who, through His Archangel Michael, would make man so strong that he will also take over and guide the civilisation he has produced outside himself. History can only make meaningful progress if the battles which are now being waged in the outer world are drawn back into the human soul. It is there that the great decisive battle must be fought. It is there that man, victorious in the struggle against his own dragon nature, must draw the strength to conquer the world-dragon without. Then, like the sun's force, scattering the clouds which billow up beneath it, man's forces will be able to conquer the powers of darkness which still rule history today, but which must be replaced by the Michaelic Sun-forces of Christ in every human being. It is that which will give renewed meaning to world history.[99]

That was the language of the 'fiery enthusiast' (Emil Bock) who guided the young people into Anthroposophy in those days. Ernst Uehli, editor of the weekly magazine *Dreigliederung des Sozialen Organismus* ('Threefold Commonwealth'), observed the effect of the lecturer Stein at the Anthroposophical High School course at the Hague: 'Dr Walter Johannes Stein held the first lecture. He spoke about the "Importance of Goethe for the whole of mankind's evolution". Stein spoke with the formal clarity, the will-imbued rhythm, the lightly-sounding undertone of feeling to which we are accustomed from him. One had the basic experience during the course of these lectures that the personality of the lecturer and the content of his lecture melted into a single living picture'.[100]

Stein, who was 31 at that time, directed his energies towards working through the contents of Anthroposophy with his thoughts and presenting it 'like a self-revelation of his own personality'. That is how Rudolf Steiner expressed it in his report of the Hague course, but he added: 'The lecturer would still be capable of giving his audience the best thing of all—the whole of his own nature'. Further steps of development on the way to the 'humanising' of his anthroposophical expositions were still needed. At first he was carried along on the wings of his success as a lecturer. He was constantly being asked to give lectures; and Rudolf Steiner had to give him a definite warning in the year 1921 to 'vigorously resist' these demands,[101] in order not to damage himself through overwork.

The artist Nora Ruhtenberg had observed the inner progress made by the Waldorf teachers:[102] 'that inner increase in their potential and abilities which brought something startlingly new to the work. The participation in the activities of the High School in Berlin and The Hague and during the Vienna West-East Congress was a kind of climax of festive experience for Stein and a confirmation of his growing ability. And he regarded it as the highest honour when Rudolf Steiner spoke to him in the Hague about his meeting with his teacher Karl Julius Schroer, illuminating the event and providing him with a key to the understanding of reincarnation and karma'.[103]

If Anthroposophy were to be presented as an organism and the anthroposophists as members of that organism, then Stein at that time would have to be reckoned among those who helped to build the central nervous system. At least, that is how the writer Andrej Belyj described him in a varied picture he drew of the Stuttgart scene in his 'memories of Rudolf Steiner'.[104] There, to begin with, are described the young academicians to whom Stein belonged: those 'eloquent "doctors" well versed in all branches of methodology, the life of thought and the fundamentals of social life'—the 'battle-eager . . . proclaimers of nothing less than world-conquest.'[105] But they stood on a foundation prepared since the beginning of the century by the continued work of Carl Unger. This long-serving pupil of Rudolf Steiner was, according to the opinion of Belyj, even 'more original than the brilliant Stein' along certain lines of thought and was able to bring conviction by means of a maturity which is evinced when the epochs of life become organs of perception and the powers belonging to the intellect, to the feeling-life of the soul and to the will-nature of the body start to be transformed into higher faculties of knowledge. It was a step by step inner development such as this which Rudolf Steiner must have had in mind when he spoke to Stein about what he might attain to in the future. The events of 1922 are unequalled in their dramatic impact. That was the year in the history of the anthroposophical movement which brought the greatest amount of expansion through Rudolf Steiner's lecture tours in the spring and the highlight of the Vienna West-East Congress at Whitsuntide, but likewise the greatest test of all in the incendiary act which destroyed the Goetheanum building on New Year's Eve. The culmination of public activity was followed at the close of the year by the tragic caesura with its dire consequences. These happenings also had an effect on Stein's own life. The pathway of his soul swung from outwardly directed activity to inwardly received spiritual reality. The work was deepened, the Grail-motive appears.

Experiences of an extremely opposite nature followed directly one upon another. On 15 May Stein was present at Rudolf Steiner's lecture in Munich, at the end of which the anthroposophical friends had to protect the speaker from physical attack by the radical opponents of the Right. After this attack Rudolf Steiner certainly completed his lecture tour, but then had to refrain from further public activity in Germany.

The situation in Austria was different. On 1 June Stein sat among the 2,000 participants who had come from all parts of Europe to attend the Vienna West-East Congress at which Rudolf Steiner presented the double theme of 'Anthroposophy and Science' and 'Anthroposophy and Sociology' on ten evenings in the context of the polarity of East and West. Stein spoke about 'The Free Waldorf School and its importance for the spiritual life of our time' and about psycho-analysis, which he characterised as the Psychology of the Unconscious with inadequate methods of knowledge. In addition he held a course of lectures on pedagogical themes together with Caroline von Heydebrand within the framework of 'specialised scientific discussions'.

In the one-time Capital of a Cosmopolitan State it was still possible to lay the foundation of knowledge for a new academy of science and to create an impulse to act out of the functioning of a geographical and spiritual centre.

The spiritual aspect which lay behind this outwardly directed activity was explained by Rudolf Steiner in a members' lecture on the penultimate day of the Congress. It was not a question, he said, of 'bringing Anthroposophy closer to science, but of penetrating science with Anthroposophy'.[106]

Such a penetration has far-reaching consequences. It makes the world of the living accessible, forms a bridge to the understanding of the Mystery of Golgotha and links up with the activity of the Christ at the present day. Thus, with the culmination of the High School courses and the congresses of 1922 an attempt was made to overcome the 'dead, unchristianised science' and to found a 'Christianised science'—a goal which is of vital consequence at a time of atomic and ecological danger.

Stein returned from Vienna inwardly stirred. After what he had experienced he saw that 'the plough had to be set deeper', the meditative exercises of the will had to be practised more energetically. A new thoughtfulness was aroused in the circle of the Dornach members by Rudolf Steiner's report from the West-East Congress. In this report—different from the character-sketches of the course at The Hague—Dr Steiner touched upon the karmic relationships among those who lectured, which Stein interpreted as a challenge to undertake karmic investigations. (See appendix.)

When, two years later, the Vorstand of the Anthroposophical Society in Dornach was looking for 'Goetheanum lecturers'—lecturers authorised by them to speak in group-meetings and in public in the name of the Society—Stein was one of the first to be called upon.

III
DEEDS AND PROJECTS

1
Tasks within the Anthroposophical Society

Some days after the school opening Stein had a conversation with Adolf Arenson about 'New directives for the Anthroposophical Society'. It was a conversation between representatives of two different generations and, as was evident later, between people of quite opposite intentions. Arenson, 36 years older than Stein, had participated in the anthroposophical movement since its beginning and had dedicated himself to the totality of Rudolf Steiner's teachings by means of systematic study. The result of his labours was a 'methodology of spiritual science', the main principles of which he explained at the first High School course in Dornach; also his well-known 'Leitfaden durch 50 Vortragszyklen Rudolf Steiners' (Reference Guide to 50 of Rudolf Steiner's Lecture Cycles). The situation was different in the case of the second-generation members to which Stein belonged. They entered the field at the time of the dramatic change in the Society's history, when the institutions were being formed, when the work was coming into the public eye and opposition was springing up. The change in the outer and inner circumstances which had been gradually coming about since the end of the war demanded a new working approach. If the main need of the older members had been to imbue the contents of the Bible with spiritual-scientific understanding and their main aim had been to train the inner powers of the soul, so, in the case of the younger members, stirred by the events of the times and living under the impression of their war experiences, it was to the realisation of Anthroposophy in the social life to which they turned. They quested after a renewal of vocation and the founding of communities in accordance with the spirit, which is a prerequisite of a truly human existence. Their hope was so to arrange practical activity that it might be in harmony with the intentions of the ruling Spirit of the Age. The tenseness of the situation came to light at a members' meeting in Stuttgart on 4 September 1921, when Rudolf Steiner, referring to the history of the Anthroposophical Society, spoke about the change of direction which took place in 1919: 'It is now suddenly a question of submerging ourselves into the stream of earthly happenings to show that we are equal to the task we have prepared for work in the stream of human evolution'.[107]

It became more and more evident that the Anthroposophical Society was not able to keep pace with the anthroposophical movement. A 'tailoring' problem had arisen, as Rudolf Steiner expressed it, and the garment had been cut too short'.[108]

A fortnight after his conversation with Arenson the 'deed-hasty' Stein proposed his 'New Directives for the Anthroposophical Society'. At the same time he demanded the 'Creation of a Science Headquarters'. The latter was inaugurated in 1920 as the 'Archive of Goethean Studies' in which were collected together not only Goethean literature but also the lectures and works of Rudolf Steiner. In contrast to this the 'New Directives for the Anthroposophical Society' took longer to materialise; for, in the every-day realities a process such as this requires the long-drawn-out negotiations of assertive egos and behind every ego stands a different karmic history. In Stuttgart in particular, the centre of activities and the headquarters of the Vorstand of the whole of the Anthroposophical Society at that time, difficulties piled up. Situations built up which Rudolf Steiner called the 'Stuttgart System': instead of a productive co-operation between people there developed a stand-offish bureaucratic attitude of those working alongside one another. One of those who took part in it has handed on an aperçu of Rudolf Steiner's relating to this: 'The gentlemen behave towards one another like the envoys of opposing super-powers'. The atomising of the Society and dissolution within the social sphere could not be avoided.

In order to create a constructive working basis for the active Stuttgart members Rudolf Steiner formed the discussion group called the 'Thirties Group'. This was where the representatives of all the departments gathered together to advise about the consolidation of the Society. Difficulties had also arisen within the anthroposophical groups. When things became acute in 1923 Stein was given the job of arbitrator in Nürnberg and other places.[109] Evidently Rudolf Steiner had assigned to him a new role in the affairs in which patience, insight and the capacity to love would be required. Opportunity for developing these attributes was provided in abundance by the endless late night sittings of the 'Thirties Group'. Here Stein was able to acquire his knowledge of karma, from which grew his understanding of history. To his systematic training in thought was now added a training in the perception of karmic connections. There was the group of doctors, there were the scientists, the teachers. Here the delegates of the two Stuttgart study groups met: Toni Völker and Carl Unger, who pursued entirely different aims in their work. People such as Friedrich Rittelmeyer, leader of the Christian Community, and Emil Leinhas, Director of 'Der Kommende Tag', tried together to find a solution to the crisis in the Society. In the centre of the dispute stood Rudolf Steiner, who, always accompanied by Marie Steiner, pressed for a ruthless discussion of all the difficulties; only complete honesty would serve as a basis for understanding and be the pre-condition to a united working together. That which took place in this circle of people was comparable to a Mystery drama. All regarded themselves as pupils of the spirit—who, though totally different in their constitution, but karmically connected to one another—were intent upon a common task. Perhaps they imagined themselves in their totality as a picture of the complete human being, as embodied in their spiritual leader. That may possibly be the mood out of which (as Hahn reported) they approached Rudolf Steiner with the request that he should take up with them again the work of the Esoteric School which he had carried out in intimate circles before the war. But a work of this kind which incorporates a spiritual reality is dependent upon certain conditions, and Rudolf Steiner was obliged to answer: 'Learn to tolerate one another. You must first learn to sit together round a table. Only then can you work esoterically together.'[110]

After endless difficulties there emerged out of the discussions of the 'Thirties Group' a call for a delegates' meeting of the Anthroposophical Society. At this meeting the working groups in Germany were asked to send 'those people who had the "New Directives for the Anthroposophical Society" very much at heart' to a conference to take place in Stuttgart from 25-28 February. [1923.][111] The number of people exceeded all expectations. The delegates who arrived from all over Germany filled the Gustav-

Siegle House in which Rudolf Steiner was accustomed to speak when he gave his public lectures. The memorable meeting—in the twenty-first year of the anthroposophical movement—was like a test of the coming-of-age of the Society. It had the task of forming a Vorstand based on the confidence of the members, which would regulate the mutual work of the older and younger generations, would clarify its relationship to the Christian Community and ultimately deal with the question of the opponents.

At that time Rudolf Steiner's work was threatened with the greatest of danger. The irreplaceable building of the first Goetheanum had been destroyed, the German Anthroposophical Society faced a test which might tear it apart and destroy it completely. On the third day of the meeting Rudolf Steiner had to advise those present to set up an organisation whereby the young people should form a 'Free Anthroposophical Society' alongside the existing Anthroposophical Society. This suggestion caused a great commotion, but the justification for this 'anomaly' (as Rudolf Steiner called it in his opening lecture at the Christmas Foundation Meeting) was able to convince those present: 'On the basis of Anthroposophy one unites with others by differentiating, individualising—not by centralising everything'.[112]

At this historic moment, when the split in the Society had become generally evident, Rudolf Steiner gave two basic lectures about the formation of anthroposophical social communities ('Awakening to Community') in which he delineated the essential concept of awakening to the other person's soul-spiritual nature, and spoke of the 'reversed cult'[113] as the aim towards a deepending of knowledge. He turned his attention towards future tasks: the esotericising of the social life and the creating of a conscious basis for a community of free spirits.

Looking back on these events which concerned the historical destiny of the Anthropolosophical Society, the simultaneity of processes in outer history was brought to mind. 1923 was the year of crisis of the Weimar Republic. The foreign and national political pressures, the economic collapse and the dissolution of traditional values put the very continuance of the German Republic in jeopardy. The general feeling of being on shaky ground and of losing control of things took hold of the people at that time and led to a growing apathy or to political radicalism.

The effect of the political situation on the work of Anthroposophy is alluded to by Marie Steiner in her introduction to the report of the meeting of the 'Thirties Group': 'Germany was an incessantly boiling pot. The infinite difficulties connected with the various intrigues of the political and social groups and the ever growing inflation made all attempts at reform of no avail. The crumbling economy threatened to stifle the spiritual life. The destructive effect of these struggles was mirrored in the souls of the people and paralysed their energy. This dismal picture faced one continually in the frustrated efforts of those who wished to work out of Anthroposophy'.[114]

With the help of Rudolf Steiner and in spite of outward opposition and regardless of all inner difficulties the New Constitution of the German Anthroposophical Society was able to succeed. A Vorstand was formed which was no longer the Central Vorstand but was the Vorstand of the German National Society. Stein, who had to report to the meeting about the 'Confederation for the work of the Anthroposophical High School' was belatedly elected to the Vorstand at Rudolf Steiner's request.

After the founding of autonomous National Societies in various European countries there followed the forming of the General Anthroposophical Society at the Christmas meeting of 1923-4 in Dornach. Rudolf Steiner's avowed intention was to 'give the Anthroposophical Society a form compatible with the needs of the anthroposophical movement'.[115] The independent National Societies should unite with the Goetheanum as the centre of anthroposophical activity. Rudolf Steiner, through whom the anthroposophical movement was expressed in spirit-reality, took upon himself the presidency of the Anthroposophical Society. He had been connected with the former Anthroposophical Society, formed in 1912, as its teacher and advisor, not as a member. Now he brought the occult movement and the organisation of the Society together. The exoteric and the esoteric sides begin to merge into one another. A type of Mystery cult arose, as it first appeared in historical Mystery practices. The Free High School for Spiritual Science, like a modern Mystery School, becomes the centre of a world-wide Society. Anthroposophy belongs in the sphere of civilisation as well as that of initiation. As spiritual science it leads to and supplements natural science, and as a science of Initiation it is the modern equivalent of former initiation wisdom.

Eight hundred members gathered in Dornach and collected in the provisionally prepared and extended workshops. The way leading to the lecture room of this wooden building went past the concrete bases of the pillars which had supported the double-cupola edifice. The burnt-out ruins adjoining the makeshift lecture hall, the heap of debris beside the wooden shack—that was the daily sight.[116] In this waste area which appeared as an image of world conditions it was intended to erect a completely new Anthroposophical Society. Rudolf Steiner started to speak of the inner reality which becomes accessible along the path of practising self-knowledge, when man gains the certainty: 'Yes, that is what I am as a human being, as a spirit-willed man on earth, as a God-willed man in the universe'.[116] A bold impulse, leading into the far future was to bind the members together in spiritual activity.

Many of the participants in the conference had just been present at the conclusion of the preceding series of lectures about 'Mystery Centres'. This historical survey of the Mysteries had ended with a consideration of the alchemistic seekers after Spirit who—like their later counterpart Faust—'had experienced the loss of the knowledge of cosmic intelligence as the loss of their own humanity'.[117] The reacquisition of what had been lost remained an open question. The Christmas meeting provided the answer to that.

It was Rudolf Steiner's intention to create a centre for spiritual research and training in consciousness from which a renewal of culture could proceed; a modern Mystery Centre and a focal point for the Michaelic Archai-Spirit should arise. The image of a Grail Castle appeared before the inner vision of Stein and he tested himself to find out if he was worthy to set foot within this territory. Then he wrote to Rudolf Steiner after the Christmas meeting: 'I feel as if I were standing on the threshold of the Sanctuary which will serve to raise human souls into the heights from this time hence and for evermore, to bring down the deeds of the gods into the depths.—I beg entry into this holy place. In so asking I promise that I will enter it with pure thoughts and with an unblemished will insofar as I am aware of it'.

After 21 years of spiritual-scientific work Rudolf Steiner applied himself to the task of creating a union which should have

Anthroposophy as its inner structural principle. 'Union implies the possibility of a higher being expressing itself through the united members. That is a universal principle throughout the whole of life'.[118] That is what he had said already in a public lecture in 1905. During the foundation ceremony of the Anthroposophical Society on Christmas morning he called upon people to 'create a true union of human beings for Anthroposophy'.[119] Such a beginning as this poses questions to those taking part, questions of knowledge and questions of the will: questions about the being 'Anthroposophia' and questions about the conditions of vital importance to the association which serves it. Stein had experienced Anthroposophy as the reality which transforms human beings and awakens their higher self as a revelation of the healing spirit; and that filled him with an unshakeable faith in Rudolf Steiner. The extent to which this therapeutic spirit can become effective in a group of human beings depends, however, on the readiness with which they accept it. Only when a communal spirit has been achieved will something like a form-structure be created which can house the being Anthroposophia. And that is a question of the readiness of will of those who receive the 'Foundation Stone' into their hearts and souls. Rudolf Steiner characterised this process as a 'laying of a foundation stone in the Spirit' and represented it in verse as a mantra, the substance of which should flow through the body of the Society like a living etheric blood-stream. 'The Foundation Stone itself must be the conviction which the anthroposophical way of life instils into its members. Out of this conviction, through a deepening of the soul forces, the will is formed to find the way to a perception of the spirit and to a life in the spirit in a way demanded by the signs of the present day'. This is what Stein could have read in the News Sheet of the weekly paper from 13 January 1924. And he could have felt that the Anthroposophical Society on its path of self-development would not be spared the difficulties experienced by the individual when confronted by the forces of opposition.

Stein was an intent listener who immediately wrote down what he heard. Friedrich Hiebel recollects that he constantly met him with a fat notebook 'wherein he probably set down much of the contents of the lectures on world history and the morning discussions'.[120] In the mornings the 'Statutes' were read through, discussed and accepted. Drafted by Rudolf Steiner they described what the members wished to achieve in the 'purely human relationship to life' of the Anthroposophical Society. The chairmanship of the meeting was in Rudolf Steiner's hands, as he had now taken over the chairmanship of the Society as a whole. During the evenings he held the lecture cycles: 'World History in the Light of Anthroposophy and as the Basis for an Understanding of the Human Spirit'.[121] The contents of these lectures put Stein into a state of high tension. It appeared to him as though his capacity for hearing increased from one occasion to the next and that the connections which Rudolf Steiner revealed presented themselves to his mind like a remembrance behind memory.— Would he also be able to speak out of the inwardly experienced word? To prepare himself for that he needed to go deeper into history. He would have to become acquainted with the forces which had built up the present and past ages—that is, to understand history from the point of view of Anthroposophy. And that meant familiarising himself with karmically connected individuals and their effect on the course of history. Thus he noted with growing interest that, after a couple of introductory lectures, Rudolf Steiner started to speak about the two figures Gilgamesh and Eabani. The karmic connection between the founders of the Babylonian civilisation—Gilgamesh and Eabani— and the two figures Alexander and Aristotle, who stand at the beginning of the Hellenic civilisation was known since the lecture cycle 'Occult History'[122] (1910-11). Rudolf Steiner now dealt with this karmic example at greater depth—just as it presented itself 'directly to spiritual insight'.[123] The stages of ego-development throughout different incarnations became visible, for individuals carry over the results of one earthly life into the next. The bow stretches from the time of Gilgamesh in the third century B.C. to the centuries of classical antiquity. It is made clear to us how the oriental founders of civilisation introduce the epoch of Hellenic world importance through their reappearance in the stream of history. A question is asked regarding the task of these individuals, the importance of their appearance on the stage of history and their effect upon the twentieth century.

A further question arose. The series of lectures was intended to serve, as announced in its title, as a 'basis for the understanding of the human spirit'. What self-knowledge could be gained by reflecting on these wide-ranging karmic studies? Friedrich Schlegal once wrote: 'The only kind of self-knowledge is the historical one. No one knows who he is who does not know who his companions are, above all who the highest of all earthly companions is, the Master of all Masters, the Genius of the Age'. The twentieth century might appear like a reflection of the time of Gilgamesh. If at that time it was a question of progressing from dreaming world-consciousness to thoughtful self-consciousness, so at the present day it is necessary to take the first steps towards extending thoughtful self-consciousness into cosmic understanding, to win through to an awakened universal consciousness. The ego which has achieved independence has become mature enough to raise itself to the spirit-cosmos to which the archaic human being was still connected in dream-like fashion. That is why Rudolf Steiner was able to speak about there being 'a mighty change taking place', a change in consciousness 'to a third world, which is really as different from the preceding one as the previous Roman world is different from the [ancient] oriental one'.[124] The realistic ground-plan of history becomes visible—the time of the Ancient Orient guided by the Mysteries; the time of the Roman, medieval and Present day epochs cut off from the Mysteries; the time of the renewal of the Mysteries beginning in the twentieth century inaugurated by Rudolf Steiner—for this world-historic deed is the renewal of a knowledge of initiation in the form of spiritual science. Through spiritual science the 'estrangement of human thinking and willing from the Spirit' will be overcome and a 'change of direction will be introduced into the process of human evolution'.[125] In this way the twentieth century will become a turning-point and the threshold of a new epoch. The usual division of history into 'Antiquity, Middle Ages and Modern times, or whatever other names the divisions may be given, call forth, basically speaking, only false impressions'.[126] Like a symbol of the dissolution of the Ancient Mysteries was the burning of the Artemis Temple in Ephesus, which, according to the witness of Plutarch, occurred concurrently with the birth of Alexander. And symbolical of the dawn of the New Mysteries is the spiritual refounding of the burned-down Goetheanum through the event of the Christmas meeting. That is why the significant words appear in the concluding New Year's lecture about the 'dawn of the cosmic turning-point to which we will dedicate ourselves, in faithful cultivation of spiritual life'.[127]

Stein took up these words as a self-imposed obligation. His own mission in life became clear to him. He looked upon this pair, Gilgamesh and Eabani, as bound up with the turning-points in history. And he wished to work in karmic relationship with the preparer of the new epoch. He was filled with the exhilaration of courage. Now it remained to bring to realisation what Rudolf Steiner had exclaimed to the participants in taking leave of them: 'the more we go hence filled with courage for the affairs of Anthroposophy, the better we shall have understood what has passed through our meeting during these days like a ray of spiritual hope'.[128]

Immense responsibilities accumulated for Rudolf Steiner after the Christmas meeting. The journeys abroad, the functions, the lectures followed on top of one another thick and fast. September marked the beginning of the three-week period which Emil Bock, who witnessed to it, describes as 'not only in anthroposophical history but in the whole of spiritual history there has been nothing like it'.[129] In three lecture courses including 'Pastoral Medicine', 'Speech and Drama', and 'The Apocalypse of St John', which were to be held concurrently, a wealth of fundamental knowledge was dispersed. Added to that were the regular members' and High School lectures, also the lectures of several years' standing which he gave to the workmen engaged in the building of the Goetheanum. Upon this there followed the sudden cessation of his lecturing activity. On his sick-bed, to which he was confined for six months, Rudolf Steiner wrote his *Anthroposophical Leading Thoughts*[130] in weekly instalments, which have become his spiritual legacy.

Stein experienced the year 1924 as a karmic turning-point. Under the soul-guidance of Rudolf Steiner he had overcome the effects of the shock which the unusual condition during the Sunday Service on 9 March had caused. Since that time his constitution had become looser. Through meditative effort in which he persevered systematically new fields of conscious experience opened out before him. At the same time he carefully studied what Rudolf Steiner had said in his lectures since the Christmas meeting about how to acquire knowledge of karmic connections. The idea of the human ego maturing in the course of repeated earth lives guided the karmic investigator. His discerning eye fastened onto the spiritual germ of man in his transformation from one life to the next and surveyed the stages of the life after death when the ego on its way to rebirth has freed itself from the past and turns to what is coming towards it out of the future. Looked at in this way world history becomes a history of reincarnating individuals and their changing relationships; it acquires a meaningful coherence, whereas it otherwise remains a conglomeration of events. Stein acquired such insights as this by studying the karma lectures, the contents of which he began to consciously recreate through his own effort. When, however, he wished to describe some of the results of his studies during a history course, Rudolf Steiner emphatically discouraged him from so doing. [See appendix.]

A chord had been sounded in Stein's soul which continued to vibrate. On 10 January 1925 he wrote a letter to Rudolf Steiner relative to the preparation for the educational conference in Stuttgart. In this letter he developed the theme about the various directions of will and groupings of destiny in the educational movement, a theme to which he had been inspired by the study of the karma lectures. He understood Rudolf Steiner's investigation of karma to be the task of working upon the perceptive involvement of one's own social circle.[131] The perception of communal destiny—so he thought—should even bring into harmony those who were separated by their past, but whose future could unite them.

2

After Rudolf Steiner's Death

The 30 March 1925 was a Monday. The Easter holidays had not yet begun, and the Educational Conference to which people had been invited, as already in the previous year, by the Vorstand of the Anthroposophical Society together with the teachers of the Free Waldorf School, was about to begin. At 11.00 o'clock a telephone call reached the school from Dornach, which Stein answered. Guenther Wachsmuth, Treasurer and member of the Vorstand of the Anthroposophical Society started to speak: 'Today at 10.00 o'clock, Dr Steiner died. Please make it generally known'. Stein noted it in his diary and added thereto: 'We telephoned the Groups. My destiny chose me to announce our Leader's death to everyone. I could not grasp it at first. Wachsmuth had to say it three times on the 'phone'.

The event was completely unexpected for those in the immediate vicinity and for all the members. 'Now we are all saying to ourselves that we were too hopeful', recollects Marie Steiner, 'but with the tremendous life-forces which Rudolf Steiner always possessed, even during his illness, he lulled us into a feeling of hope'.[132] The teachers were expecting his return, even though the letter which he had sent a fortnight previously—on 15 March 1925—to his 'dear teachers' sounded almost like a leave-taking. They could read therein that the important decisions in which he had shared as a matter of course since the founding of the school must now be given into their hands. Then followed the relevant sentence: 'It is a time of trial through destiny'.[133]

Directly after the announcement of his death had been made known the first decision had to be made. Should the Education Conference go ahead as planned, even if the programme coincided with he ceremony in Dornach? According to Rudolf Steiner's own view the decision of the teachers' conference could only be that everything should take place unaltered. Some teachers travelled immediately to Dornach in order to take part in the lyke wake. On 1 April the ceremony took place in the lecture hall of the carpenters' shop and Albert Steffen gave the funeral oration. The congregation of mourners stood closely packed together, for in order to make more room the chairs had been removed. In this solemn moment Stein felt how his soul was filled with the impulse to draw near to Rudolf Steiner in the spirit, through fidelity to his work, as he had vowed to him when he lay in state on his bier.

Arriving back in Stuttgart he wrote a long obituary notice to 'the most loved of human beings', which appeared in the weekly journal *Anthroposophy*. It concludes with the sentences: 'A human being has lived in our times, a great, pure, kindly human being. In following in his work we want to *live* his humanity. May Rudolf Steiner be born again in the hearts of many!'[134]

The 2 April was the start of the Educational Conference for which there had been 900 applications from outside. An expectant hush lay over the crowd assembled in the Gustav-Siegle House. Uppermost in people's minds was the previous year's conference at which Rudolf Steiner had ended his educational lectures with a pedagogical-meditative verse and the audience had spontaneously risen from their seats to express their gratitude. This time it was Stein who gave the opening lecture. 'The portrayal of Dr Steiner's life was presented to the crowd which was so large that it could hardly be contained in the great hall of the Siegle-House. Dr Walter Johannes Stein gave a picture, as it should be given, out of the fullness of his heart in a perfected artistic form. It was the voice of the Waldorf School itself paying tribute to its founder'.[135] This was how it was felt by Wilhelm Dörfler who belonged to the younger generation of teachers. And Konrad Sandkühler, the first teacher to be appointed to the staff of the Stuttgart School after Rudolf Steiner's death, wrote in his biographical reflections: 'What struck everybody who came to the conference first and foremost was the stamp of truth which spoke to the visitor through all the events'.[136]

Following immediately on Rudolf Steiner's death the 'time of trial through destiny' began. The social structure of the School and its relationship to the Anthroposophical Society were put to the test. With regard to the School a certain amount of stability had been achieved through the six years of Rudolf Steiner's leadership since its foundation. The Anthroposophical Society on the other hand, accessible to all and having the High School at its esoteric centre, was just in its beginning stages. The questions about the leadership of the Society and that of the High School were the occasion of conflict and separation within the Vorstand and the Society. Stein felt himself called upon to participate actively out of a sense of responsibility during this phase of the development; he took sides and became a protagonist in the discussions.

From the distance of space and time (1937 in London) Stein sought the key to an understanding of his behaviour at that time. To this end he wrote his memoirs and undertook exercises in how to recognise the facts of destiny. First he had to observe the events imaginatively and refrain from passing judgement, in order to progress to a discrimination between essentials and non-essentials. In this way a catharsis of the faculty of judgement could begin to develop, which makes it possible to attain to a realistic comprehension of relationships. Stein penetrated with retrospective vision to the karmic turning-point of mid-life. At that time he had begun to acquire a comprehension of spiritual realities along the pathway to experience free from the body. At this moment in his life Rudolf Steiner died—'and thereby great difficulties entered my life, for now I needed his help more than ever'.[9] Stein was aware of the dangers which face the spirit-seeker from the attacks of the forces of opposition after he had acquired the capacity of body-free experience. He knew that he would be exposed to self-deception and delusion if his moral integrity and spiritual discrimination were not sufficiently developed. The death of one's spiritual teacher throws every occult pupil back onto his own resources and simultaneously sets him the task of judging and acting as a member of a community. It was there that the difficulties arose. They were concentrated in the question of the continuation of the esoteric guidance of the Society by the Vorstand which Rudolf Steiner had elected. It was for a leadership of the Society based on an insight into the happenings in the spiritual world seeking entry into the physical that Stein with his 'high-riding fiery temperament' was struggling.[137] He concludes his memoirs with a survey of the crisis in the Anthroposophical Society: 'The consequence of this experience (of the supersensible) for my own life was that my connection with the spiritual world was not interrupted through Rudolf Steiner's death, so that many things could be continued which seemed lost to others. This fact, however, led—not only in my own case—to severe conflict and ultimately to a division in the circle of people which had formed around Rudolf Steiner'.[9]

Until 1928 Stein was one of the chief actors in the drama of the Society's history. What those responsible for the Society fought out among themselves was experienced by Stein as a trial of the soul. The words of Benedictus from Rudolf Steiner's Mystery Drama: 'Know that a test hath been ordained for thee by lords of fate and by the spirit powers' [*The Soul's Probation*, Scene 1] became for him the key to unlock the reality he had experienced. He enquired about the spiritual impulse behind destiny and the part played by supersensible powers, but he had to learn that barriers to knowledge pile up when he who acts is influenced by egoism.

It was the facts of destiny which came to expression in the development of the Anthroposophical Society after Rudolf Steiner's death. This free association of human beings striving to serve the life of the soul through spiritual-scientific knowledge included people of divergent inclinations of will. Would it be possible to build a bridge between these karmic opposites and to develop ways of working together? Friends of Ita Wegman, whom Stein had joined, considered this medical helper of Rudolf Steiner as his spiritual heir and based this assumption on karmic factors. Others, particularly the older members, wanted Marie Steiner to play an active role in the leadership of the Society. This difference of opinion was further intensified by the fact that Stein believed that Rudolf Steiner's will from the year 1915, according to which Marie Steiner was given sole rights over all the papers and effects of Rudolf Steiner, had been superseded by the Christmas Meeting and that consequently the whole of the estates belonged under the guardianship of the Society. Two conceptions about the leadership of the Society and the validity of Rudolf Steiner's will came into increasing conflict with one another; two currents centred in Marie Steiner and Ita Wegman strained in opposite directions.

In the emerging conflict Stein was the most eloquent amongst his like-minded friends, among whom Eugen and Lili Kolisko ranked first. What he regarded as right he advocated as the truth. He regarded himself as the protagonist of the truth who was obliged to do battle for his convictions with a holy fire. In the conflicts, which he considered of greater than personal importance, he dealt some deep wounds, but he also received some sturdy reproofs in exchange. In a conference of national Vorstand members with the Vorstand of Dornach he had begun to speak again about the question of the will, whereupon Marie Steiner left the meeting in indignation. According to the report of Carl Unger there followed a tumultuous argument; negotiations were broken off and were only resumed after the departure of Stein.[138] This incident, which had occurred immediately after the opening of the second Goetheanum on 8 October 1928, was the cause of Stein finally leaving the Vorstand of the German Society. The announcement of his decision on 2 January 1929 coincided with two completely unexpected events: on 29 December Count Carl von Keyserlingk, the initiator of the Koberwitz agricultural course, died; on 4 January Carl Unger was shot by an insane person as he entered the room where he intended to speak about 'What is Anthroposophy?' This soul-shattering symbolic language of destiny was a summons to Stein to rigorously search his conscience.

But the drama had not yet reached its conclusion. Through a decision of the general meeting in 1935 Ita Wegman and Elizabeth Vreede, members of the Vorstand who represented this current, were excluded from the affairs of the Society. Stein was not among those mentioned, he had abstained from exerting any direct influence on the development of things since his withdrawal from the German Vorstand.

After the exclusion the work in the divided working sections still continued. Ita Wegman gave the incentive for the spread of the medical and curative movement. Marie Steiner, the director of the Goetheanum stage performances, worked on the creation of a theatre for the Mysteries and helped to bring the dramatic works of Albert Steffen to effect. A high point was reached in the production of the whole of Faust in the years 1938 and 1939. Then came the outbreak of war and the Swiss frontiers were closed. Only meagre news from Dornach reached the other countries. Stein, who was in London, received news from friends that a new crisis had broken out in the Society, a second conflict

14   W J Stein with his wife Nora and his daughter Clarissa Johanna about 1929-30

about Rudolf Steiner's literary legacy. Marie Steiner had called together a group of competent members who were to carry on the administration and publication of Rudolf Steiner's literary works after her death. The institution of this 'Nachlass' Association was not recognised by her Vorstand colleagues Steffan and Wachsmuth, with whom a majority of the members sided, and her testamentary claim was declared irreconcilable with the rights of the Society concerning Rudolf Steiner's estate. Marie Steiner found herself in a similar situation to the one she was in when Stein had questioned the validity of Dr Steiner's will with his well-known arguments.

At this stage of the crisis Stein wrote a letter to Marie Steiner 'on 30 March 1948'—in remembrance of Rudolf Steiner's death. Twenty years had passed since their last stormy meeting.

These had been years of soul-searching and inner transformation for Stein. The dialectical rhetorician had turned into a lecturer who had learned how to speak out of inner hearing. The aggressiveness had given way to a mildness of manner which struck both his interlocutors and audiences at his lectures. This new note is sounded in his letter to Marie Steiner: 'I have experienced the restorative qualities of long silence. And the fruits of this silence is the present letter'.

The lavishly corrected rough copy contained in four typewritten pages and the shortened original of the letter reduced to three pages were found among Stein's papers. He never sent off the letter. What he wrote gives the impression of having been an exercise in retrospection. The rough copy shows this more clearly than the original. In this he calls to mind his meetings with Marie Steiner and recreates pictures of the past. His discerning eye rests upon these pictures and penetrates the surface to probe into soul-depths. Here he is confronted by what is essential: the true, will-related, destiny-seeking ego. Two scenes stand out from the rest holding a symbolic significance for him. He describes them at the begining and at the end of the rough draft of his letter: 'I shall never forget the moment when I knelt beside you on the stage and you spoke to me of Rudolf Steiner's death. I begged you that you would not let Dr Steiner's body be cremated and you were inclined to consider this. It was like a premonition of what was to ensue...' The other picture relates to the events of 8 October 1928 when Stein, after having once more brought up the

15   Marie Steiner

question of the will, was excluded from further discussions. 'It was a bitter experience on that day when I last entered the Goetheanum. A cordon of people were facing me. They had crossed arms with one another forming a chain which was to separate me from them, as though I were a dangerous animal, and slowly this chain of human hands pushed me towards the exit. It was the last time I was inside the Goetheanum'. Stein takes this 'bitter experience' as a self-chosen destiny and thanks those who had excluded him 'before still greater misfortune befell', namely the misfortune of the second conflict concerning Rudolf Steiner's estate. He wanted to have no part in that, as he twice repeated, for he 'was not able to visualise an Anthroposophical Society without Marie Steiner'. What he knew about Ita Wegman, that she 'wished for nothing else during the last years of her life than to be reconciled to you (Marie Steiner)', held good for him too. Stein concludes his letter with a prospect of the future: 'What we did wrong in the past will be known by each one of us at the moment of entry into the spiritual world at death'.[139] Then, from the all-embracing perspective of cosmic justice the changed view of our deeds and omissions will engender in us a determination to 'order our next life in a way which will compensate for what we have done in this'.[140] The writer was filled with the will to compensate, even though the letter remained unposted.

Stein's inner attitude towards Ita Wegman is full of mystery. A correspondence with her which can be vouched for as having lasted from 1924 to 1939 throws some light on the difficulties within the development of the Anthroposophical Society, upon the spread of spiritual science and the personal problems of destiny and knowledge. In his letters Stein strikes a note of heartfelt grateful devotion. He was well aware of the importance of this often wrongly interpreted personality and begs her to be a 'guiding, helpful friend' to him. He feels that she understands him, because his intentions are acknowledged even when his words had caused pain. And he marvels at the magnanimity and mobility of this soul which was able to grasp the spirit concretely and whose thoughts embraced cosmpolitan connections. She appeared to him as an incarnation of 'womanly spirit' to whom his manly spirit offered itself in veneration. As Wegman also served Stein's family in a medical capacity a familiarity grew up which permitted an unreserved frankness of communication. Wegman

16   W.J Stein about 1931

returned this sentiment with warmth of heart and fostered the relationship in the knowledge of their karmic connection.

Like a leitmotiv through the whole correspondence ran the question of the spiritual continuity of the Anthroposophical Society. Misunderstandings and crises of trust were not lacking between leading members working together. Stein, always ready to account for his actions, was obliged to write letters of explanation and apology to Marie Steiner and Albert Steffen, of which he gave copies to Wegman. They contain expressions of unsparing self-knowledge regarding his way of dealing which tends to severity. In the draft of a letter to Albert Steffen occur the phrases: 'My mode of expressing myself has always upset many people, they think I want to impose my opinion upon them. Certainly my intention has been to convince; I did it, however, in a way which, instead of convincing them, made them feel it was an attack!' He added thereto that he would do all in his power to overcome this bad habit in future.

The work of Stein in ferreting out scientific sources and procuring proofs was very welcome. At the request of Wegman he collected material which she needed for her study tours or for the writing of articles for the magazine *Natura* which she had founded. He sent her lists of the literature dealing with geographical medicine, with the connection of illness-producing factors to geographical circumstances; he brought references from the 'Physiognomics' of Aristotle which could sharpen the perception of the therapist, and instructed her regarding the geological structure of the Hebridean islands of Iona and Staffa, places which are of importance in the history of the Mystery Schools. He also produced a short outline 'Concerning the founding of European medicine in conjunction with the Mysteries', for the life's work of Wegman consisted in founding a new medicine based on the Mysteries in which possibilities were sought through the knowledge of initiation. The basis of this 'new medicine of the initiate' was Rudolf Steiner's last book: *Fundamentals of Therapy. An Extension of the Art of Healing through Spiritual Knowledge*[141] written in collaboration with Ita Wegman, the results of anthroposophical research applied to the realm of medicine.

'Frau Dr Wegman is a woman of action not of words' explained Rudolf Steiner at the Christmas Conference. Through her energy and world-wide connections stretching from India to America,

17   Ita Wegman

the medical movement got under way. She envisaged spiritual campaigns in which Stein was to play a special role. In 1932 he was to move to Berlin and London where she had founded medical centres, then he was to have been a lecturer and a regular contributor to journals and finally he was to have found a suitable sphere of action in America. This plan, for which she had set aside funds, had been discussed with the English General Secretary and the expenses had been worked out. The West was to be opened up for Anthroposophy. A pioneering work was to be undertaken and this 'should always be carried out by people with tremendous enthusiasm and an urge to act'. Thus she wrote to Stein on 4 April 1935, just before she was excluded from the Vorstand of the Society. She valued his combative spirit in spiritual matters, acknowledged the publication of his Grail book as being 'a great step in our work', supported the publication of Nora Stein's collection of Michael Legends and contributed the introductory text to: *Aus Michaels Wirken*[142] (About the Activity of Michael). In the foreword she emphasised that it was Rudolf Steiner's research into the spiritual beings who rule over the Epochs which had made it possible for the first time to understand the evidence of history; thereby revealing the 'true being', the 'concrete spiritual figure' of the 'Regent of the Age'.[143] She wished to help this Being to a breakthrough in its activity and found in Stein an energetic helper.

The realisation of this 'concrete spiritual figure' was their mutual endeavour. Stein approached it through the study of Anthroposophy which became for him an esoteric training. He thought of himself as a pupil of the Spirit of the Age whom he had met through Rudolf Steiner. And this meeting ignited his spiritual enthusiasm and awakened in him memories of his pre-natal experiences. Out of that sprang an impulse of will; a sacred vow to bind himself in inviolable fidelity to this Spirit-Being. Until 1924 he could still discuss with his spiritual teacher the obstacles and difficulties which beset him on the inner path. But then Rudolf Steiner became ill. Stein wrote to Wegman on 16 March 1925: 'My path is a hard one. Because I am unable to question Dr Steiner in the way that I could do formerly, I have to fight many battles alone'.

The death of his teacher confronted the pupil with the task of teaching himself, of becoming his own spiritual guide. 'It was not difficult', wrote Michael Bauer 'to address a lightly posed question to Rudolf Steiner during his lifetime and receive an answer in reply. Now, since his death, the question has to be posed quite differently in the depths of the soul, it has to become simply a clear expression of the soul seeking for knowledge'.[144]

This experience was also shared by Stein. He refers in his letters to subtle spiritual experiences and intimacies of soul life. He also indicates how he addresses a question to Rudolf Steiner out of a meditative mood: 'Under what sign is this year's Christmas (1926)?' The answer rose up in him as 'thought-experience' and as a threefold call to awaken: 'Experience the birth of the higher self, experience the widths and the heights, experience your surroundings in the marvel of the human frame, Christmas within Man', coming to expression in the threefold Adoration of the Kings, of the Shepherds and of Joseph and Mary. Stein takes up the exercises which Rudolf Steiner gave for developing an awareness of karma and arrives at impressions which he confides to Wegman. He observes changes in his dream-life and experiences spiritual intimations in illumined night-consciousness which point the direction to him for his Grail research and his understanding of destiny.

The letters become fewer after 1935. The disastrous developments emanating from Gemany were also a hindrance to anthroposophical activity abroad and to arriving at an understanding by way of letters.

There was yet another personality who had a decisive influence on the direction of Stein's work after Rudolf Steiner's death. She too, like Ita Wegman, was distinguished by her karmic closeness to Rudolf Steiner and had joined the Theosophical Society very early. We are referring to Eliza von Moltke, the wife of Helmuth von Moltke.

The discussions and exchange of ideas began in the summer of 1926 when Stein gave a lecture in Berlin about St Odilie. What their first meeting was like is mentioned by Stein in his obituary address for Eliza von Moltke who died on 29 May 1932.[145] After having come to the end of his lecture she came up to him and said that she had information from Rudolf Steiner about the subject of his lecture and was prepared to hand it on to him if he so desired. Stein accepted immediately, but remarked that he would soon have to leave. As a consequence of this the conversation took place directly after the lecture in Eliza von Moltke's apartments. After a long time she interrupted the flow of conversation to go to the window because the infiltrating light seemed so strange to her. As she drew back the curtain it became evident that dawn had already broken. That was Stein's 'first visit to Her Excellency von Moltke'.

That which he learned in the night-long conversation he described as of 'world importance'. Unusual historical connections certainly came to his knowledge then. Referring to his lecture she told him of the walk to which she had been invited by Rudolf Steiner in the cave-filled precincts of the *Erimitage* when she visited Dornach for the first time in August 1917. Rudolf Steiner described this place as the one in which Odilie sought refuge from the persecution of her father, Duke Eticho. The 'Divine Sun'—*Sol Dei* in Latin—as St Odilie was called, then founded a nunnery on Mount St Odilie in Alsace which rayed forth an esoteric Christianity independent of Rome.

But Odilie was only the starting-point of the conversation which spread out over many topics. Eliza von Moltke had had wide experience in life and as a member of the court circles around the Kaiser in which the Moltkes, as bearers of a famous name, had a prominent position, she well knew of the power-struggles which went on there. She herself had had a pathway through life which was not unusual at that time. After having passed through a materialistic phase she had turned to Spiritualism. What she had experienced during the nineties in the way of mediumistic phenomena induced her to search for an access to knowledge of the supersensible. As she was in possession of a sober reasoning power she felt attracted by the clarity of Rudolf Steiner's thoughts and joined the anthroposophical movement after the turn of the century. She, too, was one of the first to be accepted by Rudolf Steiner into the newly-founded Esoteric School in 1904. He appended to his letter of invitation of 12 August 1904 the following observation: 'I often think of the wonderful times I was able to have in your house. I have also become very friendly with your husband and have great hopes for his spiritual future. Sometimes people's lives take a special course; but there are many pathways to knowledge'. Helmuth and Eliza von Moltke were very different in the way they looked at life. Whereas she was always open to receive anything of an occult

18   Eliza von Moltke 1930

nature, he remained sceptically hesitant, borne up by a cordial belief in religion. At the urgent request of Eliza von Moltke Rudolf Steiner also accompanied her to séances, which took place in her house. From the records it can be seen that he took part in these meetings as a tolerant and positive observer who was able to understand clearly what lay at the back of the phenomena and correct the medium too. The basic difference between the methods of spiritual-scientific research and spiritualistic practices were explained by him in a public lecture on 'Theosophy and Spiritualism' a quarter of a year before the séances, held on 1 February 1904, took place. The spiritualist is also searching for information from the spiritual world, but he makes use of man's mediumistic faculties, which put him into a state of trance in which he becomes an involuntary tool of supernatural influences. In contradistinction to this the spiritual-scientific investigator searches for an ego-based comprehension of spiritual beings through elevating and transforming his powers of cognition to conscious imagination, inspiration and intuition. He is in possession of critical—that is self-controlling—consciousness and regards it as 'prejudicial to human independence, as an obstacle to the right of every human being to decide for himself, if he relinquishes the clear consciousness which has been acquired in the course of nature and returns to that condition of development which he had already acquired in former stages of evolution'.[146]

As far as Helmuth von Moltke is concerned, his relationship to Rudolf Steiner only deepened after he had been asked by the Kaiser to resign from his post as Chief of General Staff. After that there were repeated meetings and discussions between them. Moltke drew Rudolf Steiner into his confidence when in November 1914—after the tragedy of the Marne Battle—he wrote his memoirs of what happened at the outbreak of war.[147] What now transpired led to an unexpected clarification of world-historic connections. Rudolf Steiner gave him an insight into a karmic past and a karmic connection to Pope Nikolas I in the historic events which have become known to us through Steffen's drama: *The Chief of the General Staff* (1927). The mysterious saying of Rudolf Steiner in his obituary address for the deceased Moltke on 18 June 1916 points to how unusual was the constellation of this meeting: 'Therefore it is true that what flows and pulses through this our spiritual-scientific current has received just as much from this soul (Moltke) as we were able to give it'.[148]

But what had begun during Moltke's lifetime was only a prelude to the unwritten Mystery Play which began after his death. Rudolf Steiner now accompanied Moltke's entelechy on its after-death pathway and transmitted, at first orally and later in written messages to his widow, what the dead person was experiencing as a result of his past life. Now he could visualise his karmic connections: the karmic cause from his last life in the ninth century and the possibility of atonement in the near future were communicated to him through spiritual experiences. The 'inner aspect' of the ninth century was revealed, the century in which the Grail events took place, in which the Fathers of the Eighth Ecumenical Council condemned the Trichotomy and denied the Spirit, in which the separation of the Eastern and Western Church was announced. A tapestry of deeds and aims of those who create history, into whose souls the powers which form destiny are working, was now laid bare. In the centre of events stood the powerful representatives of the Papal Primates, the Roman Nikolas, his advisory Cardinal Anastasius Bibliothecarius, and their opponent, the Patriarch Photius, the Leader of the Greek Church. At the height of the Great War, when America was rising to become a World Power and Soviet leadership was stirring, the world-historical cause of the West-East problem was plainly evident. What shows forth in the twentieth century as political and economic dissension had been prepared in the ninth century in the field of religion where the dogmatic and ritualistic differences of the Eastern and Western Churches betrayed the future split. In his obituary address for Eliza von Moltke, Stein was able to say that he had 'lived for years with all this'.[149]

When at Rudolf Steiner's death the stream of spiritual-scientific revelations dried up Eliza von Moltke reverted to the methods of Spiritualism. In her circle were people who possessed mediumistic faculties and made known many things, either verbally or in writing, of a prophetic and fascinating nature while in a state of trance. It was of course known to her that Rudolf Steiner had explained that mediumism was no longer an appropriate means of gaining access to the spiritual world in our time, but she trusted in her own judgement and believed that she could discriminate between reality and illusion in this realm. Stein who sometimes took part in such sittings, was also of the same opinion. Many of the mediumistic statements perplexed him because, to his astonishment, they made reference to him and to his work and surroundings and gave answers to silent or spoken questions; answers which gave him directions which were of help, but also brought him agonising uncertainty of knowledge.

3
A Youth Conference

The conflicts which arose after Rudolf Steiner's death certainly threatened the unity of the Anthroposophical Society, but as long as representatives from the diverging parties could bring themselves to meet together at the big conferences, it seemed possible to bridge over the differences.

Thus in the year 1928, after overcoming considerable difficulties, invitations could be sent out for a world conference for spiritual science, which met in London from 20 July to 1 August. This lavishly planned 'World Conference of Spiritual Science and its Practical Applications', initiated by D.N. Dunlop, was to introduce Spiritual Science with its practical application in Medicine, the Arts, Natural Science, History, Education, Religion, Curative Education, Economy and Agriculture to the British Public.[150] Stein gave the introduction on the day devoted to History. He still spoken in German at that time and took as his theme 'History in the Light of the Holy Grail', a subject he had dealt with in his simultaneously appearing Grail book, taking the ninth century as an example.

Two months later, at Michaelmas, was the great opening celebration for the Second Goetheanum in which 2,000 members took part. Here, too, there had been painful deliberations over the drawing up of the programme on which the names of Eugen and Lili Kolisko appeared, but not that of Stein.

The representatives of the various currents were again brought together in the year 1930 over the task of arranging for a European Summer School. Ita Wegman and Elizabeth Vreede, as well as Guenther Wachsmuth, all members of the Dornach Vorstand, gave lectures and courses in the 'Kamp de Stakenberg', a camping site in N.E. Holland. An event such as this youth camp had never taken place before. The enterprise, lasting from 2 to 10

August, was a hazardous one, but it succeeded beyond all expectation.[151]

Former participants treasure to this day the memory of it as a festival of human encounter. The initiator of this youth gathering was a Dutch student who wanted to create an opportunity for members of the younger generation to get acquainted with Anthroposophy in action by meeting those of an older generation.

He had the notion of a conference in which, through the living and working together of the participants, trust founded on spiritual understanding could be engendered between young and old. The idea took hold and found spontaneous acceptance. The Dutch National Society took over the organisation of the youth camp and Willem Zeylmans van Emmichoven its General Secretary, together with the student who initiated the enterprise, searched for a suitable camping site. Finally they discovered an estate of 40 hectares [nearly 100 acres] with a roomy house among woods and moorland.

Next began an intensive appeal 'to all young people'. A 'Camp Newsletter' with explanatory articles appeared in the Netherlands, Germany, Switzerland and Great Britain. Offices for enrolment were set up in all the large cities—with the result that, instead of the expected five or six hundred applicants, nearly twice as many enrolled, making great demands on the improvised means at the disposal of the organisers.

The intentions of those in charge was expressed by Willem Zeylmans in his 'Call to the Kamp de Stakenberg' which constituted the first number of the 'Camp Newspaper':[152]

We send out this call to all young people who desire to serve the spirit of the times . . . He who would serve humanity must first know *how* humanity may best be served. He must know what is the spirit of the age, which, at a given moment, will manifest itself in the hearts and heads of those who will then assume the responsibility for the furtherance of evolution . . . We who have heard Rudolf Steiner, believe that his words have revealed to us the true Spirit of the times. We who knew Rudolf Steiner are convinced that his work stood for the service of this Spirit . . . We desire to accomplish our task in company with all those who are ready to place their youthful forces at the service of all humanity . . .

The call ended with a reference to the central theme of Anthroposophy and its significance for the immediate present:

> Do men know that Rudolf Steiner is the founder of the Free High School of Spiritual Science at Dornach, near Basel? ... Do men know of the things which have already been achieved in these spheres? Do men know with what insight Rudolf Steiner revealed the story of the evolution of mankind? What paths he pointed out to those seeking souls who desired to build up their own forces, who wished to undertake an inner training? Do men know that Rudolf Steiner taught of the essential nature of Divine Service? Of the central place therein of the exalted Divine Being—the Christ—and his relationship to humanity and to the world? or the relationship of the Christ to mankind in the near future? To tell of this is our mission ... In the working together and living together of young men and women the seeds of the New Reality can be sown ...

This fiery appeal was not intended to convert the young people to any special cause, not even to that of Anthroposophy; rather, it was intended to draw attention to the opportunity for determining one's own direction in life which could come about through an exchange of ideas with pupils of Rudolf Steiner at this dramatic moment in time. This idea was accepted and its intention understood. Leinhas reports[153] that, with few exceptions, it was young people—from Germany mainly practical people from all walks of life, from Holland many students—who followed the call. Through Stein's description the picture is completed. He arrived already on 29 July for the so-called preliminary camp and describes in his letters to his wife Nora and to Eliza von Moltke the pitching of the tents, the scenery and the people and his own contribution.

> After some days of preparation the influx began. They arrived on foot, on bikes and by all methods of transport. Seven hundred young strangers, three hundred members, a thousand in all. It was very moving to experience what sacrifice had been entailed. Taking jobs on the journey they travelled from place to place, many of them for weeks on end. Three hundred Germans, two hundred from Holland, eighty from England, and so on. One Chinese, one negress and an Indian. Never had I been able to speak so freely. I gave a course on the whole of world history and I contributed to the theme of social

problems . . . I felt—as all the others did, too—that Dr Steiner's spirit was continually present.[154]

The participating young people experienced a wholeness of ideas in the variety of the study groups, discussion circles and lectures. The unifying principle was the fruit of painstaking preparation and thorough study. Emanuel Zeylmans quoted an example: 'Elizabeth Vreede came from Dornach specially to see the grounds. She describes how on Ascension Day 1930 she went over the grounds at Stakenberg in all directions in view of the Camp taking place there in the beginning of August. In a most impressive way she quoted verses of Rudolf Steiner referring to the way that nature can be experienced during August'.[155] Those are the sayings from the great seasonal verse, the *Calendar of the Soul*, which seeks to unite the human soul with the Universal-Spirit revealing itself through the seasons. The verses for the beginning of August speak about the human soul receiving into itself the Word of Worlds and, surrendered to the Cosmic Spirit, finding strength within itself. And that was the aim of the Stakenberg venture: to stimulate spiritual experience in the certainty of awakening selfconsciousness.

Willem Zeylmans in his preparations turned his thoughts towards the Christ-Mystery of the twentieth century, which Rudolf Steiner has described. This 'Mystical Fact' has become perceptible since the nineteen-thirties by means of an experience akin to that of St Paul. As the Resurrected One appeared to his persecutor Saul before Damascus, so can He appear as a Living Comforter to the souls of those who are hard pressed. They will recognise Him in etheric form when 'their eyes have been made more acute through the study of Anthroposophy'.[156] 'The first indications of these new faculties will become more clearly apparent in the middle of the thirties of this century, approximately in the period between 1930 and 1940'.[157]

Stein's contribution to the preparation of the youth camp grew up in collaboration with Ita Wegman. He, too, lived in awareness of the 'threshold-time' of the thirties. The insight he acquired into it was published by him in a survey of the year 1930 in the periodical *Natura*.[158]

In 1930 the might of a supersensible knowledge, which has been

19   In the Stakenberg Camp 1930: W.J. Stein right foreground. In the basket-chair-for-two Elisabeth Vreede left; Ita Wegman right

developed unnoticed within man since 1899 will begin to unfold. Rudolf Steiner already described this visionary consciousness in his *Philosophy of Spiritual Activity*. In that book he calls it 'Moral imagination'. Through this faculty man, as a person endowed with supersensible (intuitive) knowledge, gains the possibility of turning this knowledge into deeds, i.e. of becoming free. He only can act freely who acts out of knowledge free from the body, that is from intuition. This knowledge is able to perceive the world in which the Christ is active as the Being in which all human and earthly goals are united.

In discussing the work with Ita Wegman, whom Stein visited in Arlesheim, the subject dealt with concerned the creating of a Persephone poem which was to renew the Greek myth. The ancient myth tells of the abduction of Persephone, the destiny of the human soul plunged into the physical body and spiritually blinded. In modern times the release of Persephone should be shown, freed from imprisonment and enabled to see again in the light of the spirit. Rudolf Steiner had spoken to Wegman about this further development of the theme and had thereby envisaged it as a task for her.[159]

Now Wegman took up this plan of Rudolf Steiner after having already published, in 1925, an essay about the Mysteries of Ephesus and the activity of Persephone.[160] What she had then begun she now extended as an elaboration of the Ancient Mysteries and of modern initiation-science, which was like the preparation for the poetic rendering of the Persephone theme. 'In modern times the whole view of nature has been lost through the decline of imagination. A knowledge of nature has arisen, which is certainly grandiose, but shattered into fragments. In such natural-scientific endeavours as this there lies, again, a first attempt to press forward to an imaginative view of nature. The total release of Persephone has again been the work of Rudolf Steiner. In his view of nature lives the complete human being, the fragmentation of the single disciplines has been overcome.[161]

It has to be shown as a dramatic occurrence of the present day how Persephone, still known to the Teachers of Chartres as 'The Goddess Natura', holds sway in the realm of the etheric forces as a spiritual elementary force. But Wegman hoped for Stein's collaboration in rendering her spiritual vision in its final poetic form (see appendix).

The result of the collaboration was a dramatic fragment: three scenes in the handwriting of Wegman and Stein, who took turns in writing it. It was intended to be performed at the Camp, but had to be abandoned because the dramatic portrayal of soul-and-spiritual events did not come up to the artistic expectations of the camp leader Zeylmans. Instead a production of Edouard Schuré's drama of Eleusis was presented; a play showing 'The History of Psyche-Persephone'.

Stein then elaborated the Persephone theme in his history course. In conclusion he spoke about the certainty that the Goddess 'would arise again in our time' and he ended with a quotation from the 'poetic fragment':

> 'Heaven and earth weave together
> in man
> When Persephone
> in your souls
> Changes your will
> into flaming deed'.

For Stein the Camp at Stakenberg was an event of incomparable importance. He divulged in his letters to Nora what he experienced as the hidden significance of it all. Immediately after an adventurous journey to the Camp 'with local trains with no connections' he began an intensive study of the history of the Greek Mysteries. He perceived thereby in a kind of inspiration: 'An Ephesus, a spiritual Ephesus must arise here. That is the motto for this occasion'.[162] Such experiences were not unfamiliar to him. When his study of the lecture cycles deepened into meditative pondering of their content it could happen that a fruitful exchange of ideas between Spirit-teacher and Spirit-pupil then arose and an inspirational experience of the words commenced. Afterwards Stein tested what he had thus received by applying it to the reality.

A meeting of collaborators took place on 31 July, after many of the participants had already arrived. This included Ita Wegman, D.N. Dunlop and his co-worker E.C. Merry, George Adams, Maria Röschl and others, altogether about thirty-five people took part. Stein reported on what took place in a letter written the same day to Nora:

Everyone gave his impression of what he thought to be the meaning of the Conference. I said: 'Of those who are gathered here only a third are anthroposophists. Two thirds of them are complete strangers. But all of them, one feels, belong to us. A great deal of will and the courage to make sacrifices led these people here to this place of woods and moorland, far from villages, towns or railways. Not one of them has come here out of curiosity. These people are following a call of destiny. Let us look upon these friends as old acquaintances who have only now found the way to us. It is not by mere chance that we have put Persephone here as the centrepiece of our programme. In looking at Persephone's destiny a kind of memory dawns in our souls. Persephone is not Eleusinian—much rather is her archetype Ephesian. Persephone reminds us of Ephesus. There, too, were woods and moorland. We are celebrating a memorial festival of Ephesus. Let us allow the people to find one another and us once more'.—That sounded the keynote. From that point an inkling pervades the communal life. No one mentions it but everyone goes about saying: 'How familiar it all is'.

It seemed to Stein that he was inhaling a breath of the Mysteries in this remote place, as if the quiet Temple precincts of Ephesus were present, the rites of which had been described by Rudolf Steiner.[163] The great temple of Artemis stood on the west coast of Asia Minor dedicated to Artemis the sister of Apollo, Goddess of fertility. In the Artemis rites the Mysteries of macrocosmic development were experienced, in the Persephone rites the inner secrets of nature. And Stein believed he could discern their whisperings. The environment of the Camp of Stakenberg had become for him a transparency through which shone the Mystery World of Ephesus.

What Stein perceived was also experienced by others. A girl student describes how she became aware of

powerfully effective pictures from the Ancient Mysteries appearing to her as spirit-memories during Stein's history lectures and in the performance of the Eleusis-Drama. How could one fail to remember when Walter Johannes Stein called to life pictures of world history during a rain storm which beat down upon the great marquee? On me his lectures about the Temple of Ephesus made the deepest impression. A quite dutifully carried out secondary education suddenly became significant at this moment. And when a thing gains significance, does not everything in life change? . . . We were swept along on a mighty current—our aim the future!.[164]

4
Journeys of Discovery

The thirties of this century were filled with a mounting unrest. Contemporary history was undergoing violent change, as though a hidden tension were building up to an explosion. During that time Stein went on extended journeys to give lectures and to study in England and Scotland; to Portugal, Spain and North Africa and Turkey. These journeys, like searching forays in quest of future and past destiny, turned into voyages of discovery comparable to Goethe's journey to Italy with all its karmic consequence. They opened up before him not only spatial vistas, but also vistas in time and pointed Stein the way to the fulfilment of his destiny in the last third of his life.

He had already practised a way of travel leading to psychic revelation and spiritual change when, in August 1925, he visited Burgenland and the eastern part of Austria, with his wife Nora and his friend Kolisko. He reports in detail about his experiences and researches to Ita Wegman, who felt herself 'irresistibly attracted' to the Burgenland and who published an essay about the history of its past Mysteries in September 1925.[165]

Unusual events occurred during this journey. The tour led from Wiener Neustadt, where Rudolf Steiner matriculated, across the River Leitha, the former border between the Austrian and Hungarian parts of the Hapsburg Monarchy, to Sauerbrunn, which lies in the north west corner of Burgenland. There the travellers experienced, at the fall of night and in the dawn, the elementary weaving of a still pristine nature, whose etheric flow of life was revealed to the boy Rudolf Steiner in what he described as 'Das Quellenwunder', the 'Miracle of the Spring'. 'One has the feeling here that everywhere around the heavens are close at hand'. That is how Stein experienced the 'unutterable peace' of the landscape.[166] Then the journey was continued in a southerly direction to Lockenhaus. In a small village inn which the party reached along a dusty country lane in a horse-drawn cart, a makeshift accommodation was found. Already on the first night after their arrival Stein began to write down the impressions of his visit to Lockenhaus Castle[167] 'by the light of a paraffin lamp that cast more shadows than it shed light'. He wanted to investigate the historical records connected with the castles of Lockenhaus and Bernstein, because they form the background for the medieval scenes of Rudolf Steiner's Mystery Play *The Soul's Probation*. The main characters of the play, contemporaries of the twentieth century, are led in spiritual vision during the course of their initiation to a life in the Middle Ages which they passed in a Templar castle or in its environment. Their retrospective experiences are connected with the tragic history of the Order of the Knights Templar which, after its persecution and destruction by the French King Philipp IV, suffered the same fate in Hungary. On the lookout for clues to the Templar tragedy in Burgenland Stein discovered evidence, in the rooms of the castle and in local tradition, for the activity of the Templars, who had also worked for antimony, that highly-prized medicament of the Alchemists, in a nearby mine; and in the manorial seat of Bernstein, which was connected with Lockenhaus, he found alchemical apparatus and proofs of Rosicrucian activity.

Unexpected help was available for these discoveries. The owner of Bernstein regarded the visit as an act of destiny and it turned out that he was 'one of us'; Nora Stein had visionary dreams which gave her important information and Ita Wegman acted, according to Stein, 'as our unseen helper consciously at our side'.[168]

But Stein was looking for a still deeper layer of the historical past in Burgenland, namely a Mystery Centre from the third pre-Christian millenium. In lectures about cultural history Rudolf Steiner pointed out that 'a colony belonging to the Hibernian Mysteries' existed there, at which Gilgamesh arrived on his westward journeying.[169] The starting-point of Stein's investigation was the astonishing fact that a Sumerian King from the 'Land of the Two Rivers' travelled to Central Europe in order to receive an answer to his question about immortality from a priest of the Hibernian Mysteries. He describes, in a paper on 'The Historic Spiritual Importance of the Burgenland'[170] how the spiritual-scientific statements of Rudolf Steiner became understandable to him through an experience of the landscape and a study of the geological conditions. In the vicinity of Bernstein, he guessed that the sought for place would be where a conical peak rises up from its surroundings. 'As though from a regal lookout post one can see from here over the whole country. Towards the South East the plains of Hungary stretch for miles in marvellous serenity. Towards the South one's gaze looks far into the Styrian landscape, even into Croatian territory. In the immediate vicinity lies the most beautiful part of the Burgenland in all its variety. One is standing here on an important place where the last ridges of the Alps stretch out from west to east. Both from a geological aspect as also from a human historic one, it is a threshold between West and East'. The region is rich in minerals, copper and antimony occur here; and prehistoric remains from the Bronze Age.

At that time trade routes led in all directions, even into England, where tin, so necessary for the manufacture of bronze, was mined in Cornwall. Finally, it is known from occult history[171] that through the receiving of metallic substances, including copper, into the human body changes of consciousness and initiation experiences were induced. From all these factors Stein drew the conclusion that this 'Regal lookout post' close to Castle Bernstein had been the Gilgamesh Centre.[172]

On 28 August a second journey to Bernstein and Lockenhaus took place, this time in the company of Ita Wegman. The Mystery Centre exerted an enigmatic attraction. The Burgenland, at the meeting point of the ridges of high ground from the west and the low-lying plains to the east, where from times past the attacks of oriental conquerors have been repulsed, served the double task of being both a boundary and a bridge, fulfilling, at the same time as being a boundary, the function of a threshold.[173] In this country, priests crossed the border as bridge-builders from the sense world to the supersensible, and there arose there, as it states on the memorial tablet to Rudolf Steiner at the Neudörfl Station building, 'the basis for the child's spiritual world'.

As always after such journeys Stein collected together in the form of essays the results of his work and the fruits of his knowledge. Thus he wrote a lengthy treatise about the Gilgamesh Epic after his journey to the Burgenland, an exposition of this earliest piece of human poetry which describes the Sumerian

King as 'a wanderer towards the goal of mankind'.

In 1931 and 1932 there followed the journeys which Stein experienced as 'soul-transforming pilgrimages'. He undertook a lecturing tour to England in February 1931. The whole stay was as stormy as the crossing itself. Already on the day of arrival he gave his first lecture in London. He spoke about Apollo and the Goddess Natura—the Ruler in the soul-realm and the Queen of the life-forces—who served the Christ-Being first as His astral sheath and then as His etheric sheath on His path of revelation prior to the turning-point of time. Although, by England standards, his lecture was 'fairly long', his audience followed with uninterrupted attention, because he did not only develop his theme with his accustomed confidence in his knowledge of the facts, but also made clear what he said with numerous examples from pre- and post-Christian occult history. After he had finished Dunlop jokingly said: 'Dr Stein speaks with such precision that some will say it was Ahrimanic; and so beautifully and with such warmth that some will say that it was Luciferic, but . . .'[174]

Next day he visited a Persian exhibition and saw 'wonderful friezes from Persepolis', the Royal Palace which Alexander conquered and burned on his march against the Persians. In reflective contemplation Stein was carried back in memory and the conviction dawned on him that he had 'seen these reliefs once before at the time of Alexander'.[175] Around visits such as these, conversations developed with anthroposophical friends who, like he, had received exercises from Rudolf Steiner for developing higher organs of cognition. Fine perceptions from personal spiritual experience were exchanged, particularly with E.C. Merry, Dunlop's collaborator, whereby the discriminatory faculty for karmic events was sharpened.

But the main theme of this English journey, so full of soul-drama, was the following up of the 'Lohengrin track'.[176] Stein was working on the continuation of his *World History in the Light of the Holy Grail*. After the portrayal of the Ninth Century, the tenth century was to have been dealt with and the activity of Lohengrin, the successor to Parzival, was to have been shown. To clarify the spiritual background of historical events, to testify to the part played therein by the 'Lord of History', that was what Stein meant as the writing of history 'in the Light of the Holy Grail'. He looked upon himself as a searcher for historical truth, creating through his knowledge of destiny an organ of historical discernment. That signified for him a self-imposed demand for knowledge which included his involvement in mankind's evolution, because man participates in history as a bearer of his destiny through repeated earthly lives. The basis of the search for truth is attachment to the earth through the ego; and from that follows 'the personal involvement of the historical investigator with his subject matter'.[177]

Stein was conscious of this 'personal involvement', but he self-critically tested its validity since his Grail Book had met with rejection from colleagues and experts.[178]

In his Lohengrin research he sought for a connection between medieval town development and the change in people's consciousness. For the time of the founding of cities 'corresponds exactly with the time of mankind's transition from the world of dreaming to that of modern economic life'.[179] The Founding of this new civilisation and stage of consciousness is mirrored in the Lohengrin Saga: in the uniting of the Swan Knight from the Round Table with Elsa von Brabant, who represents the city consciousness.[180] Lohengrin appears as the inspirer of a worldly town-centred culture—the successor to the chivalrous culture of the spirit—which, along with the growth of urban communities, seeks to replace previous overlordship by organs of self-rulership. To find out where this development had its origin, Stein carried out research in England.

On 20 February he made a journey to Peterborough in the eastern part of England, from where he was to visit Crowland Abbey. He noticed with astonishment the canals and windmills which give the countryside a Dutch character and the name New Holland. Here he met the Abbot, who gave him a personally conducted tour, after having first assured himself of his visitor's interest and knowledge in history. What Stein experienced later through his observation of the landscape, where swans were bred, through his examination of documents and lists of Abbots, in listening to the inner voice which literally pointed the way to him in decisive matters, all this went to confirm him in his conviction that: 'the saga of the Swan Knight does not have its origin in Braband, Holland or Kleve, as some would have it, but in the English Province of Holland in the vicinity of Peterborough. But in this case it is not just a saga, it is actual history. The time has now arrived, after the lapse of 1,000 years, when the story has to be freed from the shades of the legend'.[179] That was the object in view for the book he had planned to write on the tenth century.

But circumstances prevented its fulfilment. Stein was only able to write down the beginning of the first chapter. Herewith he straighway sets the stage for the spiritually dramatic events of the tenth century under the title:

The Knight of the Swan and Roman World-Domination. The tenth century is the century of the struggle between worldly town-centred culture and Roman world-wide domination. Two spirits of the Age are fighting for the overlordship. In the world-dominating power of Rome a past civilisation founded on a grandiose tradition is fighting for supremacy; in the town-building impulse the newly-uprising Age of the Cities is asserting itself. The fourth and fifth epochs were engaged in a preliminary struggle. Preliminary, because it was only in 1413 that the fifth epoch began. We must look upon the founding of the *Holy Roman Empire of the German Nations* as the bulwark erected against the fifth epoch. That was the attempt to romanise the fifth epoch . . . Into this struggle between ancient Roman power-politics and the germinally-arising town culture there gleams *The Saga of Lohengrin, the Swan Knight.*

Stein wanted to show how, in the striving after freedom and self-government in the towns, expressed through the practising of simple handicrafts and peaceful international trade, a Grail-impulse was at work which had as its aim the founding of an economic system out of a Christian spirit. As a bearer of this impulse he identified Turketul, who lived in the tenth century, was known as a Swan Knight, served as Chancellor under two town-building English kings and died as the Abbot of Crowland Abbey. From England—according to Stein—the Lohengrin or town-culture spread out, for here town-like centres were built at an earlier date than on the Continent: in order to protect the inhabitants from invasions of the Danes. What made its appear-ance at that time as the town-founding impulse seeks to be realised today in a new form. For it is now our task 'to tread the path consciously which leads from the building of towns to world economy, from the year 1,000 to the year 2,000, from dreamy vision to action appropriate to our time'.[179]

During these travels in England Stein came to see that whoever recognises that he has been called 'to serve the Grail' must work for the 'Christianising'—and that means humanising—of the economic life in the twentieth century. That is why he sought the collaboration with D.N. Dunlop, whose deeds he recognised to be guided by the Spirit.

The journey to Portugal which Stein undertook at Eastertime is connected with what happened seven years previously. Its origin lies in Stein's retrospective vision of 27 June 1924 which Rudolf Steiner interpreted and which Stein historically identified two months later on 28 August.[181] In November Ita Wegman conveyed to him Rudolf Steiner's affirmation of its historical identity with Francisco d'Almeida, the Portuguese conqueror and administrator of the Indian trading kingdom: 'That's how it will have been'.

A collection of notes in English and German were discovered among Stein's papers, from which can be seen how the retrospective vision and his identification with it came about. The notes, which occasionally sound like the minutes of a meeting, usually start with the death date of the previous incarnation: 'My last death on 1 March 1510 ca. 60 years old. I remember it Friday 27 June 1924'. On waking up the experience was visually objective. This was preceded by a process of soul which is described in an example by Rudolf Steiner in his lecture of 9 May 1924:

A person experiences that a friend tells him something which 'is not altogether pleasant', which gives him 'a slight shock', vexes him and hurts his feelings. This experience now has to be inwardly worked through and formed into a living picture and then carried forward over the next three days and nights. Then, when it has been absorbed into the feelings and the will, changes will have occurred in the soul, as a result of which the karmic cause of the event is able to reveal itself to the will, which has simultaneously become clairvoyant. Only those who are not afraid of exerting their minds and who have learned to wait—as Rudolf Steiner emphasises—will be able to receive reliable impressions along this path. Seven years later Stein set off to look for traces of a life lying four hundred years in the past. Outer circumstances came to his aid. A rich patron, the influential banker Hellmut Börnicke from Berlin, participated in the journey which was extended to Spain and North Africa. In addition to that, friendly relationships existed with the family of Leroi-Abercassis, who had economic and political influence. Alex Leroi, who later did good work in the research and combatting of cancer by founding the Lukas Klinik in Arlesheim, was a pupil of Stein and acted as chauffeur to his teacher when he visited his Portuguese homeland. His interest in history gave rise to extensive conversation about east-west conflicts in the history of mankind. Its last phase was the confrontation between Christianity and Arabism with which pupil and teacher knew themselves to be connected by destiny.[182]

The voyage started from Hamburg on 18 March. Stein took a child-like pleasure in the comfort of the huge steamer, which he described to Nora as a 'floating hotel'. The travellers landed at Vigo, the port in Northwestern Spain, in order to visit Santiago de Compostela. This city, famous as a place of pilgrimage in the Middle Ages, was built over the grave of St James—hence the name Santiago. St James was not only revered as the Patron Saint of Spain and of the pilgrims, but also as the protective Saint, next to St Michael, in the wars aginst the Mohammedans. On Maundy Thursday Stein sat in the Cathedral in front of the Saint's grave in order to reflect on the history of this place. Pictures formed themselves in his mind relating to the time of the battles against the Moors in which Almeida had taken part as a Knight of the Order of St Iago. He saw 'in his mind the knights riding through the south gate of the city. They were youthful knights who knelt down here and received the Communion two at a time: they shared the Holy Host between two. In this way they sealed their comradeship-of-arms'. In the procession of the pilgrims he also espied the figure of the Alchemist Basil Valentine, whom he encountered here.[183]

On Good Friday Stein arrived on Portuguese soil and reached Porto, the old capital city which had given its name to this country opening onto the Atlantic. He spent the night in a fishing village on the coast and watched the nightly fishing. In a half-dream the first inklings of memory came back to him, growing more vivid when he was present at a traditional bull fight. 'A piece of Ancient Rome. The arena. Thousands of people. Raving, shouting, breathless . . . these are profaned Mithras Mysteries'. He listened to the folk singers, to the veiled and haunting melodies of their songs of the sea and of the torment of love—and he felt: This is Portugal, this is how it must have been.[184] He entered Lisbon on Easter Sunday. He was overcome by the panorama of the town on the

River Tejo which rose up in terraces; the feeling of meeting again with a distant homeland rose up in him and accompanied him as long as he stayed in the country.

Of course he also held lectures. He spoke about the time of the Great Discoveries, about Santiago and the mission of Portugal. To invited guests he spoke about 'The economic crisis of the present day as a crisis of a change of consciousness'. On this occasion he became acquainted with influential people who supplied him with help for his researches. In this way he gained access to the State Archives and 'now had the possibility of holding in his hands the letters of Almeida (payment slips). A remarkable experience'.[185] He carefully copied the bold self-willed pen strokes of Almeida's signature, discovered his bust in the Artillery Museum and sought for a gravestone of which the inscription has been preserved: 'Here lies Don Francisco Almeyda, first Viceroy of India, who never lied and never ran away'. He left Lisbon on 7 April under the conviction: 'With that the way to a historical proof which I have to demonstrate has been found. I am able to say: All has now been achieved in this matter.'[186]

He remained in the land until 10 April stirred by the memories of events of the past pertaining to his own ego and to the circle of people connected with him in his destiny of that time. At the tower of Belém, Lisbon's landmark, from which the Portuguese discoverers set sail on their great journeys and from which Almeida sailed to India, Stein drew the conclusion: 'This is the point whence the spirit of the new age set forth in the fifteenth century'. Henry the Navigator, who as Grand Master of the Order of Christ, was able to provide it with the riches of the Templars, prepared the way for it. He planned the circumnavigation of the west coast of Africa to combat Islam, searched for the kingdom of Prester John, with whose help he hoped to conquer the Holy Land, and sought a direct connection with the gold- and slave-markets of East Africa in order to cut out the Arabian trade. Wide-ranging religious impulses were working through the very earthly intentions of the Portuguese conquerors and sea-captains. In the fifteenth century the spirit of the warlike Mars-Samael forces were still working—according to the chronological teachings of Abbot Trithemius—but the sword was also used in the service of the Universal Spirit of Michael whose healing impulse encompasses the whole world. And so Stein formulated it thus: 'The age was

     W.J. Stein, A Biography

under the leadership of two ruling principles: Samael, the Spirit of Deeds, serving Michael, the Universal Spirit'. The twofold aspect of the fifteenth century was revealed to him through his meeting with the being of Francisco d'Almeida. His own self confronted him as something foreign; in its martial and Michaelic bearing he recognised himself: his ego maturing through soul-changes. It was the most shattering encounter with himself he ever had.

On 10 April he crossed over into Spain. The first part of the journey had been completed. On taking leave of his 'native' Portugal he wrote to Nora: 'Destiny speaks in every place, at every step'.[187] Spain seemed 'exotic' to him. In Seville he was surrounded by the colour and light of the southern vegetation; but he felt no connection with the city whose Gothic Cathedrals and Moorish architecture he admired. It was different with Granada where he 'felt at home already with the first step'.[188] This town, founded by the Arabs, the magnificent centre of their last province on European soil, was conquered during the same year that Columbus discovered America. [1492]. The prospect of a western continent and the end of Eastern rulership in Europe mark the dawn of the new age. The Knights of the Order of St Iago contributed to this turning-point, for it was they who stormed the fortifications of Granada under the leadership of Almeida. Through his military training Stein was able to find the place where the walls had been breached; this was such an important discovery for him that he added a plan of the layout to his letter of 12 April. His last stop in Spain was at the port of Algeriças. From there the travellers crossed over to Tangiers, where they caught a bus which took them by way of Marrakesh, the most southerly point of the 2,000 kilometre journey, to the Algerian port of Oran. After the experience of his quest in Santiago, Portugal and Granada there now followed the enjoyable sight-seeing tour, dipping into the world of Arabian culture in North Africa, where Gahmuret, the father of Parzival, withstood his trials. The Mediterranean crossing to Marseilles and the long train journey to Stuttgart were the last stages of the undertaking which ended— after barely four weeks—on 22 April. [1932].

After his soul-shattering experiences at the age of 40, Stein acquired new strength. From the middle of February until the beginning of april he was on lecture tours in Berlin, England and Holland and gave 42 lectures in as many days. His public activity culminated then. The reports of those who heard him at that time all concur in speaking of the 'fire' of his lecturing. They experienced how, in the flow of his speech, gripped by the spirit, he drew near to intuitive knowledge. Some of those who revered him as a teacher of Anthroposophy explained the effect he achieved as being the result of his closeness to Rudolf Steiner. The love for his Master had ignited the fire of the higher ego in the pupil so that—like the prophet Elisha receiving the cloak of Elijah—he was able to perceive the 'inner word' and begin to speak out of its strength.

The lecturing tour to Berlin went by way of Bremen, where Stein had to speak to a public audience of party members and education officials about 'the background to the world conception' of the Waldorf School—its concrete idealism which made the pupil into a person able to deal with the affairs of life. The lecture was amicably received, but at the decisive meeting of the Bremen citizens there was no majority in favour of giving permission for a Waldorf School owing to opposing extremists from left and right. In Berlin he soon got to know the political intrigues and economic difficulties. The vote for the Presidency was pending and political radicalism was growing. The number of those out of work in Germany rose to six million and the Government reduced wages and salaries. The hopelessness of those concerned and the lack of ideas of those in charge produced a mood of crisis and catastrophe. This vacuum-situation demanded ideas which would carry forward into the future if the development were to be given a positive turn. Stein accepted the challenge and answered it with the presentation of two main themes: the transformation of the human being as described by Rudolf Steiner in his book of inner training *Knowledge of the Higher Worlds*, and the transformation of society as it is explained in *The Threefold Social Order*. As the German catastrophe was beginning to show itself in 1932 he wanted to speak about the truest and most radical form of revolution: the change in consciousness in the sense of an enhancement of the powers of knowledge. And he found people who would listen to him. The halls in the various districts of the city were full, in the city centre even overflowing. As a result of the putting out of placards a very mixed audience turned up, to which he first had to accustom himself. 'I said just about everything twice over: once in a

20   W J Stein 1932

scientific form, and once in an extreme and humorous manner. It was a complete success in front of a completely new audience never reached before.'[188a] The whole undertaking had been carefully prepared by the banker Börnicke. He 'also brought it about that Stein was able to speak to a group of prominent industrialists and politicians'. He wrote about this to his wife Nora: 'I gave a talk of more than an hour about the threefold social order which was well understood; and afterwards there was an excellent serious discussion till one o'clock at night. Many expressed their interest in a most cordial manner . . . some others were less demonstrative but friendly, a few were dismissive but also friendly. At any rate everything turned out better than we could have hoped for'.[189] A former manager of the Daimler works who had known Rudolf Steiner at the time of the Threefold Movement in Stuttgart gave unexpected support in the discussion and Emil Leinhas, a leader of the business enterprise 'Der Kommende Tag' gave further support with his experience of management. A National Socialist leader of industry also took part in the meeting which was held in the 'Hotel Kaiserhof', the lodging of the top members of his party. In a turbulent time in which everything was pressing for a decision this influential body of people—the 'Herrenklub', which was founded as a political-scientific union of conservative-minded industrialists and politicians—was to be informed about the perspectives of anthroposophical social science. The most suitable advocate was Stein, who at that time had come into the foreground through publications dealing with questions of social renewal, monetary affairs and world economy.[190]

The strenuous Berlin weeks with their daily lecturing duties—there were even two lectures on the programme for 21 February—ended on 27 February, Rudolf Steiner's birthday. For this occasion Stein was to give the festival lecture, which was to be held in the Herrenhaus, the seat of the First Chamber of the former Prussian Diet. He spoke about the life of Rudolf Steiner and the spiritual background of contemporary history. It was the climax and summing-up of the previous lectures which he had delivered on wide-ranging subjects, including Rudolf Steiner's spiritual nearness, the inspiration of the Time-Spirit and the commencement of a new age which will break through the boundaries of sense-perception. The nurturing of Anthroposophy—that was the gist of his words—is not an academic, but a practical affair: the effort we have to make every day to open the flood gates to allow the true Time-Spirit, the individuality of Michael, to work in a manner suitable to the present day.

One year later—to the day—the Reichstag building in Berlin was burned down. The rulership of the demagogue began and the scattered seeds were choked by the dangerously spreading weeds.

Stein arrived in London on 1 March. He travelled via Ostend because this was the only route on which you could travel third class all the way. In England, too, where he stayed till the end of the month, a full programme was awaiting him. The regular letters, which bear the character of a diary, allow us to make a reliable reconstruction of events. Besides lecturing in London, he also held lectures in Oxford, Bristol, Sheffield and Birmingham in which he not only dealt with historical and social questions as in Berlin, but also spoke on ethnological and even medical subjects. Starting from the fact that mankind is growing together into a single whole at the present day he described the conditions for a global ordering of life. Its basis is the knowledge of man's being, of people of different countries and races and an understanding of the way in which what is essentially human expresses itself differently in the different groups of people. Following on to Rudolf Steiner's ethno-psychology he sketched a spectrum of the races which demonstrated how the peoples of east and west stand in polar relationship and are balanced one against the other. He elucidated this by the examples of England-India, France-China, Japan-America, Italy-Russia and of Germany which contains a polarity within itself; for in Central Europe the polarities of East and West meet in the 'enigmatic' country of Germany itself. 'Therefore the special position—tragic too—of the German people. They are the Folk of the Ego and in the ego all the soul-forces intersect one another, the interests of all nations intersect there'.[191] The aim of such an enquiry was to build up a framework of knowledge for the construction of a world economy in which the egocentric attitude of a national economy would be replaced by a global-geocentric feeling of responsibility.

As concerns the medical lectures, he had gained such compe-tence at that time that he could lay the results of his labours before doctors 'quite calmly, as though I were a doctor'.[192] His interest in medicine had been awakened early in life. In April 1921 he had taken part by special invitation in the second medical course which Rudolf Steiner held in Dornach. When, ten years later, on the journey through North Africa, he became aware of the misery of those suffering from tropical diseases, the decision to some day become a therapist ripened within him.

On 22 March, the centenary of Goethe's death, he lectured to a full house in Rudolf Steiner Hall about the Fairy Story of the Green Snake and the Beautiful Lily. The lecture became, as he wrote to Eliza von Moltke, 'A Goethe Festival of Germans in London'.[193] Under the impression of contemporary events he set himself the task on this memorial occasion of applying to historical reality, the picture form of Goethe's 'Fairy Story', which was a mirroring of supersensible happenings; for he wished to show to his audience that spiritual powers tread the stage of history as actors in the twentieth century.[194]

When he was not lecturing Stein regularly used the time for historical research for which the London Museums gave him ample opportunity. This time he concentrated on Buddhistic Esotericism at the centre of which stand 'the three mysteries': a doctrine of meditation, mantric verses and gestures. The curator of the Indian section of the Victoria and Albert Museum, with whom he became acquainted through E.C. Merry, introduced him to the teachings of the gestures and explained, through pictures and statues of Buddha, the cultic significance of the various arm and finger positions. Through that Stein experienced the 'bliss of the historian': to be somewhere where everything is known and one can ask questions to one's heart's content.

He could follow such conversations without an interpreter and could also answer in the foreign language. He felt this as the conquest of a new realm of the soul which he wished to make his own. He noted in his diary whilst in Birmingham on Easter Sunday: 'That is my Easter experience for this year, that I now have a wide circle of culture at my disposal and I am firmly determined that I shall cultivate and study the English language'.[195] He then succeeded in acquiring a complete mastery of English with its subtle means of expression; but his pronunciation remained unmistakably German, which was the cause of many a joke.

It became ever clearer to Stein that basic changes were about to take place in the personal circumstances of his life, but also in the situation with regard to the conflicts within the Anthroposophical Society. Insofar as it affected him the journey—in spite of a bout of sickness from which he recovered in London—'brought him added strength' and a new confidence in the intended direction of his work. 'I am more and more conscious of my right path, and will pursue it in spite of all hindrances,' is how he expressed it in the last letter he wrote [to Nora] from England.[196] And with regard to the Anthroposophical Society the deepening rifts had already been the cause of long drawn-out discussions in Berlin. The position had become so obdurate that Stein expected to be excluded from the Society by the Dornach General Meeting. Instead of that the attack on his teaching and lecturing activities took place, which he countered by handing in his notice at the Stuttgart school.

Other threatened members from England, Holland and Germany saw themselves endangered by a possible exclusion. In face of the critical culmination of events Dunlop had prepared the foundation of a 'World-Economic-Union' and announced it officially on Easter Sunday in Birmingham, where Stein was staying for lectures. A Union directed towards the field of economics was planned, 'but so that at any moment the new Anthroposophical Society could develop out of it'.[197] Ita Wegman, Jules Sauerwein, the journalist known to Rudolf Steiner and representative of the Anthroposophical Society in France, and those members from a distance who had heard Stein lecture in London were present when the announcement was made. Whether the plan of the 'World Economic Union' was ever put into practice is doubtful.

After Stein, with his remaining strength had finished lecturing in Holland, he set off back to Stuttgart at the beginning of April. He was filled with gratitude towards his destiny when he reviewed the stages of this six weeks' journey. What he had experienced and achieved seemed to him the high point of his life till this moment. He had formed connections in Berlin and London, centres of politics and economy, which opened up to him undreamed of possibilities for work. But it would have required a super-earthly fantasy to imagine all the things which were in store for him.

When in December he set off for Turkey the separation from Stuttgart had been completed, but the step to England had not yet taken place. During this transitionary period he tried with increased vigilance to understand the language of his destiny in order to act in harmony with his guardian spirit. Therefore he reflected upon the moral quality which lies at the root of accord with the higher self, which he wished to follow. He was conscious of the fact that in the age of freedom the spiritual guidance of mankind imparts a true thinking which includes feeling and willing or—as Rudolf Steiner expresses it—establishes an 'inner trust in the guidance of the Spirit'.[197a] The quality of selflessly practised faithfulness can enable a person to gain intuitive experience, the content of which creates order in the chaotic world of the senses by means of knowledge. In just such an experience as this Stein became aware of a guiding motto which he applied to his own life: 'Everything I experienced on this journey has a significance for the future, although it has been determined by past events'. He confided it to Nora in his first letter and assured her that he felt 'quite self composed' and knew himself to be 'under good guidance'.[198]

Stein originally intended to visit not only Turkey, but also Damascus and Jerusalem. For this journey, too, a patron and companion had turned up: his Dutch acquaintance Christian ten Noever de Brauw, whose gift of languages proved indispensable throughout the journey. Their first goal, which they reached in a two-day voyage from Brindisi, was Constantinople. Stein experienced the contrast between the dark sea of Marmara with its gloomy, almost uninhabited coastal scenery and the brightness and the human bustle of the then capital city. He felt as though 'he was coming home after a long journey'.[198] Everywhere he came upon a German element, which had continued to work on since imperialistic times, when the Empire of the Wilhelms had exerted an economic influence on this land-bridge to India. But in a deeper sense than that he felt this land to be familiar, for here he was confronted with the spirit of the ninth century. It was in the Hagia Sophia that the Eighth Ecumenical Council had sat, which rejected the trichotomy and paved the way for the great Schism, the split between the Eastern and Western Church of 1054. The world antagonism which had been fought on ecclesiastical grounds in the ninth century appears in the twentieth century as the political-military rivalry for supremacy between East and West. In this field of tension lies Turkey: the creator of this State who adopted the name Atatürk, Father of the Turks, stands at a crossroads according to Stein: 'Will he pay homage to his gigantic Russian neighbour, will he ally himself with the West?'[199] At this time, which for Stein was one of decision, he sought to make a connection with the Head of the Turkish State, just as he had done to Gandhi, whom he had provided with an English copy of Rudolf Steiner's *Threefold Social Order* and to Mussolini, to whom he sent a copy of his own booklet: *Gold in History and at the Present Day* in an English translation.

Stein's visit to Constantinople did not keep him more than two days and by 14 December he had already arrived by express train in Ankara, the new capital, where he immediately called at the Austrian Embassy. He introduced himself as a writer, gave proof of his identity through a letter of recommendation from Jules Sauerwein and explained that he wished to write about modern Turkey and therefore hoped to gain an audience with the Ghasi. Stein made use of Atatürk's title of honour, Ghasi (meaning victorious warrior) which was reserved for Sultans and Generals of the army. The answer of the Legation Secretary sounded encouraging—and oriental. An audience with the Ghasi is not impossible. 'Here one is in the desert and is still human. He gladly receives writers when he is in a good mood'.[200] Now began the wait for an appointment for an audience, which turned into a hard test of patience. Certainly the recommendation of a valued publisher opened the way for him to the ministries and ministers themselves, but not to the State President.

From his interlocutor Stein received a varied picture of the achievements and personality of Kemal Atatürk. This man of action with an astonishing depth of perception built up a Turkish Republic as a Europeanised National State after the collapse of the Ottoman Empire. No other country under the influence of Islam broke so radically with the tradition of the Muslim Divine State as did Turkey. In the centre of Atatürks's great reforms was the abolition of the Caliphate, an office which had last been held by the Sultan of Constantinople. The Caliph, who was deemed to be the successor and representative of the Prophet Mohammed, combined in his person both spiritual and temporal authority. Only after this 'unity' had been abolished two generations previously, at a time when the Islamic revival was still a long way off, could secularisation with its intervention into ancient Islamic traditions begin. Clothing, orthography, jurisprudence, the place of women and even the national consciousness underwent a change; for according to the will of the reformers the Turkish people were to receive not only a new future, but also a new past.

His letters to Nora log over many pages the course of the conversations which he was able to have with the Foreign Secretary and on two occasions with the Minister for Education. A complete programme was drawn up which envisaged visits to all the important resorts, artistic events and scientific educational establishments. 'The Turks are full of good will to report and to show as much as possible'.[201] He was also received by the French Ambassador, alerted by Sauerwein's recommendation, who wished to learn of his intentions. Stein offered the following explanation: 'Firstly, I am interested in the development of a consciously created young nation from a national economic point of view. Secondly, I wish to gain a personel impression of His Excellency Kemal Pasha, because he has a particular conception of the relationship of East and West, a problem which I am studying, and I wish to find out what it is. Does he only want to carry western civilisation to the east, or does he wish to impart to the term "Turkish Nationality" a real content of its own?' Upon this the Ambassador answered:

He, Kemal Pasha, who, by the way, is the most interesting person alive, feels himself to be the successor of Alexander the Great and wishes to make Alexander's methods his own. Just as Alexander carried western civilisation to the east, Kemal Pasha wishes to do likewise; but, just as Alexander was more Persian than the Persians so must he be more Turkish than the Turks. Actually, though, he is a western Conqueror-in-Chief. . . he resists with all his might becoming a successor to Attila. He does not want that and so he builds up new sciences, constructs new language derivations, in order to prove to himself and others that he is the successor to Alexander the Great who was a Greek from Asia Minor, in short, of all those who are not barbarians but civilised human beings. But he himself doubts if that is the case.

The audience ended with an amusing exchange of pleasantries. On taking leave the Ambassador wanted to make sure that he had got the name of his visitor right. ' "Stein or Steiner?" "Stein" I said. "Oh, just Stein" he answered oblivious to the meaning of his words'.[202]

The explanations of the Ambassador gave Stein food for thought. They supplemented what he had heard from the Secretary to the Austrian Legation: that Kemal Atatürk attached importance to his 'descent from Gilgamesh and the Sumerian Civilisation'; from which Stein drew the inference: 'He is actually searching for Anthroposophy'.[203] At any rate he decided to make another advance in order to gain audience with the State President. He composed a memorandum which should serve to demonstrate his conception of modern Turkey and be a basis for discussion. The Foreign Secretary offered to hand on the leaflet and, after glancing at the text, added thereto: 'The Ghasi prefers to read German rather than French'.[203]

The four-page essay with the title 'The New Turkey and its Creator Ghasi Kemal Pasha' is still in existence. In addition there is a synopsis dealing with 'the Basis for an Understanding of the New Turkey', which was apparently originally intended as an explanatory prelude to the above. It contains the official view of the 'cultural ancestry of Turkey', its pre-Islamic, Central Asian past which was reported on by the Minister for Education and the Director of the 'Society for the Research into Turkish History', founded in 1931. The theory of the Asian cradle of culture had been modified by Stein in his conversation with the Minister by a reference to the researches of Rudolf Steiner into pre-history: the spiritual-scientific description of an Atlantean Civilisation and of the migration from the West—the submerted bridge of land between Europe and America—to the centre of evolution in inner Asia that only later became the radiating point of Post-Atlantean civilisation.

The exposition which was intended for Atatürk begins with the concise statement, 'The New Turkey is not a continuation of the old Turkish Empire, but a completely new creation of Ghasi Mustafa Kemal Pasha. The work of Kemal Pasha is characterised by the political reconstruction and cultural extension of the most ancient and valuable stream of civilisation and its adaptation to modern life'. What is decisive for this creation, continues Stein, is the question of its spiritual content, which seeks to establish an autonomy in the midst of the antagonistic interests of the Great Powers. That is the reason why the Ghasi refers to an oriental past history of Turkey which now has to blend with western civilisation. 'Western civilisation and eastern soul force must now become united. That is the will of the guardian at the threshold between East and West'. Stein puts this 'guardian of the threshold' Atatürk into a time perspective by interpreting his intention of creating an East-West partnership as a reflection of the Gilgamesh journey to the Burgenland. He connects it with Alexander's Asian campaign and compares it also with the Renaiassance Popes who rediscovered Classical Antiquity because they recognised therein the true Ancestors of Civilisation.

Well, those are daring statements, particularly the last one which draws a comparison with the Popes of the Renaissance. But a karmic impression lay at the back of it which Stein had received from a description of Atatürk. How did such impressions of karma come about? Stein was a meditative man who endeavoured not only to immerse himself—according to Rudolf Steiner's instructions—into the life-stream of plants, but also into the dream-like course of history. It might happen that this dream of history unexpectedly became illumined and was taken hold of by the consciousness. But whether or not what was thus illuminated corresponded with reality remains to be tested.

But the writing in question had the desired effect; Stein was received by Atatürk. Perhaps the latter had a feeling for the truly unusual train of thought and desired to make the acquaintance of the writer. Certainly there played into it the fact that only a short while previously a conference of Turkish historians had discussed the new historical situation. And, to conclude, what Stein calls 'the will of destiny' may have played a part. The basis of the discussion was the paper which had been handed in. Thus the conversation soon turned to Gilgamesh and the submerged Atlantis. Stein did not hold back with the knowledge he had received from Rudolf Steiner about 'Our Atlantean Forebears' and their wanderings to Central Asia. He spoke with such conviction that the now reflective Ghasi exclaimed that if what was said were correct then he would have to revise his opinions about the origin of culture being in the East, for a pre-historic epoch of high civilisation on the legendary West Continent had not been taken into account by him in his view of history.

On the long return journey to Holland during the first days of the New Year Stein was stirred by what the inner voice had told him of the 'significance for the future' of his oriental journey. That he had experienced a 'foretaste of later deeds' became for him a certainty which was to guide him in his future dealings.

The last of his 'journeys of discovery' was his visit to Italy. In a state of complete exhaustion he sought to recover through the medium of art. Serious symptoms of illness had developed as a result of many years of overwork; and in the spring of 1937 his state of health had worsened to such an extent that he lost his voice. Then well-wishing friends made it possible for him to spend four weeks in Italy, which he used for recuperating by means of a change of activity. 'A month without speaking was a good remedy'.[204] A month silently and intensively accustoming himself to the Vatican picture sequences of Raphael, the frescoes of the 'Villa dei Misteri' in Pompeii and the mosaics of the Capella Palatina in Palermo helped him to find a new balance.

He stayed longest in the 'Stanze' rooms of the Vatican which had been painted by Raphael and his pupils. There he experienced a guided history-of-art tour which aroused his opposition because the over-rapid explanations prevented a real comprehension of the subject and on top of that it only dealt with the technique of art. Stein regretted the fact 'that his destiny allowed him no opportunity to take over the guidance of the tour in order to say quite different things'. He would have drawn the attention of the visitors—it was the Dutch royal couple Princess Juliana and Prince Bernhard—to the objects portrayed and to their composition. He would have enlarged on the view that the 'Mysteries of the Eucharist' were portrayed in the frescoes. 'The might of the eucharist—that is the common basic theme running in a more or less hidden way through these paintings'.[205] That which has to do with the preparation of bread and wine which turn into holy substances through ritual celebration—already in the Demeter and Dionysus Mysteries of pre-Christian times—is the common theme. And in the 'Disputa', a painting familiar to him since early childhood, he experienced what stirs within the innermost centre of the history of salvation and mystery: 'The wise men of all times have struggled to understand the Mystery of Transformation, the Transubstantiation . . . the essential quest of mankind for the highest of all secrets'.[206] In what these pictures conveyed he found what he experienced as his 'highest secret': the hidden connection between knowledge and ritual; for he knew from Rudolf Steiner: 'Knowledge must become an inner sacrament within the soul of man'. He knew the sacramental element in the sphere of knowledge and arrived at the experience of communion along his path of development. Those were the spiritual experiences to which Rudolf Steiner had alluded. From this time onwards he had an understanding of what is meant by the archetypal sacrament: the Word becoming flesh, the Incarnation of a Divine-Spiritual Being which transformed the human sheaths. And he was touched by such a transforming, healing power through the language of Raphael's pictures at a moment in his life of which he was obliged to say: 'I could not go on'.[207] In this helpless state the healing process began. He felt as though he were being rejuvenated and surrounded by pictures from his childhood. At that age the Last Supper of Leonardo and Raphael's Disputa were his teachers of religion, and religion was for him 'the respectful adoration of something which made the world loving and beautiful'.[208] Now he had come to the end of his stay in Rome, rejuvenated in soul and strengthened in his ego he was called to new productiveness.

But it was not only the testimony of art with which Stein had become acquainted but also Italy turned fascist. The marshalling of troops and the uniforms, the pompous theatricality and anachronism of the movement, which at that time had not yet come under the spell of German power-politics, appeared to him as the expression of a 'youth movement which never grows up', moreover—what he did not foresee—it leads into its own abyss. He noted the external side of fascism, which corresponded with the exhibitionistic urge of a nation behaving in a youthful way. He contrasted it with the observer-role, that taken up by the politically experienced Englishman. 'I was deeply aware of the difference between the older English person observing the comedy and the younger Italian who enjoys joining the show in fancy dress costume. Two attitudes of soul with a contrasting history.'[205]

The situation which confronted Stein on his return to London was 'again materially difficult. But the public which had at first dispersed now came together again, and so life continues. I have also started to write for other papers which pay me, e.g. *The Modern Mystic*.[209] He started out on his new tasks with renewed vigour and could have said with Goethe when he arrived in Rome: 'Although I still remain the same, I believe that I have become changed right through to the marrow of my bones'.[210]

21   D N. Dunlop about 1930

5

The Collaboration with D.N. Dunlop

Stein received Dunlop's offer of work in May 1933. Two weeks later came the provisional residence permit and the work permit, and he arrived in London on 29 June. He regarded it as a new turn in his destiny that he should move into the world capital of Britain to which at that time a world empire still belonged, for his entry into the circle of western culture and into the milieu of a different language, meant a completely new adjustment of his life. Already on 12 July he reported to Stuttgart that he was now a Londoner and 'would only occasionally pay a return visit'.

I have changed over to business life. I am director and organiser of a research office of the World Power Conference, that is to say of a union of electrical engineers of 45 countries. My office is next to the British Museum, 21 Bloomsbury Square—a good position. What do I do there? Well, I write letters to 107 countries and gather news about industry in order to publish it. The sort of news which tells you what is going on in the world. Thus, for instance, I study the circulation of paper money, the wholesale and retail trade prices. And by that means I can tell what is going on, where there is a blockage, where the stock accumulates, the demand dwindles, where something picks up. Or I study the individual wares; let us say coffee. What the prices are, what is destroyed, whom it affects, who has to do without, how one can arrange it better. (In 1932 large amounts of coffee were destroyed in Brazil owing to marketing difficulties.) Therefore I study and feel the pulse of commerce. And immense London, and the Great British Empire with its resources, provides all the answers. One only has to ask. Now, where I begin, I have to learn how to put the questions. I have just finished working out on paper the organising of the news service. Everything will have to go by air mail. People can be of help to me in my work, however, if they send me statistics of bank returns, newspaper cuttings or the addresses of people who have particulars of certain materials, let us say aluminium. For every commodity there is someone who has the overall picture. Everything is now becoming quite concrete and all who want will get something to do . . . It is becoming a great network consisting of nothing but voluntary service throughout the world. Here is a list of the commodities with which I have started.

Then he enumerates in detail the things about which he needs exact information: foodstuffs and luxury goods, raw materials, precious metals, fuel; but also financial matters, services, transport, working hours, etc. Widespread knowledge must be collected and published in order to form a basis for the building of an associative opinion to consciously steer the course of the economy without the intervention of the State or of politicians. During the economic crisis of that time Stein wished to contribute to bringing about a change of consciousness through self-enlightenment of the economists, by providing international statistics giving information about such questions as: 'What does industry produce? How does it distribute the goods? What does it destroy? How do national characteristics play into this?'[211]

The directing of his activities to the new opening provided for him by Dunlop was a decisive break in the course of Stein's life. What he now had to do seemed to him to be the reverse of what he had done before, the reverse of his lecturing and teaching activities which had begun 14 years ago in Stuttgart. The watershed of life had been crossed, his time as a teacher at the Waldorf School directed by Rudolf Steiner had been left behind him. Now, at 42, he stood at the threshold of the last third of his life, which was to bring him unexpected fulfilment. A new prospect opened up and he was filled with the urge of discovery. Now it behoved him to live towards the future and to take up what life offered. He knew from the spiritual-scientific teachings of biography: 'What a person develops inwardly in advanced age will contribute to the forming of organs and the building up of the body in the future; that will also work later on in the outer cosmos'.[212] During the last third of his life there began what Stein called 'the trial of the will'. He had to pass this test in order to find the meaning of his life. His progress would certainly entail difficulties, but from now on what was striven for counted for more than what was left unfinished or was unsuccessful.

The conjunction of Stein and Dunlop is a remarkable chapter in the history of how things work in Anthroposophy. The collaboration lasted for two years, during which time both parties contributed their abilities, as opposite to each other as they were outstanding in themselves. Two mighty individuals—Dunlop from the Celtic west, who excelled on account of the maturity of his spirit-guided actions, Stein from Central Europe distinguished by mobility of thought and by the richness of his ideas—united in their work during the historically important year 1933. Stein recognised a fatherly friend in the 23 years older Dunlop, acknowledged his sovereign qualities and found his own abilities enhanced by the work they did together; for he experienced the fact that Dunlop's forces flowed into him when he took up the latter's suggestions and followed his advice.

Daniel Nicol Dunlop, in praise of whom Stein had said that his example had 'so to say educated him', was an outstanding personality. His far-reaching activity and spiritual distinction have been portrayed by Thomas Meyer in his comprehensive biography.[213] At an early age Dunlop developed a directness and ability of spirit. He became the co-editor of a theosophical magazine in Dublin, and after his stay in America he attained to a leading position in the English electrical industry. Inspired by his encounter with Rudolf Steiner and acquaintanceship with the Threefold Commonwealth idea he started to work constructively in his surroundings out of the spirit of Anthroposophy. In 1924 he founded the World Power Conference which was intended as a precursor to the World Economic Conference. Through his initiative technicians, engineers and scientists met together from 40 countries in order to discuss energy problems and prepare the way for international co-operation. The participants decided upon the formation of national committees and the establishment of the Conference as a permanent Institution. The World Power Conference, created as a private organisation and known today as the World Energy Conference with a membership of as many as 80 states, has certainly changed its name but not is original ideals of promoting 'national and international help towards the development and peaceful use of the sources of energy for the greatest benefit of all mankind'.[214] After Dunlop's death the determination to enlarge the scope of the Conference to include all branches of industry and bring about a reorganising of the whole system in the sense of the Threefold State was no doubt lacking.

In conjunction with the World Power Conference Stein undertook the task which Dunlop had already delineated in his note of invitation: 'To establish a research institute for the gathering of data and statistical information in respect of world economy and, indeed, with the double purpose: (a) of preparing an international conference and (b) of publishing—in suitable form—the various conclusions arrived at by means of the accumulated data and information'.[215]

For such an undertaking as this the London of the thirties was the most suitable place: a centre for world trade and international banking, the re-shipment port for all raw materials and riches of the world and, at that time, the centre of a world encompassing empire. It was here then where Stein began his research work in accordance with a strict plan of campaign. He regarded himself as a pupil obligated to learn over again the oft taught lesson-material of the twelfth class: 'a universal comprehension of the universe and the earth'. He writes to an acquaintance in Germany about his task and his learning experiences:

> I am studying the earth in respect of its geology, botany, zoology, climate, history and economy and am every day amazed at the things I do not know. But nevertheless, one comes at last through all this abundance to things which have not yet been worked upon. At first one deems it to be impossible with all that fullness of material. But then gradually the gaps start to show and one's own work begins. During the first weeks I studied the underlying nature of economy. At that time I was often in the wonderful Greenwich Observatory. There I held in my hands the original works of the great astronomers and saw slides of them. And so I could follow how the planets imprint their circuits, their rhythms into the sphere of the sun's radiant light.[216]

He noted the cosmic influences upon the whole planet earth and arrived at the conclusion: 'Seen from a particular aspect economic life is the imprint of the sun and the planets. But on the other hand there is man with his arbitrariness and the State with its traditions. And into that work the folk customs'. Such studies as these, the letter concludes, are the preparation for future deeds, 'even if only in another life'.

But Dunlop had a more immediate goal in mind in the planning of the third World Power Conference in Chicago in 1936, where Stein was to have given the main lecture on the subject of World Economy. For this occasion a 'Year book of World Economy containing comprehensive statistics was to have been made available to act as a basis for further planning and to prepare the way for extending it to a World Economic Conference, which was now due to take place. The realisation of this project was, however, prevented by the untimely death of Dunlop in May 1935.

The first years in London were a time of unremitting self-assessment. Stein was searching for a spiritually conformable interpretation of economic data which he laboriously compiled. But the abundance of material was so overwhelming that the task appeared insoluble. Exhaustion and renewed attacks of loss of consciousness and breakthroughs in knowledge alternated with one another. He refers to his path as 'hard and stony, but nevertheless satisfying. The world which I have to contemplate is beautiful. The means by which I carry out my work are such that one is almost continually in a state of losing one's consciousness. But one accustoms oneself in time to the saturnine atmosphere. And as in all lead mines there is silver present, one admires the wisdom of nature and of destiny.'[217] He acquired perseverance through the practice of meditation, at the heart of which was the contemplation of the ego as the innate innermost being. By means of meditation he gained a deeper experience of the 'higher-self', which is the bearer of the higher faculties of knowledge and moral responsibility. What was acquired on his way to this reality he epitomised in a verse which has been preserved in a letter written by Stein: 'I will write to you about a few things which I now meditate myself again and again. The first is the meditation about the ego. It is quite wrong to think of the ego as being separate from other egos. To do that leads to error. The egos overlap one another. Large parts of one's own ego are in other people and much of the ego of others is in us. Ultimately one discovers that one's own ego does not at all belong to oneself exclusively, but is something by which one distinguishes oneself from every other person. When that begins to become a concrete experience then one knows that one cannot express it otherwise than by saying 'Christ in the Cosmos' and 'I am': It is the same thing. That does not merely apply to human beings, it also applies to whole States. They are all different, but nothing is owned. If one can recognise that fact in all its details then there lights up behind the egos overlying one another in myriad colours the stars of all individuals which together constitute the whole of the starry heavens. That is the one thing. The other is love. It rests on becoming conscious of one's connection in the ego. When one is conscious of one's difference, then one knows. When one is conscious of one's union, then one loves. On this depends the whole rhythm of the cosmos. Birth and death, too, are only one expression of it—words are very poor in describing something of that sort. But in world economy and in the single States this double aspect is also present. States are individualities. But one cannot think them within their own boundaries because the latter overlap one another. That is why Dr Steiner taught about the threefold division, but it is nothing but the overlapping into the other ego. What he called the 'Rights State' is living in isolation, and the economy is where everything is held in common. And if one has understood that one will see that the economy is astronomy, the States are the star-constellations and man is that which interweaves from one constellation to the next. Others will perhaps formulate it differently, but that is how it is'.[218] There speaks in these stammering words the struggle for knowledge of the basic order out of which world economy proliferates in manifold appearances and interlacement—comparable to the struggle of Goethe to realise the basic form, the archetypal plant, which manifests in the unlimited variety of the single plant forms. Shaken in soul Stein experienced, through his study of the phenomena, the moment in which the reality of 'co-ordinated economy' stood before his inner vision. This experience is indicated in the verse-like summary which comes at the end of his letter:

> Weaving life
> In the garment of rays
> Of the stars
> Art thou, O man,
> Before God's countenance:
> Living, yet in isolation
> Distinguished from others

Art thou, O Folk
Thy group-ego
Before God's wisdom-filled
Justice.

In mutual weaving
Awakening,
Flames up
Love
Of cosmic becoming
In God's astonishing
Wonder of creation,
When human beings and peoples
And peoples
unite
For reciprocal support
For mutual creative work
For individual communal deed
In the earthly business
Of co-ordinated economy.[219]

During this time his views about the activity of the spirit in history and nature become consolidated. Stein mentions the subtle experiences by which the awakening to the world of the living etheric forces announces itself: 'It is as though the thoughts which previously had been centred in the head now waft around it, fluttering around, so that we project into new worlds, new spheres and new possibilities of knowing and acting. And in the world which our spirits enter in this way a being appears whose streaming light and body of warmth radiates selflessness. The time for serving one's own ego is over. Thus sounds the call of the Spirit of the Age, heard by all, though differently interpreted according to the power of comprehension granted to each one'.[220] Stein recognises the 'clarion call of the spirit' as the Christian-Michaelic summons to the individual to become aware of his growing responsibility towards nature, which is the basis of his physical existence, and to work for the building up of a world economy, the aim of which is brotherhood. But the 'call for selflessness' turns into its opposite if it is stated: 'Human beings have to serve the nation rather than themselves as individuals—

or, as the national slogan would have it: the individual is nothing, the community is everything. In the unremitting factual language of history, predicted Stein in the year 1933, will be revealed, 'that impossible ways will have been embarked upon, so that they will prove themselves to have been absurd'.[220] Thus catastrophe may become a way to salvation.

A lecture which Stein had to give unexpectedly on 30 March 1934 in commemoration of Rudolf Steiner's death day provided him with new insight into the sequence of contemporary history. He has preserved the main gist of it in a very much shortened version which he wrote down after the event. Through the advent of spiritual science the twentieth century is divided into three phases. The subject of the first phase is 'Instruction', of the second 'Incorporation', of the third 'Action'. In the first third of the century Rudolf Steiner developed anthroposophically-orientated spiritual science; in the second third spiritual science must come into the possession of the civilised world; in the last third the conditions of life must be altered to fit in with it. In the second phase, which is now just beginning, continued Stein, the step in consciousness must be made from the experiencing of an ideal to the experiencing of a spiritual reality, which would correspond to the step from *The Philosophy of Spiritual Activity* to the book *Knowledge of the Higher Worlds*. But the sudden change to an alertness for spiritual perception which is now due produces a crisis in consciousness 'which represents no less than a cry for help from those who are unable to cross the threshold before which we now stand'. In a situation like this in which a decision is required the world-wide spread of the anthroposophical movement is a necessity demanded of the age in which we live and Stein regarded his new homeland England as the starting point for this development.

Out of these experiences of the times and the bases of events there arose, as the fruits of his co-operation with Dunlop, the book *The Earth as the basis for World Economy* and the monthly periodical *World Survey*. Stein described to a Dutch friend where and how this book originated. 'Banned for a year in complete isolation in the British Museum Library', where long before him Marx had carried out his economic studies and Soloviev had beheld the countenance of the Sophia, he became aware of what 'the cosmos was beginning to say' in the language of silence.[221]

The individual facts which he had collected fitted harmoniously together and a picture of the whole earth organism and its processes arranged in cosmic order appeared before him. His hand was led and he discovered in French and Russian specialised journals 'the proofs that the world is a unity'. The papers of a Leningrad researcher drew his attention to the 'connection between the planets and the harvesting rhythms'. He arrived at the view that 'humanity had received Anthroposophy everywhere in scattered portions and that it is our task to tell these isolated searchers what it is to which their portion of research belongs, whereby he immediately began with the Russian author.[222]

The first part of the book was finished in August 1934, first of all only in rough and in German. 'Now it has to be polished up. The English expressions often call for a change-round of the whole train of thought. One cannot translate', he says in a letter from 16 August 1934. Eight chapters were then published in his magazine *The Present Age* in 1937 as a special issue on this particular theme. In his foreword dated 30 May 1937, the death-day of Dunlop, he explained the motive for the publication by saying: 'The far-reaching plans' of this man to co-ordinate industry on a global scale by means of a permanent world-wide Economic Conference have lapsed into oblivion. Therefore 'I have planned to make this uncompleted plan known, in order that future promoters of a World Economic Conference may make use of the foundations which we have worked out together'. The heading of the first chapter 'The Earth as a Star among Stars' is derived from Herder who, in his *Ideas regarding the Philosophy of the History of Mankind* describes the earth as a planetary body in the cosmos. This fragmentary work combining within itself both nature and history, which Goethe had also helped to create, moved Stein to 'write a continuation, however imperfect'. He saw himself as being in a comparable situation: 'Herder had the remarkable courage to introduce concrete factual observations and investigations by cosmological thoughts. A researcher who would undertake to compare the way in which the world of the twentieth century develops, as opposed to the world of the nineteenth century, would have to develop the same courage'.[223] And Stein proved to have this courage. He reckons the economic life to the breathing and circulation processes of the earth-organism in which man's participation is not without effect. It is only a knowledge of the laws of life and a feeling of ecological responsibility which can prevent a world catastrophe and overcome the present anarchy in economic practices. As Herder, in the final note to his *Ideas*, hopes for 'common sense and strengthened social activity among men', so Stein, too, at the end of the last chapter which deals with 'world-wide economy'. He trusts in a growing sense of reason which does not merely take account of 'what is' or 'what ought to be', but of 'what wants to be' and he closes with an apocalyptic prospect: 'Only when the earth is regarded as something holy and regains its say in the great universal questions will the salvation of mankind come about. But the earth does not speak. It is the dumb God among the Aesir [Widar] of whom the northern Saga speaks when it tells of the Twilight of the Gods; the god who outlasts the war of all against all and who, after the great chaos, orders everything anew. The chaos is here. The God of the Aesir survives, the Earth keeps its faith with us. Should not men be found who will loosen the tongue of the dumb God, who will live and work together so that salvation and peace and harmony can grow up through honest struggle for the highest good?'[224]

In the first part of the book Stein deals with the 'natural-scientific aspect of the connection between economy and the earth'. In the second part the 'historical-psychological aspect' was to have been dealt with. That, too, was at the suggestion of Dunlop. But only a few rough notes were produced, for after Dunlop's death which followed shortly afterwards, Stein was unable to continue the work. Nevertheless the following direction of thought is discernible. In our present cosmopolitan age the view is becoming widespread that mankind living on the earth represents a complete organic whole. From this there follows the necessity of comprehending the structure of this whole and the significance of its parts. For the races, peoples and tribes are vital parts if mankind and the earth form a single organism. Therefore for a peaceful living and working together the self-knowledge of the races is indispensable, but a self-knowledge in the sense of spiritual science which recognises the Folk Spirits and the Spirit of the Age as individualities of a higher order. This step forward in knowledge is what the book is meant to stimulate. 'Self-knowledge of the Nations is necessary if every nation is to make its contribution to the common field of human decisions according to its particular abilities'.

In this connection his sketch of the 'Characteristics of the English' is examplary.[225] By way of numerous examples of cultural, political and economic phenomena, Stein brings to expression the activity of the English Folk Spirit which, proceeding from the British Isles, carries out its world mission by developing a language and form of thought compatible with its nature, stamping upon it its national characteristics and habits.

> The English are predominantly an Island people. Islanders have a different psychology from mainlanders or even to those living on peninsulas. The Islesman on the one hand always has the inclination to expand, on the other hand he has a tendency towards asserting his self-enclosed personality. Both of these traits are characteristic for the Britisher. He is not aware of any lack of modesty when in his letter-writing style he introduces the word 'I' with a capital letter. For the assertion of his personality comes naturally to him and does not include any presumption. By writing 'I' with a capital letter the Englishman does not signify any sort of ambition he may have, but merely denotes therewith his own body from which he surveys the world. The English language confirms in many ways that it is the body which is meant; for instance in its use of the word 'every*body*', 'no*body*'. The basic thing about the Englishman is that he has an especial talent for sense-observation and a matter of fact way of describing events and can rightly be seen as the most typical representative of the modern consciousness soul. From this soul power there developed under British leadership a world economy which then, however, degenerated into an instrument of rulership. At the present day it must be transformed in such a way that an approach can be made to he ideal of brotherhood.

Stein spent the last 24 years of his life among English people, gaining British nationality in 1939. His way led him from Southeast to Northwest, from the interior of the country to an island; Vienna, Stuttgart and London were the stations along the route. The Hungarian element of fiery attack, which he inherited from his father, he laid aside in England, but he did not wish to adapt himself to the phlegmatic Folk-temperament of the English.

The monthly bulletin *World Survey* began its appearance after thorough preparation in 1935. This organ had the aim of contributing towards extending the World Power Conference into the domain of World Economy, for which reason it bore the inscription on the title-page: 'Published under the auspices of the World Power Conference for the exchange of economic and technological information and the preparation of a World Economic Service and international bibliography for energy and fuel'.[226] A world economic service such as this demanded of Stein not only a comprehensive correspondence with foreign commercial institutes, but also the forming of personal contacts. He was able to form influential connections through his acquaintanceship with the director of the International Board of Statistics in the Hague; nevertheless it was 'exceptionally difficult' to produce international statistics, as he remarked in his survey, 'The Situation in the World Copper Market'.[227] National interests were at variance with integration and hindered the formation of an economic system which would bring about a division of labour throughout the whole world. 'In the economic field', wrote Stein, 'two forces are at war with one another, the force of national groups and the force of the world-wide economy which has not yet come into being?[228] This continuing tension—well enough known today from the history of European integration—must be reduced by means of comparative observation of world-economic conditions and through the dealings of experts. Stein and Dunlop set their faith on the productive co-operation of responsible individuals, capable and willing to arrive at serviceable agreements. The interchange of international information was not a panacea, but was regarded by them as a 'very practical and directly effective measure', very well aware of the fact that the necessary 'change must take place *within ourselves*'.[229]

In the third number of the periodical, appearing in June, the death of Dunlop was announced. Already by the end of that month Stein received notice to quit. The Economic Institute and the *World Survey* were brought to an end 'on account of the necessity for strictest economy which, to our regret, has been laid upon us'. That was the explanation offered for the liquidation and dismissal which deprived Stein of his work and living.[230] Doubtless this explanation accorded with the facts, but it also provided the welcome excuse for not proceeding further with the line of activity taken by Stein and Dunlop of extending the World Power Conference into a World Economics Conference. What Stein had factually achieved and contributed was impressively acknowledged in his testimonial: 'Dr Stein has proved himself to be an exceptionally conscientious investigator in connection with the economic and statistical studies and analyses published by *World Survey*. Apart from that his international connections have proved to be of tremendous value. Dr Stein is a hard worker and one can rely upon his enthusiastic co-operation with his colleagues. . .'[231] These possibilities of development had been foreseen by Dunlop. But after Dunlop's death, two years after his new start in England, Stein was standing before an economic void.

In an obituary article for Dunlop intended for German friends Stein characterised the intentions of this personality with which he had karmically united himself: 'The idea was: to bring together not only for *technical* reasons, but also *in a human way*, economists and industrialists of all countries on a non-political basis on which, because of the freedom which it pervades, truly valuable impulses can arise. Dunlop was the first person to invite Germany to take part in an international conference after the war . . . he loved the German Spirit because he saw in it a hope for mankind'.[232] And he loved Stein as a bearer of this Spirit. What grew out of the English-German co-operation was full of future meaning for Stein. He felt that seed had been scattered the fruits of which would only ripen at a future date.

The move to England also brought about changes of great consequence in Stein's personal circumstances. After the death of his elder brother Stein had married his brother's fiancee, Nora von Baditz. Now, shortly after his forty-second birthday, another person entered the circle of his acquaintances. Their first meeting was like a hieroglyph of destiny; he describes it as folows.[233] 'I met Johanna Lungen on 1 March 1933 as I was getting into the Continental train on my way from England to Holland. I sat opposite her and knew from the very first moment that this was my destiny . . . We soon progressed from everyday discussions to serious conversation. About former lives, the existence of a spiritual world and about ourselves. I learned that she had been in Java and was going to Holland and we exchanged addresses'. The conversation continued during the night-crossing to Holland and was echoed in the dedicatory verses which Stein entered into his Grail Book which he sent her 'In friendly memory of a night-conversation on the high seas'. It was two years till he saw her again after lectures in London where she worked in the Natural

Therapy Institute. By inner agreement a collaboration arose which led to a life-partnership. According to Johanna Lungen their marriage formed the basis, out of certainty of soul, of a mutual responsibility towards the continuance of the anthroposophical movement, the destiny of which—according to the 'Michael prophecy'—was to be decided at the end of the century if its representatives in the various fields of activity could join together in the great synthesis of karma. In September 1936 Stein wrote to Nora, who was recuperating in Ascona from the suffering which the estrangement had caused her, that he saw no way of retreat and 'divorce would be the right thing'.

Throughout the storms and stresses of soul of these years Stein kept his inner balance by means of newly undertaken and enhanced activities. He saw himself as a 'free-travelling learned man-of-God' who earned his living by the production of spiritual wares.[234]

And this production was many-sided and included almost all fields of Anthroposophy. That can be gauged from the subjects of his lectures and his contributions to the periodical he founded *The Present Age*. How this undertaking came about is mentioned in the dedicatory article in memory of the life's work of Dunlop with which the first number begins: 'The publication of this journal was Mr D.N. Dunlop's idea and the title "The Present Age" was his choice. He wanted me to create this journal and he hoped to write the introductory article . . . The last thoughts which he communicated to me before he passed away on Ascension Day 1935 were dedicated to this journal and it became an absolute duty for me to overcome every difficulty in creating it'.[235]

In fact the difficulties seemed insurmountable at first. Stein had no money to pay for the publication of a magazine and no helpers either. He was then given a printing press which he tried to work himself. But then he decided he would prefer to sell it to pay for the printing of the first number. Without capital and lacking the usual advertising facilities the continued publication from one month to the next remained an open question. He dealt with the correspondence on his old typewriter, he did all the editorial work and for each number he wrote several articles which were often a resume of his regular study courses, which explains their compressed character. In addition to that, he mentions in his retrospect of the first half year, that three years previously he had not even been able to write an English letter correctly.[236] Only the trust he enjoyed as a teacher of spiritual science and the concept of *The Present Age* as a universal journal for culture worked convincingly and attracted a growing number of subscribers from the English speaking world.

What was successful in this way and continued as a periodical until the outbreak of war, was a 'monthly magazine with high pretensions which dealt in a comprehensive way with the latest developments and currents in education, medicine, history and religion, natural science and technology'.[237]

The age in which we are living, our 'present age', was for Stein the epoch which began with the end of the previous century, bringing with it new challenges in knowledge and demanding new answers from the will, for, since it began, the Spirit of the Age and of Humanity, Michael and Christ, have become available to the human souls as their companions. The motto for his work was taken by Stein from *Anthroposophical Leading Thoughts*: 'Michael will give the right directions with regard to the world which surrounds man in his knowledge and actions. The way to Christ must be found in man's inner being'.[238] Stein wanted to make his readers into 'Companions of the Spirit of the age', to become conscious of the clairvoyance of thought which has to be achieved as a world-historic fact in the twentieth century and begin to act socially out of spiritual experience. The uniqueness of this present-day transformation of human consciousness only becomes understandable when we look at the whole of human history. That is why Stein constantly deals with mythological subjects, because he recognises that myths portray a higher form of history-writing in which the interplay of supersensible powers is still perceived and an outline of future development is indicated. Thus the destiny of Merlin, the teacher and guardian of the Round Table, becomes for him a key to the understanding of the present day.[239] Merlin still possessed the old pictorial consciousness through which the spiritual side of nature was revealed. But he then experienced the tragic destiny of the spirit in human evolution as his own personal destiny. He learned how to 'transform his universal present-day consciousness into a consciousness of the future'. And that is a picture of the present-day task: after having acquired intellectuality, to attain to a clairvoyance compatible with the contemporary stage of development. 'This new clairvoyance, unlike the old, does not reveal the secrets of nature in cosmic imaginations, but in prophetic pictures no less significant, foresees the future evolution of the social life.—So that the true quest of the Grail begins only at the point where Merlin dies. It is the quest of the spirit in the crystal cup of matter, it is the seeking of that social love the coming of which cannot merely be awaited, but must be brought forth by our creative action. The newly awakened love is not the love of antiquity—the love of nature and of the nature spirits—it is the love within the human kingdom, linking man with man, nay, more, linking whole groups of human beings one with another. Through this alone shall we find the way back from matter to the stars'.[240] Thus it is man's task to create the social world as 'a second nature'. 'The original nature was created and enspirited by Divine Powers. This second world will be created by human beings in whom the divine spiritual world, after having once become flesh in a human being, will manifest ever more strongly through creative individual activity'.[240] The social world which must be built is the threefold social organism which, like the future within the present, like a prophetic vision of a future regime worthy of humanity, is revealed to visionary thought.

The range of subject matter stretches from the mythological accounts to the consideration of current affairs with which Stein had begun the first year's publications. The outer occasion for this choice of subject matter was the simultaneous occurrence of two events in 1936: the coronation of the English King George VI and the invitation to a peace conference by the American President Roosevelt. Stein considered this moment propitious for introducing to leading Statesmen in a form suitable to the changed situation and comprehensible as a goal for their practical application, the ideas of the Threefold State, explained by Rudolf Steiner to the Statesmen of Central Europe in 1917. For this reason England should submit the following suggestions to the Peace Conference: (1) The founding of an International Parliament for Culture by two named representatives of the spiritual life; (2) The institution of a Ministry for World Economics; (3) The restructuring of the League of Nations to form a political gathering restricted only to the jurisdiction over rights.

Only the separation of the three spheres: Culture, Economics and Politics—so runs the argument—will ensure permanent peace, and the Coronation provides a suitable opportunity for making such an advance.[241]

This suggestion, which, as was to be expected, had no repercussions, rested on the life's work of Dunlop.

In addition to that Stein had called upon the representatives of the world religions, present at an International Congress of Religion in London in July 1936, to form themselves into a permanent Ministry of Culture with the task of overseeing the self-government of the whole of the spiritual-cultural life.[242] Taught by his experiences of the Threefold Commonwealth time with Rudolf Steiner, he fought simultaneously on two fronts: for self-government of the economy and for self-government in the cultural life.

A source of strength in this war of spirits was to have been the 'School of Spiritual Science', founded on the initiative of Eugen Kolisko and opened in London at Michaelmas 1936.[243] Stein, too, was involved in this attempt to bring to realisation the idea of the School of Spiritual Science. By means of a deepened study of Anthroposophy in this Mystery School, ways were to be sought to an esoteric knowledge which would lead to an enhanced activity in the various fields of work. But after an encouraging start the enterprise miscarried on account of outer and inner difficulties. Stein bore such developments with growing equanimity since being in England. From observation and experience he knew the difficulties which were bound to occur when people tread the spiritual path leading to a union with spiritual realities, or when people with different karmic backgrounds work together; and he interpreted this failure in the light of a self-chosen test which brought what was hidden into the open.

In the drama of current affairs the contrasts became sharper, too, and alreay by 1938 the political tension led to the edge of the abyss. 'European history is like a film run backwards' commented Stein in April 1938 to the German invasion of Austria.[244] The development towards a radically nationalistic state-leadership in Germany and its aggressive policy of expansion are unseasonable and have to be countered by the West through activities which ensure the future. Now it behoves us, after having achieved freedom of religion and equality before the law in modern times, to take advantage of the world-wide division of labour and facilities for distribution of goods to bring to realisation an economic order based on brotherhood. That is what Stein saw as the world-mission of Britain and America.

But what reason demanded remained unfulfilled. 'The catastrophe which we feared and against which we fought has come upon us ... nevertheless, we believe in an evolution, which will lead to the freedom of the individual'. With these words Stein introduced the last number which he was able to publish in the autumn of 1939—after the outbreak of war.[245] After that circumstances forced him to cease publication.

Four years of *The Present Age* appeared, to begin with under great difficulties. Stein's articles on natural science and the history of religion, on economics and medicine gave it its particular character. Its readers valued its wide scope of thought and reference to practical things—both German and English components of these contributions. The reminiscences of his life which describe the road which led him to Rudolf Steiner as 'an opening of his soul towards the spirit', he published under the heading: 'an aid towards the understanding of our time'.[246] They connect the recounting of outer facts with a description of occult experiences, because life today cannot be brought under our control without a knowledge of the supersensible. Following on that was the life's retrospect of Count Ludwig Polzer-Hoditz.[247] The circle of authors increased and Stein was able to build up a staff of European colleagues to which belonged Eugen Kolisko, Caroline von Heydebrand, Herbert Hahn, Count Ludwig Polzer-Hoditz, Jules Sauerwein, Karl König, Fritz H. Julius, Max Stibbe, Hans Hasso von Veltheim-Ostrau, David Ferguson, among others. Their names are still known today and many of them published their articles in the form of books after the war. The latest reprint was of the memories of Rudolf Steiner by Ludwig Polzer-Hoditz.[248]

During the fateful year of 1939 the circumstances of Stein's life underwent another profound change. It began with his divorce from Nora. Then followed the acquisition of British citizenship, the suspension of *The Present Age* and the search for further employment; at the end of the year came the sudden death of Eugen Kolisko. Stein had known his friend for 35 years and gave in his obituary account a loving and impressive picture of him.

'Dr Kolisko represents a type of ability and knowledge and a life style which is only possible on the Continent in the Central-Europe of pre-war Vienna where he was born. For this kind of person study begins where there is interest; but in order to be truly interested one must have a love for the object of one's studies. That means that one gives oneself up entirely to the subject in hand and that creates unlimited enthusiasm. Enthusiasm together with complete honesty—that was the spiritual atmosphere in which Kolisko lived—an atmosphere which he conveyed to everyone with whom he came into contact . . .'[249]

Kolisko avoided the conventional way of greeting and saying goodbye and his friends experienced 'a kind of continual presence' which also continued after his death. In the part of Stein's life which now commenced this 'presence' was an inspiration to him.

Stein had reached his forty-ninth year, at which age, according to Rudolf Steiner's knowledge of destiny, the epoch of karmic fulfilment comes to an end. If, during childhood and youth, karmic demands are inscribed into man, then, during the twenties, karmic demands and karmic fulfilment are in balance with one another, so, in the following period there comes about a fulfilment of karma, a discharging of karma'.[250] Stein's destiny in the demands and fulfilment of karma stood under the sign of Mars. His main trait of character was unmistakably the 'militant knightly', the 'noble-martial' one.[251]

But out of the warrior emerged a healer; and beyond the age of karmic fulfilment the individuality traced its future under the sign of Mercury-Raphael—thereby awakening once more to a forgotten motive of his youth.

Stein's therapeutic work, which began during the war, grew out of his producing of medical remedies. He reported on it to his former co-worker in the Stuttgart 'Archive of Goetheanism', Emmy Mattes: 'During the war when we began to lack medicaments I organised the production of these remedies and discovered many more by following Rudolf Steiner's indications. Wonderful remedies for cataract, for glaucoma, for epilepsy, many, many remedies, also a new injection and homeopathically potentised penicillin for hypertrophy of the prostata. That involved me in a kind of medical activity and I held medical lectures. Oculists sent me their incurable patients and it branched out into a widespread activity'.[252]

The inspired wish to heal which had made the pioneers of anthroposophical medicine into artists in medical skill, had also gripped Stein. He was thoroughly prepared for the job when he took up the task of a therapist which he carried out for the rest of his life, jokingly referring to himself as a 'quack doctor'. The proof of his many-sided studies is a long series of compositions and the 'plan for a medical book' which was to have served as the basis of an extended art of healing. A division into seven chapters was intended: as an introductory chapter the discussion of the historical aspect, the changes in the form of medicine during the various cultural epochs; then the treatment of physiology according to the indications of Rudolf Steiner's lectures on *Occult Physiology*.[253] Further, a description of spiritual-scientific psychology; as a central chapter the characterisation of the individuality and its maturing during the course of incarnation; in the last three chapters the extension of the perspectives of folk-psychology; of the world-wide effect of the founders of religion in uniting mankind; finally of the 'social diseases' which are the result of rampant overproduction. History was to have been portrayed from the therapeutic point of view with reference to health, illness and healing. It was a comprehensive attempt to 'really understand the principle of healing, of the great historical therapy which came about through the Mystery of Golgotha'.[254]

Stein's most extensive composition relates to *The Spiritual Basis of Medicine*. In this he explains that the old art of healing (and also the alchemistic doctors such as Paracelsus) were in possession of an original universal wisdom such as is to be recaptured today through Anthroposophy. 'Ancient traditions of healing which still contain something of the cosmic origin of man must come together with modern rational therapy. It will at the same time be a meeting between East and West. The East has already set about studying in the West; the time has now come for the West to show that it understands the ideals of the East, but has to realise them in a different way to the latter'. A universal knowledge embraces the supersensible world and comprehends the wholeness of the human condition as a rhythmical interweaving of polarities, of opposing fields of force, which Rudolf Steiner calls the members of one's being. Their harmonious agreement with one another manifests as a constantly threatened, but ever to be re-established balance. From this it follows that illness and health are to be understood as loss and restoration of balance, which is upset by one-sidedness and the preponderance of the one or other factor. Whoever would cure disease from such a point of view will have to take the physiological and moral aspect into account and grasp the connection between the two. He will prove equal to the task of healing the illnesses of his patients if he himself sets out on the way of practice to become a human being seeking to attain a state of balance between polarities through moral effort. And that was the method which Stein applied.

6
King Leopold's Plan

Stein published his report 'King Leopold's Plan' in *The Present Age* in autumn 1937.[255] This seven pages long contribution at the beginning of the September/October double number of his magazine, contains the wording of an open letter which Leopold III, King of the Belgians, sent to his Prime Minister van Zeeland on 24 July 1937. It is accompanied by a commentary by Stein. The King of the Belgians had chosen this form of an open letter in order to make known to the public his initiative aimed at establishing a permanent World Economic Council. He refers to the suggestions of England and France, accepted by Belgium and also looked upon favourably by America, to prepare a World Economic Conference. He stresses, however, that such a gathering as this would have to be 'as independent as possible of national influences'. To be effective its 'universality, permanence and independence' would be an essential part of it, that is, a willingness to undertake a world-wide continuous co-operation independent of the means of enforcement of the Government. The plan—so concludes the letter—would follow humanitarian and world-wide human ends; in pursuing its aims the West would be offering a proof to the East that such a universal co-ordinated world economy, built up on objective criteria, is engendered from 'a genuine feeling of brotherhood'.

Stein sets this plan in a world historic setting. He compares the age of town-building and the rise of city culture of a thousand years ago to the establishment of world economy as the preliminary to an international peace plan in the twentieth century, and sums up: 'It is obvious that the appeal of the Belgian King has not only an economic, but also a moral side ... Every peace movement may glimpse its own fulfilment in what is planned here, for that which makes war superfluous is certainly working for peace'.[255]

This open letter, which is markedly different in style and content from what had been the thought and custom until then, was the result of an exchange of ideas between King Leopold and Stein. The pianist Walter Rummel had arranged their meeting out of which an intensive working relationship developed. Rummel, an anthroposophist of many years standing and a pupil of Rudolf Steiner, lived in Brussels and had access to the King. The course of their first conversation and what happened afterwards is reported in detail by Stein:

On Sunday 26 June 1937 I travelled with my school friend Dr Eugen Kolisko from Vienna, to Ostende and from there to Brussels, where we were the guests of a well known pianist Walter Rummel in the Rue aux Laines 54. Frau Rummel, an impulsive and very interesting personality, was there too. We were invited to an evening meal by King Leopold III of Belgium. It was my first meeting with the King. He came towards us down the steps of the Palace at Laeken and walked through the park with us. Herr Rummel proposed that the King should go with me alone for a while, and that is what happened. I spoke about the plants and also explained their shape as the effect of cosmic forces working upon them. He was interested and listened to the explanations of the geological epochs as well as to the origin of the kingdoms of nature. While I was silent he repeated what he had heard. He allowed me to correct him and fill in the gaps. He then spoke about two friends of his father, Lagrange and Brück, who had also looked at the universe mathematically. I knew the works of both of them and could answer his questions about the connection between the cosmic rhythms which I described and those of the latter. He was very satisfied about the fact that the two views did not contradict one another. Referring to Lagrange he came to speak about the leadership of nations, about the position of Christ and the contrast between the Old and New Testaments, finally about reincarnation. He said: 'If I could become conscious of who I am and where I belong I would be able to find my way'. At table I talked about my meeting with Kemal Pasha and about his interest in the question of the origin of civilisation in the West or in the East. We also came to speak about the Destiny of the Duke of Windsor who abdicated from the English throne. The King wished to see me again; I should first see Bouillon and d'Owal, however. I actually drove there in Herr Rummel's car and was back again on the evening of 29 June. That was the day of the decisive conversation on which we drew up a kind of programme of the possible actions to be taken in Europe. The outcome of this conversation was the open letter of the King to his Minister van Zeeland. A real friendship soon sprang up with King Leopold and I visited him regularly. The idea of founding a Research Institute for World Economy in Brussels took on with him and led to the appointment of David Ferguson, my long-standing colleague in Dunlop's office in London. He soon drew after him J.K. Montgomery from the Roman Agricultural Institute. I was thus able, quietly and without pushing myself forward in any way, to organise an instrument suitable to setting World Economy onto the right lines.[256]

The destiny of the man and the Regent Leopold throws up questions which are still awaiting an answer. 'In him lived the same "why" which has accompanied me throughout my whole life', notes Stein in a biographical study. Leopold had to undergo hard trials in his life. In 1934 his father, King Albert I, died as the result of a mysterious mountaineering accident. In 1935 the car which Leopold was driving at the Vierwaldstätter Lake had an accident, as a result of which Astrid, the Swedish Princess whom he had married in 1926, died. In this situation in life the conversations which he had with Walter Rummel and his wife brought him the answers of spiritual science to the great question 'why?'

The new turn taken by Belgian foreign policy is connected with the reign of Leopold, who gave a public speech about it on 14 October 1936. After German troops had occupied the demilitarised Rhineland in March of that year and doubt had been cast on the international safety guarantees, Belgium relinquished its bond with the West entered into after the Great War and returned to a policy of neutrality—and, indeed, to a free voluntary neutrality, not imposed on it by the Great Powers. A policy such as this was intended to increase the safety of the country which was strategically endangered by being placed between France and Germany. 'We must carry out a pure and exclusively Belgian policy' explained the King in his speech: 'The aim of this must be to keep ourselves apart from the conflicts of the neighbouring States'. But now the question arose as to what spiritual task a strictly neutral Belgium could undertake in order to create a space between the opposing great powers. This was the position of affairs both humanly and politically when the conversations

22　King Leopold III about 1930

between Stein and Leopold began in the summer of 1937.

Stein now saw an indication of the way he had to go. Through his collaboration with Dunlop the foundation had been laid on which to build further with the help of the King. The contemporary situation had certainly become more acute through the militarisation of Germany, but so much the more necessary were the activities in the economic field. Belgium, one of the most important industrial countries, the 'England' of the Continent, seemed to be the ideal starting point for such a planned undertaking.

To begin with—as already in England—a research institute had to be established in order to prepare for a world economic ruling. Stein became more and more conscious of the difficulties facing the project on account of the whole situation. The world economic crisis and the collapse of the gold standard in 1931 had led to chaos in the economy and currency. Mass unemployment, decline in world trade, devaluation of the currency, foreign currency control, protectionism were the results of this development. The nineteenth century theories of political economics proved incapable of controlling the complex economic processes. A full recognition of the earth as an economic entity complete within itself would be needed before one could intervene to regulate and steer the development; but, according to Rudolf Steiner, that would entail 'a deep and thorough specialised knowledge such as no branch of science or naturestudy provides'.[257] With the help of the Research Institute Stein wanted to tackle these tasks and he was able to win over the King for this plan. He also succeeded in interesting certain sponsors; an American banking magnate and adviser to the President put a considerable sum of money at the disposal of the Instiute.

In November 1937 there followed the State visit of Leopold to England which was announced as a 'peace mission'. Political and economic themes were discussed: the plan of a new West European security treaty and the project of a closer world economic collaboration with the declared object of reducing the risks of an armed conflict, which, since the open letter, was known to be Leopold's main concern. In a speech at the Lord Mayor of London's reception the King made special mention of two important factors: Britain's task of leadership and the economic realities. Through the extent of its Empire Great

Britain holds responsibility for humanity as a whole, especially in the economic field. 'Politics concern only a part of humanity but a better regulation of economic life is important for everybody'. Of course international economic measures come up against the opposition of national economic interests. 'In order to overcome these difficulties we need a clear insight into economic realities, which have to be looked at quite dispassionately and independently of all other considerations'.[258] It was a restrained allusion to the necessry separation of the political and economic spheres. The speech derives—according to Stein—'in all essential points' from his suggestions. It was not the only time he had provided the King with such projects.

Stein had quickly gained the confidence of Leopold, as can be gathered from his notes and hand-written letters of the King to 'Dr Stone'. After his visit to England there was an opportunity for a detailed discussion in the Laeken Palace on 23 December 1937. The King handed Stein the report of the Prime Minister van Zeeland (who had meanwhile resigned) and begged for Stein's opinion and suggestions. Stein explained: 'He (van Zeeland) does not understand how to separate politics from economy and because he does not understand it himself he cannot get others to be enthusiastic about it. For him it remains an idealistic phrase not leading to any practical application'. There had even been a question of Stein becoming an authorised negotiator in economic affairs.

The greatest difficulty, of course, was to work out concrete suggestions for producing a world market that would function. A new line of thought, born out of spiritual science was needed to put right the economic and currency situation. 'What is at the basis of economic life', explained Rudolf Steiner, 'must be sought for in the regulating forces of initiation science . . . it is particularly the economic life which is most in need of the influence of spiritual life . . . The salvation of future humanity depends upon that'.[259] These regulating forces emanate from the idea of the Threefold Social Organism and may lead to the solving of problems among freely acting human beings and others who collaborate associatively together. When individualities arrive at their decisions out of a knowledge of superimposed social laws then the force of circumstance ceases to exert pressure upon them. In the sphere of economy the motive will no longer be to obtain the greatest gains and growth, but to trade economically out of social understanding which will prove to be both intelligent and practicable. Stein saw the historic prototype of such a way of thinking in the way that the Templars managed their money and dealt with their business affairs. They sought to reconcile 'eastern religious feeling with western striving after reality. Each one of them on their own was poor and destitute, but they had the management of vast resources of gold. Their Order functioned like the organisation of a bank, acting selflessly'.[260]

The regulation of world economy to which they aspired was, to start with, the wheat market. Here the four most important countries of its production, U.S.A., Canada, Australia and Argentina had started to negotiate about terms of sale and minimum sale prices. The well-known practice of manipulating the market was discussed: curbing production in order to keep the world price high—in spite of the fact that millions were starving. The discussions in the Wheat Advisory Committee ran their course fruitlessly, it is certain, because the conflict of interests were irreconcilable. But this process, which could not be justified either economically or morally, roused Stein's indignation and drove him to act: 'The Wheat Advisory Committee seems to think that the stabilisation of the price of wheat justifieds starvation . . . It is necessary to unmask this dragon and slay it'. The wrong way of thinking of the producers consists of not taking the consumer's standpoint into account. The economy is not out to serve the consumer, it dictates the price out of a desire for profit by making use of a position of power.

In this situation the endeavours of the Brussels Institute were directed towards urging the introduction of an economically justified price. As can be seen from the draft of an international agreement on wheat it was to be determined by a form of exchange appropriate to the time and by agreement within a panel of experts. The intention was, first of all, to build up a fund 'to be used to stabilise prices through buying and selling stock'. By a process of learning the participants would then develop an objective sense for others which would bring about just conditions worthy of life.

The Brussels proposition was the outcome of long years of study. Since the social upheavals at the end of the First World War Stein had been working on questions concerning the economic and social order and since the world economic crisis he had been engaged on the complex problems of the currency. The changed times demanded new insight to make new solutions possible. After most countries had abandoned the gold standard it was high time that the processes connected with money should be reconsidered and the whole structure of currency put on a different footing.

Stimulated by Rudolf Steiner's explanations of 'a healthy currency' and the necessity of adjusting the money to its true level, Stein, and more particularly Ferguson, developed the idea of a 'Gold-Wheat-Standard'[261] after having made a close study of the markets. The value of gold was to be regulated according to the price of wheat and by that the exchange rate should be fixed. An international currency agreement on this basis would then do away with obstacles standing in the way of free trade.[262]

For the further progress of the work it now depended upon getting the co-operation of other economic institutes and making contact with personalities with political and economic influence. In May 1938 Prince Bernhard of the Netherlands twice invited Stein to his summer residence in Soestdijk. The latter suggested that the International Statistical Institute in the Hague should divide its work with the Brussels Institute of Economics. In detailed letters Stein describes the intentions of this undertaking which reckoned on the free initiative and enlightened will of the participating individuals: 'An Institute is being formed in Belgium organised by King Leopold. This Institute is planned as a World Institute. It will not give advantage to anyone on a one-sided way, it is there to introduce reason into the complexities of the economic problems. On the one hand it is a research institute, on the other hand it will lead to practical steps in the form of suggestions. It sends an invitation to Holland to participate in it. This participation is not thought of as an inter-State affair, but as something which makes an appeal to the good will of single individuals and is occupied, to begin with, in the economic and not the political field. Now it must be said, with all propriety, that it is up to you, Your Highness, to decide to use your own powers, in the form of your own person and with the support of the Institute already existing in Holland, to organise the Dutch contribution to this work of humanity'.[263]

The conception of the 'Royal Institute' was so divergent from the usual way of thinking that it was at first met with distrust. The danger of war due to the planned invasion of Czechoslovakia also had a paralysing effect on the intentions. On 29 September, the day of the Munich agreement which brought a short respite, Stein reported to the Prince about 'those things which could still be discussed with King Leopold with regard to the Institute'. The King was of the opinion that they should 'work on undisturbed by the alarming world situation, because positive and constructive things which would outlast all crises could only be achieved over a long period of time'. He was prepared to receive the leading participants of the International Institute of Statistics (among whom was the later Nobel Prize Winner Tinbergen), 'so that there should be no further mistrust of the fact that anything other than a truly honest wish to build up something constructive and helpful for humanity lay behind this undertaking'. Finally, what financial contribution Holland was willing to make had to be made clear, for 'every human concern is, to begin with, something which requires sacrifice.'[264]

In spite of opposition the work showed promise of success. Stein was full of an urge to act and was very confident, especially since in the spring of 1938, he had made the acquaintance of the owner of a gold mine from Rhodesia who was reckoned to be the presumptive President and who was willing to become financially involved in the Brussels Institute in a big way. At Stein's instigation a meeting came about between the mine owner and the King. But in later proceedings the transactions of the South African became so dubious that the compromised King had no other option but to close down the Institute.

The proceedings cannot be reconstructed in detail. Leopold, who in any case was endangered by his working association with Stein, was unable to take on any further burden in the political tension of the summer of 1939 which led to the outbreak of war, and so he gave up the Institute. Stein vacated his office in Castle Bellevue and after his two-year working association with the King he transferred the centre of his activity back to London. A similar fate had befallen him as he had experienced at Dunlop's death when his activity had come to an abrupt end.

What King Leopold and Stein brought about in conjunction with one another seems like an episode of modern history. But their action, which was under the guidance of the Spirit of the

Time, had far-reaching consequences, which became evident seven years later. In July 1944 one of the most successful economic and currency conferences of the century took place in Bretton Woods, a spa in the north eastern part of the USA. More than 730 experts from 44 countries, among which were representatives from the Soviet Union, discussed the reforms of the post-war economy. The time in which the conference took place, from 1 to 22 July, is notable. Three weeks before it began the Western Allies had opened a new front through their landing in Northern France, which was the preface to the end phase of the war. Made wiser by the catastrophe which had shattered Europe and destroyed the national economies, there met together 'people full of idealism to draw up a plan for a new international economy'.[265] Dunlop. Stein and Leopold had followed the same objective, but their insight into the process of historical development had taught them a lesson and they were filled with a certainty that only an action springing out of spiritual-scientific knowledge of reality could prevent the threatened catastrophe. Nevertheless, the architects of the Bretton-Woods agreement made it possible, through the founding of the International Currency Fund and the World Bank, that freedom of movement in the monetary field was restored and that trade restrictions for the transport of goods were lifted. After the outbreak of war Stein's life story became more consolidated again, for at that time he was nearly given the post of a mediator between the Belgian King and the English Government. Stein remained silent on this subject. All we have are the entries in a large diary, acquired specially for this purpose, seemingly intended to serve as an aid to memory for a later report.

Since the time of his collaboration with Dunlop Stein had been able to establish connections with politically authoritative personalities through his publishing activities. In this way he also got to know Winston Churchill through the British Admiral Roger Keyes, who was a friend of the Belgian Royal Family, and he found an opportunity of talking with him about the occult background of National Socialism; which caused the rigorous opponents of Chamberlain's 'appeasement policy' to remark that nothing of that should reach the public.

But Stein was not merely an observer of English politics, he also observed the labours of the Western and North European countries which, in the field of tension between the German land-power and the British sea-power, respectively its French forces on the Continent, had to keep a watch in both directions. These so-called 'Oslo-Countries' — Belgium, Denmark, Finland, Luxembourg, the Netherlands, Norway and Sweden — attempted to establish themselves as a third force between the axis powers of Germany/Italy and the two West European democracies, and to offer their diplomatic arbitration services. At the end of August 1939 there was a meeting of these seven neutral countries in Brussels at which King Leopold handed in a declaration framed by Stein. Those present agreed to appoint the King as their spokesman in the peace negotiations, whereupon he, together with Queen Wilhelmina of the Netherlands, took on the post of mediators between the opposing parties, which both the Monarchs renewed after the German invasion of Poland.[266] Both in Belgium as well as in Holland peace-keeping efforts were made in which pupils of Rudolf Steiner were involved. Stein had some influence in Brussels on account of being adviser to the Belgian King who was aware of the importance of Rudolf Steiner; in the Hague, a few months before the outbreak of war, Willem Zeylmans van Emmichoven along with two other anthroposophical friends, appealed directly to the Queen 'with the suggestion that she should call a World Congress for the general settlement of spiritual, economic and political questions throughout the World'.[267]

Such initiatives leave no trace behind them in the historical archives, they are not recorded and they count as irrelevant if ever they are even known about. But, in the light of spiritual reality, it is the quality of consciousness and will which counts, even in positions in which there is not the slightest chance of success.

The situation of the neutral countries was radically changed by the rapid overthrow of Poland. Now it was particularly Belgium and Holland who had to ask themselves what value they could attach to the Franco-British guarantees of protection when they were unable to protect either Czechoslovakia or Poland from German occupation. When would it be their turn? As a land of transit between Central and Western Europe and the gateway to France for the Germans, Belgium was in the greatest danger. The King, according to the opinion of the Commander-in-Chief of the Belgian troops, found himself in a precarious position. Through his military sense of responsibility he wanted to have strategic discussions with the Western Powers, as the Head of State he had to follow a strictly neutral policy. Everything had to be avoided which could give the Germans, who had infiltrated innumerable agents into Brussels, the pretext of a violation of neutrality—all the more so as the public opinion of the country was pro-Western.[268]

That was how Stein interpreted the situation when, at the end of September, he received from the Foreign Office the exit permit he had applied for to travel to Belgium. Without doubt he hoped to be received by Leopold, but the King declined to accept him as a mediator in political and military affairs and declared that he had only had conversations with him about economics. Even though the desired discussion never took place, Stein was, nevertheless able to successfully sound out Ministers and political representatives through his connection with the Royal House. Arrived back in England he immediately paid a visit to Roger Keyes, an account of which is reported in the latter's biography as follows: 'After nightfall an unexpected visitor, who proved to be an emissary from King Leopold, arrived at Keyes' house in Chelsea, and told him what the King wanted to know'.[269] Upon this, Churchill, at that time First Lord of the Admiralty in Chamberlain's Cabinet, was consulted and Admiral Keyes was entrusted with the mission, as Leopold wished. He was to function as 'unofficial link between King Leopold and the British Government'.[269] Certainly he could only carry out this task for a short while, because the Belgian Government, which was concerned about its neutrality, protested. It was only after the start of the great offensive in the West that Keyes again took up his post, this time as a personal liaison officer between King Leopold and the new Prime Minister Churchill. He was recalled immediately prior to the Belgian capitulation. The King had refused to follow his Government into exile. As Commander-in-Chief he remained with his troops and declared himself a German prisoner of war. On 29 May, one day after the capitulation, Stein sent a letter to Roger Keyes, who had now returned, asking him the reason for Leopold's decision. The answer is not available, but it is known that Keyes strongly supported the King who had been accused of treachery because of his capitulation, and called his action heroic. The King's decision was final and was known to the Allies: to end the fighting insofar as there was insufficient guarantee for an immediate and effective support of Belgian troops. As the latter was not forthcoming he ceased to offer resistance, which, in face of the superior force of military machinery, had now become meaningless. He thereby spared his country still greater devastation.

Stein kept up correspondence for a while with Keyes, through whom he hoped to secure a new post, for he was unable to carry on with his journal after the outbreak of war. On 12 July he laid before Keyes his view of coming events: what had to be done out of necessity and what was to be achieved out of free initiative. At that time, after the English troops had been evacuated and the French had been defeated, the position of German power had reached its zenith; a liberation of the Continent seemed impossible for years to come. Then Stein explained that the only way to end the war was to occupy Germany. Then it would become evident that a large part of the population rejected the ruling government. This part could be won over to a new European Economic Order, for which useful preparatory work had been done by *The Present Age* and the Brussels Institute. What was meant was the de-politicising of the economy in the sense of the Threefold Social Order and a reform of the currency whereby not gold, but the goods and services of production should be taken as the basis and measure for the foreign rate of exchange. England's mission was to prepare peace-time economy during the war and the accomplishing of this task 'would draw the population of Europe onto our side'. 'Is there nobody in this country who could make this possible?' With this question, which remained unanswered, he ended his letter.

In 1941 Roosevelt and Churchill formulated the 'Atlantic Charter', a declaration of the basis of the future world order, which would include the participation of all countries in world trade. Upon this the fascist Dictators announced a 'New European Order' which was to do away with Bolshevism, put an end to 'plutocratic exploitation' and found a peaceful co-existence among European nations. The time for new social and inter-state forms of co-existence had long been due, at the latest since the First World War had brought to light the hidden tensions and Rudolf Steiner had laid before the Central European Statesmen his 'factual programme' for a Threefold Order of Society. Stein, who experienced contemporary history consciously, felt his co-responsibility for the destiny of the twentieth century and future evolution; he was smitten by the 'historical conscience' which impelled him to activity wherever the opportunity presented itself.

The new 'European Economic Order' which Stein wished to work out would most certainly have been very different from the measures which brought about a stabilisation of the economy and politics of Western Europe after the war. The instrument by means of which this policy was carried out was the 'European Recovery Programme', the American economic aid for Western European States known as the Marshal Plan. In face of the increasing East-West confrontation the American plans were directed, from 1947 onwards, towards binding the German potential to a Western political-economic system. Instead of a de-politicised economy, acting freely, there arose the economic military concentration of power of a political economy of East and West—and with that the conflicts of the present day which threaten humanity.

The time for action in the larger social sphere was now at an end. The quiet years of seclusion began, in which Stein certainly continued to give lectures, but in which he had to confine his activities to his more immediate surroundings. His contemplative gaze rested on his past destiny out of which—after the miracle of transformation—would grow his future destiny. The three phases of his life, during which he had trodden the stage of contemporary history, stood out ever more clearly: the years in Brussels, as the result of the Committee instituted by King Leopold which the Boer General and politician Smuts and the English Prime Minister Chamberlain used to attend: the far-reaching activity as colleague of Dunlop in the World Power Conference; the Threefold Commonwealth time in 1919 as, called by Rudolf Steiner, he made known the new social ideas with combative zeal in Stuttgart and Vienna. And, as the prelude to these stages of his life, the instructions he received personally from Rufolf Steiner about the Threefold Social Order in the summer of 1917. 'We are the preparers of the preparers' Stein once heard his spiritual teacher remark. Everything which happened in the first half of the century remains a beginning and a project; but in order to prevent a catastrophe of mankind, it will have to be carried further in the near future. Till that time arrives the work done with Dunlop and

Leopold 'will continue to work on in the developing economic institutions'.[270] Stein can rightly lay claim to the fact that the customs- and economic-unit of the Benelux Lands, planned since 1944, can be traced back to the impulse given by the Brussels Institute which he directed. To prepare himself for the new cultural inspiration of the next century was the task he set himself for the remaining years of his life.

7
Rudolf Steiner as Comforter

During the last years of his life Stein made several attempts to write his memoirs. But he did not succeed in producing a connected account [see appendix]. On 5 December he remarked in a letter to his daughter: 'The writing of my memoirs does not proceed very fast, it is a very difficult task'. Twenty years earlier the work had flowed easily from his pen as he wrote his life's story for *The Present Age*. What he now started to write down on Christmas Day 1951 and, adorned with 'My Life' on the title page, broke off after the fifth page. And for this he had planned a work the size of a book, not because he thought he himself was so important, but because many important people had entered his life; it was of them that he wished to speak, more particularly of Rudolf Steiner as his soul-guide.

The age of 'confessions' introduced by St Augustine, the age of the great 'life-penance', is a thing of the past. Stein wanted to direct his comprehending gaze towards the entelechy of man which, in the realm of the life before birth, is already at work on the sheath of the earthly personality. Stein's father had confined himself to noting the weight of the new-born babe and his mother had only described the difficulties of feeding the infant, whose life was saved by a wet-nurse; he himself adds to that that his individuality left its 'heavenly home' prematurely because his 'desire to come down to earth' was so overwhelming. Thirty years after the birth of Rudolf Steiner it was able to dip down into the stream of heredity, which it had followed already for generations, so that it could become a contemporary of the spirit guide to share with him his life's work.

In contemplative reflection the survey of his life's history became clearer to him. It appeared as a soul-drama, the scenes of which Rudolf Steiner described as 'changing the direction of

23   W J Stein about 1950

one's will, experiencing supersensible knowledge, participating in the destiny of one's time'.[271] Ever since he read the first pages of *Occult Science* his will had been directed towards comprehending the spirit; on the pathway of 'exercises' his experience of supersensible knowledge had become deepened; and in constant progress—noticeable since his work on the Threefold Commonwealth in Stuttgart—the participation in the destiny of our time had become the destiny of his own soul. There had been upswings and downfalls, nodal points and turning-points, doldrums and storms. In 1945, so Stein felt, a new epoch commenced both in outer history and in his own life. Two generations had gone by since 1879, the start of the Michael Age. Central European development ended in catastrophe, in emaciation and self-immolation. The 'moral cataclysm' and 'destruction of Europe' foreseen by Rudolf Steiner—if human initiative could not break through to prevent it—had already come about.[272] Would the construction of a new civilisation succeed in the 'atomic age' of division and disintegration which started in 1945? Rudolf Steiner wanted to create a centre, aware of itself, which would master the art of balancing polarities. But the centre had annihilated itself, the enfeebled Europe became divided in two and a system of international connections was instituted which rested on the twin military poles of the super powers. It was not peace which reigned but cold war, threatening to degenerate into an armed combat. What could still be done in such a situation? Stein asked himself; and in many a dark hour resignation came upon him.

But then, he reasoned to himself, he had to prepare the ground for a realisation of the things which he would not experience himself.

There was something shadowy and unreal about the post-war years as compared with the eventfulness and crowded experience of the preceding decades. At that time things had taken place on the stage of history which can only be compared to the conscious experience of the spiritual seeker after truth when meeting with real supersensible powers. Stein experienced the destiny of the times as the initiation of mankind, as a sojourn in the abyss. The trials of the Mysteries had been enacted in public, the ego of man had been led beyond the threshold—knowingly or unknowingly. Central Europe had delivered itself over to the enemy of its spirit in the frenzy of self destruction. But the spiritual seed had already been sown before the year of downfall approached. At the end of the century—according to the 'Michael prophecy'—the decision would be made, when Rudolf Steiner, along with the circle of his pupils and collaborators, would continue and renew the work for humanity which had been begun. What the teacher had told the anthroposophical friends on his last visit to London, by way of leave-taking, was stored up by Stein as hope and certainty: 'Every anthroposophist should be moved by this knowledge: Here I stand. I have in me the impulse of Anthroposophy. I recognise it as the Michael impulse. I wait and am strengthened in my waiting by the true activity in Anthroposophy at the present time in order that after the short interval allotted in the twentieth century to anthroposophical souls between death and a new birth, I may come again at the end of the century to promote the Movement with much more spiritual power. I am preparing myself for the New Age leading from the twentieth to the twenty-first century . . . It is thus that a true Anthroposophist speaks. Many forces of destruction are at work upon the earth. All culture, all civilised life on earth must fall into decadence if the spirituality of the Michael Impulse does not so lay hold of men that they again become capable of bringing upliftment to the civilisation that is hurrying into the abyss today'.[273]

But to what would Rudolf Steiner connect up in his future activity at the beginning of the next century? To the Society founded by him at Christmas 1923? The state it was in at that time gave Stein cause to doubt this. He desired to prepare the future by making souls ready to receive the spirit and moving their dispositions to accept what was to happen. That is how he looked upon his lecturing and therapeutic work after the war had ended. At that time the direction of his gaze was altered: he set his sights towards the end of the century and the increasing resumption of anthroposophical work in a forthcoming incarnation.

Measured by the former intensity of his destiny they were twelve peaceful years which rounded off Stein's life: years of a 'mild growing light', as it appeared to visitors from the Continent who could remember the aggressive eloquence of the speaker at meetings before the war. It was now mostly to small groups of people that he held lecture cycles about subjects of anthroposo-phical cosmology and the history of the Mystery Schools, of

Christology and research into destiny, of the spiritual knowledge of mankind and of soul development. The notes from members of his audience have been preserved, lecture outlines in Stein's handwriting and comments by friends in letters giving their impressions of what they had heard. Thus, one of those present at a lecture he gave in Amsterdam shortly after the capitulation of Germany brings to mind that quite new insight had been given him about 'the connection of wheat and gold in the West and rice and silver in the East'.[274] But Stein's appearance at that time, during which the brutality of the German attack on the Netherlands, the harassment and deportation during the time of the occupation was still present on all hands, caused 'surges of emotion' to occur. The anti-German mood broke out against the naturalised British Austrian, who was only able to start his lecture after he had called his audience to order.

At the centre of his reflective investigation stood the puzzling questions of the common destiny of the Anthroposophical Society and Rudolf Steiner's identity; questions with which he was intimately bound up through his personal encounter with the great teacher and through his own interference in the history of the Society, which had such dire consequences. A threefold task was given him: to practise self-knowledge as it is reflected in the karma lectures, which characterise a duality in the streams of destiny; to be able to recognise these currents and their representatives again in the development of the anthroposophical movement; finally, to prepare the future collaboration for the founding of a spiritual civilisation. This direction which his questioning took and the tasks which were set him had started to become clear to him during the Stuttgart years while Rudolf Steiner was still director of the Waldorf School. At that time Stein, who had asked about his past lives and his karmic connection to the Waldorf School, had received the key to his further investigations. Rudolf Steiner said to him: 'The teachers were Aristotelians and the pupils were Saxons from the time of Charlemagne'.[275] This surprising statement which points to the karmic environment of those concerned, was a double challenge; to comprehend oneself in the living stream of Aristotelian cognition of the world and of man, which Thomas Aquinas christianised; and to recognise in the school movement issuing from Stuttgart the spiritual counterpart to the monastic schools of the Carolingian age, a study which demands a historical synopsis of the ninth and twentieth centuries. The occasion for Rudolf Steiner's piece of information concerned what happened during a lesson which Stein reported: 'I described to the children how Wedukind (the Saxon Duke) came in disguise into the Cathedral on Christmas Day and, when he beheld the monstrance, shouted "Saxnot". Charles the Great embraced him, his enemy, and was reconciled to him. The children were most impressed. Dr Steiner said: "It is no wonder, it was the Saxons who were present"'.[275]

As Stein grew old he became more and more aware of the fact that his life was moving towards a future which revealed itself as a metamorphosis of the past. He now tried—led by the thread of spiritual-scientific knowledge—to follow Rudolf Steiner's individuality in its stages between death and a new birth, as he had previously investigated the life between birth and death and its changes. It was through Rudolf Steiner that he learned to understand the ancient word of exhortation: '*Memento mori*' as a summons to 'accompany the destiny of the dead'.[276] And the service of the Grail, to which he had committed himself, was for him the association with 'the specially selected living Dead'.[277] Familiarity with the results of his investigations about the after-death experiences then brought him the certainty that the individuality of Rudolf Steiner had passed the 'World Midnight Hour' in the Saturn sphere and that the decision to incarnate had occurred at that moment in which the Christmas Foundation Meeting was celebrating its thirty third anniversary. He writes about this to a friend in Germany on 6 January 1957, half a year before his own death:

Dr Steiner has now already passed the World-Midnight hour and again draws near to the earth. One has got to understand that the direction of his activity has changed . . . The thirty third anniversary of the Christmas Gathering must not be sought on earth, but there where he himself resides: in his World-Midnight. Everything comes to *fulfilment* there which was a *seed* in 1923: namely, the descent begins. Thus we have to discriminate in our feelings between essentials and non-essentials. The essential thing is in the *spiritual world* . . . In 1957 we must look up with reverence and devotion to the spiritual world which is rapidly approaching us . . . Thus everything comes about as it was prophesied. Truly everything is in the best order. There are no grounds for being depressed. The great decisions will come at the end of the century and we shall be there.

Stein was able to express himself thus in anthroposophical circles during the last years of his life. His listeners noticed the changed style and interpreted it after his death as the announcement of his 'leave-taking'. He spoke at that time in a simple and impressive manner out of a deepened experience of anthroposophical truth which he drew from his study and from his intuitive spiritual faculty. Unmistakable was the urge to elucidate the karmic connections of the anthroposophical movement by means of obtaining knowledge through spiritual science. But the karmic connections of individual personalities he only touched upon in private. There is no doubt about the fact that he had acquired a spiritually intuitive ability in the realm of insight into destiny; nevertheless, his friends sometimes asked themselves whether these statements of his were derived from information given him by Rudolf Steiner or whether they were personal impressions of Stein which needed checking. But the predominant impression remained that there was an important teacher of Anthroposophy active here. A friendly-critical observer such as George Adams who 'sometimes had difficulties with Stein in spiritual matters' wrote to him in a Christmas letter in 1949 that he had always noticed 'how many people you are able to help by speaking so calmly and naturally, so substantially and at the same time so lovingly about the great facts of spiritual life. There are very few among us who have this vocation... You are a true pupil and friend of Rudolf Steiner; you have helped us throughout the years with devotion and calmness, always giving, always bestowing gifts'.[278]

When Stein received this letter he was in an awkward position. He had formed a new life partnership and in November 1949 he left the house that he shared with Johanna Stein-Lungen. Visitors were received in his new house, where he also carried out his therapeutic practice, but he always introduced visitors to his new home where, until his death, a friendly caring relationship persisted. The changes in his private circumstances meant that he was no longer able to hold lectures in Rudolf Steiner House in London and had to find other facilities for this. But the difficulties could be overcome because his audience followed him to the

24   W J. Stein in Kensington, London, about 1955

new lecture rooms. He could continue lecturing, not only in London, but also in other anthroposophical institutions in the country, such as in Clent and in Stroud, in Wynstones and Michael Hall schools.

Stein's way of life accorded with his individual disposition and not with convention. To the question as to what he considered his professional activity to be he would answer: 'I can only give lectures and spread Anthroposophy and I have been doing that now for many years with everything in my power. Whether one calls that a profession or not I do not know. I hold about 330 lectures a year. Besides that I see many people whom I try to help. That is not a profession either, but it is a task which completely fills my time'. To add to that there was the prompt attention to his widespread correspondence which, in special subjects—as, for instance the ninth century—could be very extensive. 'One does not know where to start and where to finish' is how he finished his nine-page-long letter which was the continuation of a lengthy epistle from the previous day.

He wrote a single article for the magazine *Beiträge zu einer Erweiterung der Heilkunst* (contributions towards an extension of the art of healing), the last thing which was published during his lifetime.[279] In it he described the occult-physiological aspect of the Argonaut Saga on the basis of Rudolf Steiner's indications. The Greek heroes sail to Colchis, on the eastern shore of the Black Sea, under the captaincy of Jason in the ship Argo to bring the Golden Fleece to Greece. They are in search of the Mysteries which guard the secret of the sun-like archetypal human being. The astral body of this being is not yet penetrated by the ego or darkened by egoism, but is irradiated by divine spiritual beings'.[280] The mystics of Colchis knew of the pains and dangers connected with the gaining of the Golden Fleece, the restoration of the 'light-radiating astral body'.[280] And Stein's cryptic account also made it evident that he was familiar with this sphere. He concludes:

Jason's end is a tragic one. 'Disharmony with one's surroundings is the fate of those who are the bearers of a Divine Being' said Dr Steiner. It is a word bearing great weight which has often comforted me. 'The World', said Dr Steiner 'hates every initiate'. It also crucified Christ. Jason had to forsake Medea, because she represented a stage of consciousness which he had outgrown. Medea kills her children and escapes in the dragon chariot, Jason then falls on his sword ... Dr Steiner says in comment to this passage: 'The initiate has to live in his *ego* only, he falls upon the sword of his divine self, which penetrates all and before which nothing base can endure'.

During the first three days of the week Stein held regular consulting hours. He regarded the everyday therapeutic practice as something which complemented his lecturing activity. Because of his familiarity with the anthropological and cosmological aspect of Anthroposophy he longed to turn his knowledge into deeds. His patients felt that his power to heal had developed along the road of initiation-science; and they experienced the process of recovery as being gently led to the World-Healer.

There is no doubt that Stein drew nearer to his life's end consciously. He had, after all, a clear picture of the form of his life-history and its exact centre-point in the year 1924, at the time when that eventful turning-point of consciousness took place which Rudolf Steiner had interpreted for him. His friends observed 'the stages of his leave-taking': ... how he cut himself off from the topical events of the moment and how the whole world began to lose its interest for him; how he, nevertheless, gave a new structure to his lectures and spoke about things which he had previously kept to himself. During the last months, however, that had changed still more. Everything became more intimate and more delicate, as though every human contact was a gentle leave-taking. Whoever had known him in Stuttgart would hardly have recognised Stein today. The erstwhile warlike spirit had disappeared and he rayed out benevolence in a completely unsentimental, but practical fashion'.[281] Like a dissipation of his life-forces was how his audience experienced his lectures, which remained alive in the memory, not merely on account of their content, but also because of the challenging intensity of the words. In the circularised letter to the Waldorf Schools in which Herbert Hahn announced the death of Stein, he mentioned the last lecture which Stein gave in Michael Hall School: 'On the 30 March of this year (1957), that is on the 32 anniversary of Dr Rudolf Steiner's death, Stein spoke to the pupils of our largest English Sister School, Michael Hall, about Rudolf Steiner's inner being and spiritual stature in a way which gripped the hearts of all who heard him. It happened that I came upon an echo of just this lecture on two occasions while I was on an Easter trip through France and Portugal'.[281]

He held his last lecture at Wynstones School on 21 June, five days before he was taken ill. He spoke on the subject which Rudolf Steiner had started to speak about in his last address: about Lazarus-John, the important Disciple who stood apart from the circle of the Apostles, the author of the Apocalypse, the one initiated by Christ. One of the participating teachers spoke in a concluding conversation about the reverberations of what he had heard: 'I spoke to him afterwards and mentioned the intimate, warm and personal tone of the lecture. "You seem to have a special personal connection to him?" Then a light came into his eyes, which had been gazing inwards so much, and a smile, like that of a happy young lad spread over his features. "He (Dr Steiner) loved him (St John). So I must love him" he said'.[281]

Closer observation could not fail to notice that Stein had appeared over-strained and exhausted for some time. A nurse, who got to know him a few weeks before he was taken ill confirmed the fact 'that he is not well'.[282] On 26 June, Wednesday evening, he was overcome by such a strong attack of illness that a doctor had to be notified immediately. Next morning he was taken to the Middlesex Hospital where the doctor in charge diagnosed coronary thrombosis and ordered complete rest in bed and a four weeks treatment in hospital. After sleepless nights an easing of his condition came about and Stein, who was aware of the seriousness of his condition, seemed to gather hope. An unusual, almost tropical heat, which was hard for him to bear, rendered his circulation more difficult. On the twelfth day after the onset of the illness, on Sunday 7 July, death set in. It was twenty or twenty-five minutes past one at night. He lay in a ward. No one noticed his passing; it was the Night Sister on her rounds who first confirmed what had happened. The corpse was then taken to Mrs Stein's house and was laid out in state. At his head burned the candles of the candlestick which had also been placed on the coffin of Eugen Kolisko. In front of it, in the centre, stood the picture of the youthful Christ which has been ascribed to Leonardo, which was known to him from the children's service at the Waldorf School. To the side of it was a photograph of Rudolf Steiner. The countenance of the deceased beneath its still dark hair gave the impression of being narrow and emaciated, severity and earnestness were engraved upon it, a painfully bitter expression lay at the corners of the mouth, the energetic chin spoke of a will-force which strove towards 'thresholds of fulfilment'. It seemed as if he had already gone far away in order to follow after his spiritual comrades at arms who had gone on before.

The cremation ceremony took place on 10 July. The service was held by Alfred Heidenreich as priest of the Christian Community. Robert Killian, the former colleague of the Stuttgart Waldorf School, spoke for the German friends, George Adams for the English ones. All the speakers concurred in emphasising his heart qualities: his courage, his love for his Master, his simplicity of heart, his modesty. Particular points were put forward: He felt himself to be alone in the world, for his friends had preceded him; 'he did not want to shirk his duty at the end of the century'.

The most important contributions towards an understanding of his death were given by George Adams and Willi Sucher. 'Adams said that in the few days after Stein's death one could experience with wonder and astonishment how actively Stein had already begun his work in the spiritual world. Sucher, who was an investigator of the cosmic aspect of birth and death in the sense of spiritual science, said that in the whole of his practice he had never met an individuality who set out so directly on his way to the gateway of the sun'.[283] Out of the instructive communication of the Living Word Stein had summoned the profound forces of his individuality to his aid in order to become ripe to enter the sphere of Him Who makes free. His soul-development depended upon this meeting. A fragmentary note with the title 'Rudolf Steiner as Comforter' bears witness to this:

There are moments in life in which one is suddenly surrounded by light, in which one radiates a love of which one is certainly not capable oneself; a love which is so powerful that one cannot even imagine it later. In such moments the soul can feel the might of Christ. It lifts one out of a consciousness of the body, while one certainly is still in the body, nay, more than ever in the body, for one becomes aware of powerful currents pulsating through it. St Paul had such experiences which he described. The unexpected thing about these Christ experiences lies in the fact that the figure of Christ does not appear outwardly, but rises out of currents within one's body and bears one in its love. Christ said to the one possessed whom He healed: 'Go to thine own people and make known to them the love by which I bear thee up'. This 'being carried by Christ's love' can be experienced. I would like to say: What one can thus experience through Grace in festive moments of life was present continually in Rudolf Steiner. He was a personality borne by the love of Christ.

A generation has now passed since the death of Stein. The contentions between the forces which would destroy culture and those which would renew it are moving towards a decision. Will the principle of social renewal which springs from individual spiritual experience be able to win through?

Towards the end of the century one's searching gaze falls on the individualities who will be fighting by the side of Rudolf Steiner in the decisive battle for the future transformation of human consciousness. Among these pioneers of Anthroposophy is also Walter Johannes Stein to be found. He lived and worked in the certainty that the work which has been begun now stands at the threshold of the Millenium. He had often pointed to these things, for the first time, perhaps, and possibly in its most pregnant form when, during a 'terrible meeting' of members of the Anthroposophical Society in Dornach on 6 February, 1926, his thirty-fifth birthday, he laid the following words on the hearts of Rudolf Steiner's pupils: 'Perhaps only at the end of the century will it be possible to bring into complete harmony what today confronts us as differing directions of will. In spite of that, however, we shall have to succeed in preserving the continuity of our movement until the time when our leader again appears among us and we shall be there, too, to work at our common task. Then will truly take place what Doctor Steiner describes in his Mystery Drama in the words: "I see in much that hates only the germ of future love"'.[284]

APPENDIX

1
Autobiographical Sketches by Walter Johannes Stein

Several fragmentary sketches were found among Stein's papers bearing the title, 'Rudolf Steiner as Comforter'. The complete text is given below:

'Anthroposophy is your sun; all other things are only planets' said Rudolf Steiner comfortingly at an awkward moment. And on another occasion in another difficult situation, he wrote on a piece of paper:

What life has set itself to present to my spirit out of the depths and from the fountain head of world destiny: the courageous soul will find the right way to encounter it when it puts its trust in the gleaming warm ego.

And again, on another occasion, he said:

Follow your star. Before falling asleep visualise yourself placing a pentagram before you; delineate it in your mind so that the lines stretch out brightly in space and remain there, follow this star into the universe. In so doing think the following thought: 'Convey the spirit of my will to the spirit of the world through Thy strength!'. And with that fall asleep. And in the morning, on awaking, visualise to yourself that this brilliant star is suspended above your head. But now it does not merely glow, but it also sounds. Allow it to sound forth from where it hangs there above the human being, let it sound into your heart, into your breast, and imagine to yourself that the star is now speaking to you: 'Spirit from Eternity I bestow upon thee. Receive it through me'.
   And then, before such meditations, practise the following: 'Watchfully waiting, while waiting watch'.

When one practised in this manner, or gratefully recalled

Rudolf Steiner's advice, one could become aware of the fact that he was accompanying one during this practice with his warm bright personality.

That could be experienced as something so bright and warm that he appeared to be in front of one as in life. And so lively and living was his picture as he stood before one, just as one had known him in life, that this picture started to speak.

I was under heavy artillery-fire during the First World War. I thought my last hour had come. A large grenade was in front of me, another behind me, one to my left, and one exploded directly to the right of me. I thought, now there are only a few seconds left. Then he was standing before me, smiling so kindly with sun-like calm and said: 'The fifth will not come.' And when I heard that in the spirit an endless joyful peace flooded over me.

That took place while he was still alive. His picture was always there. He could always get through to you. But it is still the same today after he has been living in the spirit for such a long time. 'If someone has only read one line of my book *Knowledge of the Higher Worlds*, I shall be obliged to accompany that person through all subsequent lives on earth' he said. I am quite certain he accompanies his pupils in spirit-body. He is able to do so because he has united himself so closely with Christ. There are moments in life in which one becomes suddenly as though illumined, in which a love streams forth from one of which one is certainly not capable oneself; a love which is so powerful that one cannot even imagine it oneself in retrospect. In such moments as this one can experience Christ's power in one's soul. One is lifted out of the body in one's consciousness, even though one certainly remains within the body—yes, even more within the body than at other times, for one is conscious of mighty currents which flow through one's body. St Paul had such experiences as this and described them. The surprising thing about such an experience of Christ lies in the fact that the Christ figure does not appear to one from without, but arises out of the currents of one's own being and bears one up by its love. Christ said to the one possessed, whom He healed: 'Go to thine own people and make known to them the love by which I bear thee up.' This act of being upheld by the love of Christ is something which can be experienced. I should like to say: 'What one can thus experience as an act of grace in solemn moments of human existence was present all the time in Rudolf Steiner. He was a personality continually upheld by Christ's love.

And by endowing us with his thoughts we are supported by the tremendous force residing therein. When we experience the upholding love of Christ in this way and turn to look back upon ourselves, we can also become aware of the figure of Christ.

In the scene on Easter morning, Mary Magdalene experienced just this. She had to turn round in order to see Him whom she addressed as Master. Rudolf Steiner leads the way to the inner Easter morning. He enables us to experience that the soul is the Magdalene to whom the Risen One appears.

After one has experienced this one can readily believe that seven devils dwelt within this maiden. For there lives within us in a seven-fold way what—according to our nature—only turns into Christ-perception after it has been overcome.

Rudolf Steiner as teacher, soul-companion and guide would so much like to lead us to this experience. He comforts one. For one is in need of comfort when one stands face to face with one's seven devils.

But when one complained to Rudolf Steiner about one's own imperfections he said: 'You must not be discouraged, get on with your work.

I had the good fortune to meet Rudolf Steiner when I was 21 years old, he himself was 30 years older than I. When I saw him for the first time I had already read some of his works. On 18 June 1922 Rudolf Steiner gave a lecture in which he described how I came to Anthroposophy. He said: 'Dr Stein came to Anthroposophy as though by matter of course and in him there works what was carried out by the Cistercians.'

Such a simple statement as this is surprising because I was educated by Benedictines (in the Schottengymnasium in Vienna) and have never met a Cistercian. With these words Dr Steiner was not characterising an actual relationship which took place in this life, but was giving a characterisation of a particular soul and spirit which he wished to depict in this way.

The connection which he indicated points to a former life in which, indeed, I was not a Cistercian myself, but belonged to an Order of Knights which had been founded on Cistercian principles. That is the reason for the expression, 'works carried out by the Cistercians'.

One gains an insight into former lives through grace. When I spoke to Dr Steiner about such an experience he said to me: 'In this case you have experienced your last death'. And he drew a diagram for me. He said: 'That is the current of your life:

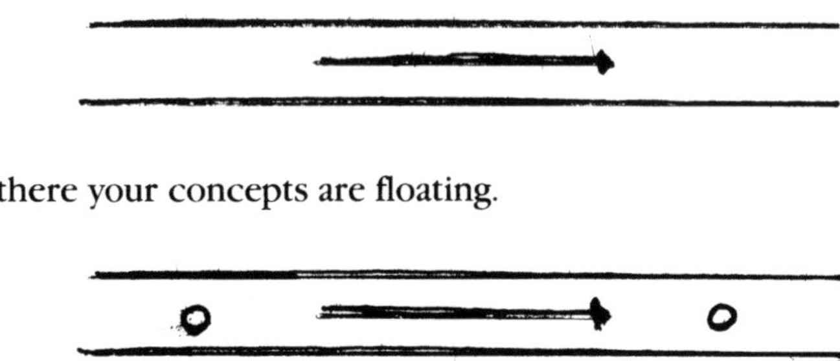

there your concepts are floating.

Now, however, you have a concept which does not float in the current of life, but which has emerged as the whole current of your life itself'.

An experience of this sort holds many surprises. One might think it would be a terrifying experience to relive one's own death (I mean the last death before one's present life). But that is not so. It is a joyous experience I experienced the murder of an old man. He was a ship's captain and met his death as he emerged from the hatchway onto the upper deck. There, between ships cables and the masts, he was struck down by the spear of his enemy. It was a strangely shaped ritual spear, the blade of which had a wavy outline. This spear struck him above the teeth of the upper jaw, and killed him instantly. I experience this in all detail. The landscape—it was sunset—the uniform of the old man with its ornamental metal buttons, the heavy tread of the old man as he climbed up the companionway.

My interest centred more on the wonderful ease with which I streamed out of my body than on the person who had thrown the spear. Nevertheless, my love went out to him in gratitude. One would not expect that one would be grateful to the person who kills one. And yet it is so.

True spiritual experiences are always quite different to what one would expect according to the practices of ordinary life, in reality one usually feels it as a liberation.

What I felt I can best express by quoting Empedocles:

> 'When, released from your body,
> you rise up into free etherial spaces,
> you become an immortal god,
> escaped from death'.

One can truly love one's enemy. But this is easier after death than during life. When one spoke about such things to Rudolf Steiner he was always kind and helpful and explained the things by which one was perplexed.

The two following autobiographical sketches were first published in: *In Memoriam Walter Johannes Stein*, by Herbert Hahn, Stuttgart 1959. The essay: 'How I found my guide, Rudolf Steiner' appeared for the first time in *Das Goetheanum*, Year 4, Nos. 16 and 17.

Rudolf Steiner enters my Life

I saw a book lying on my mother's writing desk. I opened it and read the words: 'What is said in this book about heat processes... would not have been said by the author had he not, at a time which now lies some 30 years in the past (1879), made a study of physics branching out into the various domains of this science. In the domain of heat phenomena the explanations belonging to the so-called mechanical theory of heat formed the centre of his study at that time. And the mechanical theory of heat was even of quite particular interest to the author. The historical development of the relevant explanations which were at that time attached to such names as Julius Robert Mayer, Helmholtz, Joule, Clausius, etc. formed part of the author's constant study. Through this he has acquired during the course of his studies a sufficient basis and possibility to follow all the actual advances which have been made in the realm of the theory of heat up to the present day (1909) and has found no barriers to an understanding of what science has achieved in this domain. If the author had been constrained to say he was unable to do so, it would have been a reason for leaving unsaid and unwritten what has been brought forward in this book. He was really made it his principle in matters of spiritual science to speak or write only about such things of which he can say that, according to his opinion, he is sufficiently informed of what modern science has to say on the subject'.

These remarks occur in the preface to Rudolf Steiner's *Occult Science*. They were written by him in 1909. (They are still pertinent with regard to the state of science in 1956 as I start to write this book.)

I knew when I read these words in 1912—I was a student of mathematics and physics at the Vienna University at the time—that I must undoubtedly get to know what Rudolf Steiner had to say about heat processes'.

I had the feeling that a wonderful conscientiousness and objectivity was here expressed which allowed the author to refer to himself in the third person. I noticed, too, that Rudolf Steiner talked of speaking and writing, but not of printing. I said to myself, he does not mention printing because it represents a mechanical reproduction and he only wants to go so far as moral responsibility is concerned. Here, I told myself, speaks a modest human being who is nevertheless conscious of his own worth, for he says, 'in a way which seems adequate to the author'. He therefore makes his own judgement about what seems to him to be the duty of conscientiousness.

Rudolf Steiner's character revealed itself to me in the first sentences of his which I read. Here, I said, was not only knowledge but an exemplary scientific morality. I felt myself inevitably attracted by it.

The first encounter with the writings of Rudolf Steiner took place in 1912 and I was at once deeply touched in the depths of my soul. I read the whole book through immediately several times from beginning to end. In the book *True and False Paths in Spiritual Investigation*, lectures given in Torquay, 12-22 August 1924, Rudolf Steiner says in the ninth lecture that he had worked on the writing of *Occult Science* between 1906 and 1909. He there states that during these years he had imbued his soul with the ideas of Natural Science, not in order to gain knowledge from them, but to use them as an inner activity in order to carry them up into that sphere which is otherwise occupied by the imaginations. 'You see, I tell you about this way of gaining knowledge so that you will understand how such things come about. You may say: That is a personal matter. But in this case what is personal is completely objective. And if there is anything which people have found fault with in this book it is that it is written like a mathematical textbook, that I did not attempt to introduce anything of a subjective nature into it, but have written the whole thing, as I have now described it to you, with mathematical coolness.'

It was this coolness, the factual conscientious exact description which attracted me. I first read the book for the sake of its contents, then a second time in order to comprehend the way things are described in it, and since then I have not ceased to read it from all differing points of view over the last 44 years.

Even at that time in 1912 I could have said: 'What is Anthroposophy?' and I should have been obliged to reply: 'conscientiousness, conscientiousness, conscientiousness'. Steiner says himself in the introduction to *Occult Science*: 'Yet, with regard to these statements, it is certainly not so that something has to be communicated, the important thing is that what is communicated is done in such a way that it is in conformity with a conscientious approach to the relevant domain of life'.

That is what I felt, that is what moved me so when I first became acquainted with Rudolf Steiner's writings.

I had to read through 127 pages of *Occult Science* before I came to where he speaks about the heat processes. Steiner speaks in a different way than does a physicist who is content to describe the effect of heat on solid, liquid and gaseous bodies but who, in describing the movement of heat in these bodies, not only does not describe the essence of heat itself, but does not even notice that he does not do so.

Heat is not the movement of molecules but the movement is the effect of what heat brings about in a three-dimensional body. Heat itself belongs to a world which cannot be encompassed within three dimensions. Heat possesses one dimension more than the mechanical theory of heat admits. This opened for me the gateway to an understanding of a physics with more than three dimensions. A physics in which the fourth dimension is not time but inversion. An inversion in which the inside becomes outside and the exterior becomes interior. The expansion of bodies brought about by heat in the three dimensional world is only the next best thing to the inversion which takes place in a circle or a sphere. In the latter case what is inside becomes the whole of outer space. Warmth can penetrate three dimensional bodies because it is something which has more than three dimensions itself.

'In the world which is presented to our physical senses heat is certainly present as a condition of solids, liquids and gases, but this condition only represents the outer aspect of warmth, or at the same time its effects. Physicists only speak about these effects of heat, not about its inner nature.

In order to experience the four-dimensional aspect of heat one should direct one's attention to outer space, a thing which one does unconsciously every night in sleep. At night, namely, we are outside our bodies with our consciousness of ourselves and of our surroundings. But it is not sufficient to describe this in a negative way and say that self consciousness and consciousness of our surroundings, are lacking during dreamless sleep. One has to learn to be there where they are. That is to say, we must learn to become conscious of what is outside ourselves during sleep. Then we have ourselves become inverted and we are able to observe our own body-warmth from outside our bodies. Our body-warmth then streams out towards what is four-dimensional, where we ourselves are, and this refined kind of evaporation from what is three-dimensional appears to us like a diffused scent.

When one has once learned to observe this (from four dimensions) and is able to recall it in the three-dimensional world on waking, then one will be able to understand what Rudolf Steiner describes in the lecture which he gave on 15 October 1921. 'Der Mensch in seinem Zusammenhang mit dem Kosmos' (*Man in his relationship to the Cosmos*, Vol 3, lecture 5). There he says: 'For instance man lives in warmth, you see. Just as a person becomes aware of the world of colour through his sense of sight, so too he becomes aware of the world of warmth through his sense for warmth. He experiences warmth through what I should like to call his inner bodily nature in as far as he is bounded by his skin. But he makes an abstract of it in the process of perceiving it.

Warmth perceived in the outer world can actually only be described when it is comprehended in its totality. But there is also always something present in warmth which in human experience can only be expressed by pointing to the sense of smell. Warmth, experienced objectively in the outside world always has something of a smell attached to it. And now read the chapter in my *Occult Science* about that event in world evolution which took place mainly in warmth, in the description of which, at the same time, sensations of smell are spoken about'.

Living outside the body in deep sleep and having learned to carry one's full extra-bodily consciousness into this experience, a perception of warmth as described here is obtained.

One will find an exact description of this experience and also a hint about its four-dimensionality in a lecture by Rudolf Steiner on 25 August 1918. (*Die Wissenschaft vom werdenden Menschen*, Vol 2, Lecture 2). [The Mysteries of the Sun and of Threefold Man]. In this lecture, too, he points out that it is described from this aspect in *Occult Science*.

'What is described in *Occult Science* as Saturn-, Sun-, Moon- and Earth-evolution . . . that lies . . . on the far side of the globe . . . (I really ought to draw this four-dimensionally)'.

One can see how much is contained in every line of *Occult Science*, which Rudolf Steiner further elaborated in later years but which, nevertheless, is already contained in *Occult Science*. And by taking what one has thus learned into one's sleep one's consciousness lights up and gives shape to the problems which one then has to face in the further course of one's life.

My first meeting with Rudolf Steiner's spirit was experienced through the element of heat. It burned on the altar of humanity like a holy fire with the summons to read in the flame what can illuminate the evolution of mankind and of the world.

In the Mystery Play, *The Soul's Awakening*, words occur which are spoken by the representative of the Element of Fire in the Egyptian temple belonging to the time of Echnaton:

> Let all the errors of thine own ideas
> be burned in fire that this rite lights for thee.
> Let, with thine errors, thyself also burn.
> As flame of cosmic fire thy being seek;
> Bind to thy semblance that which thou dost find;

Its fire will give thy being unto thee.

And in the same play, a little later in the same scene, the Chief Hierophant speaks:

> O human soul read now what through the flame
> The cosmic word declares within thyself...
> And now from out the cosmic vision wake!
> Declare what can be read from cosmic words!

The Word: I hear Rudolf Steiner lecturing

Before I became personally acquainted with Rudolf Steiner or heard him lecture in Vienna I had read for a whole year all that was available in Vienna at that time in the way of printed or typed lectures. I read for ten hours every day for a whole year. Thus, a large part of the spiritual treasures were familiar to me before I met Rudolf Steiner in real life. He visited Vienna on 18 January 1913. He gave two public lectures which I attended: On 19 January 1913 'Die übersinnlichen Welten und das Wesen der Menschenseele' (Supersensible Worlds and the Nature of the Human Soul) and on 20 January 1913 'Geisteswissenschaft und Naturwissenschaft in ihrem Verhaltnis zu den Lebenstratseln' (Spiritual Science and Natural Science in connection with the Riddles of life).

I had not only read a great number of Dr Steiner's works, I had also seen pictures of him (photographs). I therefore knew what he looked like.

But when he now actually appeared in person in the lecture hall I was nevertheless astonished to meet someone who seemed to my feelngs to be a friend of such long standing. It was like returning home after a far journey. Even his movements, his gait, seemed familiar to me, even though they had something infinitely original about them and no other person walked or made gestures such as he.

It was then that I realised for the first time that the word, the diction of the thought sequence, contains the gesture *within* it. By reading Rudolf Steiner's works I had already experienced his gestures, even his gait. I only was not yet aware of it at the time. But now I had him before me—alive, mobile, moving about and peripatetic.

What a wonderful revelation of his inmost being is a living human being! I said to myself.

At that time I knew nothing of the previous lives of myself or Rudolf Steiner. But that I was not meeting him here for the first time, of that I was absolutely and firmly convinced. That was no mere theory which lived within me. At that time I was not interested in reincarnation. But it stood before me as an experience: 'I know everything about this person'. Not *actually*, of course; I know nothing about him. But his appearance, all that is about him, I know that through and through. 'That is my erstwhile teacher and friend', said something deep within me. 'What a festival to have him present!' And this mood was generally present in this hall. What a great and wonderful feast!

And then I heard his voice. Every tone was a gesture. He spoke so naturally, but his every word contained the whole of his being. Again there was this wonderful conscientiousness in every expression he used. He spoke in High German with here and there a Viennese term by way of illustration. Every vowel was filled with soul, every consonant was a gesture. His voice had about it somethig dark and warm like velvet. It was uttered as though from depths of earth. But those depths were filled with love. Here speaks someone who loves the earth, I said to myself. This was also present in his tread. He placed his feet on the ground like someone who becomes conscious of the earth when he walks on it. It was a free and lively tread. But whilst he spoke he did not stand quite still. At one time he put his weight more on the front foot, at another time more on the back one. That coincided with what he was saying. He appeared to advance or to retreat. When he was illustrating something he approached closer. When he was filled with awe at the grandeur of the world he stepped back. Other folk express themselves through the play of their features. He expressed himself with his whole body. If he wished to emphasise something he had just said he made a gesture which I have never seen anyone else make. The fingers of both hands crossed and touched one another in front his breast. Then they described a semicircle outwards to the side. The hands came together again, crossing again. And now he moved them sideways with a quick movement downwards and to the left and right away from each other. It was as though he were tying a knot or making a stitch. A wonderful movement of emphasis. As though one were to say: 'Yea, so be it.'

He had dark eyes. Actually he had brown eyes containing many dark brown spots in them. An eye specialist diagnosing them would have found a whole world within them. Dr Steiner once said that these spots did not indicate illness but over-exertion in his youth. But during the time he stood there lecturing his eyes gave a dark and fiery impression. Dr Steiner had nothing of the fanatic about him. He could be humorous, kind and serious, but never fanatical. Some, who do not know him have described him quite wrongly. His eyes were filled with soul. But as he spoke, when turning his gaze towards the spirit, his eyes would become for some moments as though blind. One could see that he was then looking inwards and not outwards. And then in the next moment he came out of his momentary absence and turned his gaze on those who were present. And that was a quick and often unexpected change. In later years it was more seldom that he allowed his spirit absences to be outwardly noticeable.

His hair often fell to one side across his brow and across his eye and he brushed it back if it fell forward whilst he was speaking.

When arriving or departing he greeted with both hands. He waved heartily with the backs of his hands towards the onlooker. I have never seen him remove his hat in greeting. He always greeted in the manner described. On a silk cord hung an eyeglass. He held it up to his eye when he wished to take a closer look at someone arriving late. Otherwise I hardly ever saw him make use of it.

That was how I experienced Rudolf Steiner when I first heard him lecture and on countless occasions since.

At the close of one of these lectures there was a time for answering questions. One was allowed to write questions on a piece of paper. At the end of the lecture, after a short interval, he gave the answers. I had read a book by Lazarus Geiger, a learned language scholar, (born: 21 May 1829 in Frankfurt-am-Main, died: 29 August 1870): *Ursprung und Entwickelung der menschlichen Sprache und Vernunft* (Origin and development of human speech and reason), Stuttgart, 1868. The book had made a great impression on me. I gave it to Rudolf Steiner seven years later in the Waldorf School in Stuttgart. He did not know it at that time.

On the basis of this book I wrote my query: 'What came first, human speech or human reason?'

Dr Steiner, to my disappointment, answered from the point of view of the *child's* development. They developed in conjunction with one another. But I had hoped he would have answered it by dealing with it from the point of view of *mankind's* evolution. When he had finished answering my question he laid my note down on the speaker's desk. At that I said to myself: How can it be, Dr Steiner can read in the hearts of men; he must know that my question was asked from the point of view of the evolution of mankind! How does it come about that he answers from the point of view of the child's development?

Today I know that Dr Steiner had already seen in me the teacher I was to become later when I taught at the Waldorf School. But at that moment I was simply disappointed. Dr Steiner took up my note once more. He looked around the hall. Then he said: 'I did not completely answer this question. One can also answer it from the point of view of mankind's evolution. That is what is actually meant.' And now came an answer to my question. That was very important to me. Ultimately it was the test by means of example. I was sure that he could read in human souls. I was extremely happy.

At the end of the lecture and questions I went up to him. He looked at me. I said: 'I know who you are and I would very much like to become your pupil.' I thought that he was one who could read the thoughts of others. He said: 'You are the son of Mrs Stein.' He saw that I looked like my mother.

I have to thank my mother that I was able to find my way to Anthroposophy. She introduced me early to Grimm's Fairy Tales, to the Greek myths and to the North Germanic Sagas of Gods and Heroes.

My father died early, in 1908. He was gifted in languages and spoke German, Hungarian, French, English and Italian equally well. He could read Spanish. He did all in his power to give my brother Friedrich and me the best upbringing and education. Gustav Mahler, as a student, had been my mother's piano teacher and important people had been visitors to our house in Vienna. My father was lawyer in the Imperial and Civil Courts and a certified interpreter for the various languages he spoke.

My mother—I belive—came to Anthroposophy through the

wife of Councillor Bittner, the mother of a gifted composer, Julius Bittner, whose operas were performed in Vienna. Julius Bittner taught me the theory of harmony and counterpoint. But my world was that of physics, mathematics and everything which had to do with technology. But Dr Steiner introduced me to Philosophy and education and to the study of history.

My mother died only in 1928, my brother fell in the First World War. He was to have taken over my father's Chancellery. But it never came to that. He died early, in 1915, at the age of 29.

Before seeing Dr Steiner again important decisions had been made in the anthroposophical movement. A decision had been made to transfer the Goetheanum building, called at that time Johannes Building (after Johannes Thomasius, a character from Dr Steiner's Mystery Plays) to Dornach in Switzerland. Originally the building was to have stood in Munich, but the Authorities made difficulties about granting permission, even with regard to what was only interior architecture.

Whilst Dr Steiner was giving lectures in Helsingfors [Helsinki] and Stockholm I was absent on call-up for a military exercise. This practice was held in places where Dr Steiner spent his youth (the surroundings of Wiener Neustadt). On returning from Stockholm Dr Steiner gave the course of lectures in Munich 'Secrets of the Threshold' (24-31 August 1913).

My mother came to Munich on 16 August and I arrived there on 17 August. I very much wanted to see the performance of the third Mystery Play, *The Guardian of the Threshold* and the fourth one, *The Soul's Awakening*. The performances took place in the Volkstheater [People's Theatre] in Munich.

The first two plays *The Portal of Initiation* and *The Soul's Probation* were known to me in book form. But the performance was only for members of the Society and I had not yet been able to make up my mind to become a member.

That might cause surprise that I had found my way to Rudolf Steiner but still hesitated to become a member of the Society. But Dr Steiner himself was also not a member. He was the teacher. The Society had been founded by Dr Carl Unger, Michael Bauer and Marie von Sivers in the form it then had. As such it had grown out of the German Section of the Theosophical Society of which Rudolf Steiner was the General Secretary, but not a member. When later Rudolf Steiner with his audience had been excluded from the Theosophical Society because he did not wish to participate in the veneration of Krishnamurti, the difficulty arose that he was excluded from the Society, but, as he told me, had never been a member.

Already during the founding of the German Section Rudolf Steiner had had to be absent for a few hours in order to hold lectures elsewhere about Anthroposophy. When he was then excluded from the Theosophical Society along with his friends he returned once more to this current and called his movement the 'anthroposophical movement'.

One of the leading friends of that time told me that it was he who had taken the initiative in 1912 of asking Dr Steiner to found the Society anew. Dr Steiner declined. He did not want people to tell him what to do. He knew it himself and so that friend took the initiative on himself. But Dr Steiner never was a member even of this Society.

This latter statement was made to me by Rudolf Steiner himself.

How I discovered my Guide, Rudolf Steiner
On my mother's desk lay *Occult Science*. When I opened the book and read the words about heat I knew: There is expressed a world view which is either true, in which case I must make it my own, or else it is wrong and I must oppose it violently. But I felt immediately that I stood before a vital decision. I read the book *Knowledge of the Higher Worlds?* It was as though I were returning to my long lost home. Oh, if it were only true! It cannot be, it would be too beautiful! Thus spoke the voices within me.

Rudolf Steiner spoke in Vienna. I was present. I do not know what he said. I observed his figure, I listened to his voice, I looked into his eyes and all within me rejoiced. There he is once more, the one from whom you have been separated for so long. And a conversation in the spirit began during the course of the lecture. I said: If you are really he who lives in the spirit then you will hear what I am saying to you in the spirit. And I began, in the middle of the lecture, to ask questions in my thoughts. And Dr Steiner answered every question. He answered in the course of the lecture.

How shall I describe the joy which surrounded me? Afterwards people were allowed to write questions on pieces of paper. I wrote: 'What came first, human speech or human reason?' The question arose in me through reading Lazarus Geiger's wonderful book on this subject. Rudolf Steiner answered the question from the point of view of the growing child. I was terribly disappointed. He had, so I thought, not understood my question. Doubt rose up in me and said: My former experience was self-deception. But suddenly he said: 'One can also look at this question from the point of view of mankind's evolution,' and then I got my answer: speech and reasoning developed together: reason is awakened through speech.

When I was at home again I said to my mother: 'Get me all the writings of Dr Steiner.' She did so to the best of her ability. I interrupted my studies and read for a whole year, often for ten hours a day, in the lecture-cycles, lectures and books, until I had read everything which existed in Vienna at that time. At the same time I made a note of everything which appeared to be contradictory. But in reading on the contradictions disappeared.

At first I said to myself: Perhaps it is only imagination. Then I said: But it runs according to rule. All religions, myths and fairy tales show the same conformity. And finally: Nature, too, can be understood by means of this spiritual approach. If it is only imagination then *this* imagination is what has created the world. Therefore it is the truth. With this determination to build a bridge between Natural Science and Anthroposophy I came to Munich for the performance of the Mystery Plays. But I was not yet a member and was not allowed in. Countess Kalkreuth informed me of this and said: 'The bridge to Natural Science has already been built, you come much too late!' But I was in no way minded to go away without having seen the plays and I appealed to Dr Steiner. He came out of his consulting room with unending good will: 'Yes, Herr Stein,' he said, 'the performances are only for members. But you can become a member and immediately after the performance you can resign.' I was satisfied with that. And so I was able to take part in that wonderful performance and to live in that delicate atmosphere of soul warmth by which everything was borne up during these days. After the performance Dr Steiner came to me and asked: 'Now, Herr Stein, how did you enjoy it?' I answered: 'I am no longer such an ass as I was before the performance. And I shall never more resign from the Society.' That is how I became a member.

How wonderfully kind, how understanding was Dr Steiner in

face of my inner difficulties which had prevented me, without more ado, from wishing to become a member.

I had the rare good fortune to be given advice by Rudolf Steiner for my studies, yes, for all the affairs of my life, from then onwards. To begin with he advised me about my course of studies at the university. He said to me: 'Carry out your philosophical studies as I did: Start with Johann Gottlieb Fichte and supplement Fichte with Aristotle. Fichte was the one who recognised the act of cognition most clearly by describing how deeds are performed. But the fullness of the universe was shrunk by him into a mere non-Ego. Aristotle, however, had the fullness of reality in minerals, plants, animals, etc. in place of the non-Ego! I was to become acquainted with Aristotle through the writings of Franz Brentano and Vincenz Knauer. I was to read *The Theory of Science* by Fichte. Those were wonderful starting points for a young student of philosophy. Alongside this I was to continue with my mathematical and natural scientific studies which I had already begun at Grammar School.

At the end of a lecture in Vienna I was allowed to ask Dr Steiner for a theme for my philosophical dissertation. He said: 'Create a theory of knowledge for spiritual cognition. Start with a study of Locke and Berkeley.' After having received this advice I came to Dornach where work on the building was in progress. I was allowed to help with the carving of one of the architraves. I heard there the wonderful lectures by Rudolf Steiner and shared in the anthroposophical life. Then came the World War. When post stopped arriving I said to Dr Steiner: 'The call-up papers cannot reach me any longer now. I feel I ought to travel.' He answered: 'Follow what your feelings say to you.' I travelled. On Basle station it suddenly struck me that I might never return, that it would end in death. During the last quarter of an hour before the train departed I wrote to Dr Steiner that I could feel how the spirit of the German nation was awakening; I knew that it was a tremendously historic moment. I would remain faithful to him throughout all time, to him and to his work. This letter was read out by Dr Steiner in the carpenter's workshop. When I arrived in Vienna mobilisation had in part begun. My brother had already left. I never saw him again. He fell in Przemÿsl.

During the war I had Dr Steiner's books with me. A rucksack with laundry and one of books hung on the gun carriage. I dragged this gun with special affection through all the bogs. Once when it was quite hopelessly bogged down and nearly all my horses were dead another anthroposophist, Captain Karl Rössel, came along and dragged it out with his horses. Once I lent my Theosophy to a comrade. It returned to me after a long circuit round a part of the front. My *Cosmic Memory* accompanied me in my saddle-bag in all the battles. *The Calendar of the Soul* copied by my mother into a little booklet was my constant companion. When I was once under heavy fire in one of the front trenches and death seemed imminent I suddenly grew quite quiet and calm. Dr Steiner stood before me in my inner vision and I knew I should survive. This picture never afterwards left me and the strength of his peace is with me still. During the war I grew so intimately together with everything of which Anthroposophy is composed. My brother fell on 22 March 1915. He had come to Anthroposophy through me and had participated with intense interest in the Vienna lecture course about the inner development between death and a new birth. Dr Steiner wrote an epitaph for him: 'In life his senses were directed towards the spirit, so may he find in death the life of spirit'.

I came once more to Dr Steiner in Berlin while it was still wartime. My dissertation had been completed in the trenches. I wrote it down during my ten days leave in a small Hungarian village where my wife lived. Its contents stood before my mind's eye in twelve pictures which I then transcribed into philosophical terms. I brought this dissertation to Dr Steiner. For two days he worked through it sentence by sentence with me and removed everything which was too anthroposophical and which might have given offence. But during this conversation, lasting many hours, a whole world opened up before me. At that time Dr Steiner explained to me the principle of the twelve senses, about which he had only published indications. He gave me a book to read on this subject 64 pages long which was printed but had never been distributed. I must at this point gratefully acknowledge my indebtedness to Frau Dr Steiner, who provided me with a written reply to the questions about the sense of sight which I had addressed to Dr Steiner in a long letter of enquiry.

After the war I was able to be in Dornach again. Already during the war, in Berlin, Dr Steiner had said to me: 'Your gifts do not lie in the mathematical but in the pedagogical realm.' But before my life led me to teaching a different epoch came in between.

My friend Dr Kolisko had travelled to Stuttgart. I had for long been intimately connected with him. His brother, who died early, was the school friend of my brother. He himself became my school friend in the third class in the Grammar School. It was a happy stroke of fortune which forced me to repeat the third class owing to bad accomplishments in mathematics and Greek. Through that I came into contact with Eugen Kolisko. The latter had travelled to Stuttgart to Dr Steiner. He handed Dr Steiner a long letter from me containing innumerable questions. 'Nobody can answer that in writing,' said Dr Steiner when he had read the letter. 'But write to your friend and tell him to come to Stuttgart to take part in the course which I am going to give here for the future Waldorf teachers. Perhaps some of his questions will then receive an answer.' A few hours later somebody (Herr Molt, I think) told me on the telephone to come to Stuttgart. I set off immeidately, took part in the course and then was about to return home. I was already hurrying down the school steps when I was called back. Dr Steiner asked me: 'I have just heard that Miss von Mirbach is unable to be present for the beginning of school. Would you care to take over the first class for a few weeks in her stead?' 'Yes.' At this moment an important event had occurred in my life: I was a teacher. And I remained a teacher and am still one today. Out of deputising arose permanent employment. After one year my wife, who belonged to the Dornach eurythmy section, was called to Stuttgart by Dr Steiner. We had married in 1918. We had become more closely acquainted with one another in Sauerbrunn, the neighbouring station to the place where Dr Steiner had spent his youth. I have walked countless times with her along the ways where Dr Steiner went to school from there to Wiener Neustadt, where I was stationed as a young officer, where Hermann von Baravalle became my pupil and I became his instructing officer. I began my teaching activity as an instructor in the school for reserve officers in Wiener Neustadt, in Vienna and in Brünn. But now, for the first time, I was a real teacher of a first class.

It was a wonderful time, this first time in the Waldorf School, when there were only 14 teachers, when we sat together with Dr Steiner at the conference table, which was then very small, and discussed everything, really everything, with him. How he attended to each child and to every regulation with his great love. As I was still there after Miss von Mirbach's return and became a proper teacher, even acknowledged by the State as such, then Dr Steiner entrusted to me the history teaching in the top classes, the eighth being the top class at that time. I stood facing the void. To begin with I had to acquire everything through effort. For a couple of hours of teaching I needed ten hours of preparation. But it succeeded. Dr Steiner helped. He gave countless pieces of advice and help. And the course of my history lessons grew along with my own path of spiritual knowledge. Weighty and great were the instructions Rudolf Steiner gave. He once said: 'If you wish to portray something historical then ask yourself: "What do I first have to become in order to be able to portray it?"' It was a path of becoming, of work on oneself which he showed us.

Then the day arrived on which Dr Steiner called my friend Eugen Kolisko to the school. It was a difficult decision for Kolisko. He was a medical assistant at the University at Vienna and wanted to become a primary school [Waldorf] teacher. He also had a mother in Vienna who needed him. It was a night-long discussion between us over things affecting the whole of life. Afterwards Kolisko hurried out into the night, climbed the Uhlandshöhe and then came down again with his mind made up: 'Yes, if Dr Steiner calls me, then I will come.'

So we two friends were united once more. Out of that grew great spiritual wealth for us. It was destiny which brought us together. Dr Steiner often smiled about this friendship. Once at an academy course we gave a lecture together without preparation. First Kolisko said a few sentences, then I, then he again. We were so attuned to one another that this was possible. Dr Steiner laughed at us and called this lecture a 'dwarf's theatre'. But when we lectured together in Gottingen to 2,000 students our performance was tested in earnest.

The planet Mars played a special role in my life. Really, with my whole soul I had been a soldier. During the war I discovered Nature. How splendid it was to sleep out of doors at every season of the year. Above me the glittering starry heavens or the grey snow clouds. How close was the sprouting nature when one had plants at eye level before one in the trench. How well I could observe the animals: the rabbits, the birds, the squirrels. For me the war was a great exercise in meditation and concentration. Now in the Anthroposophical Society war was once more my lot. And a first, most serious experience was my encounter with Professor Traub. As I wrote to my wife in Dornach after the event: 'It was a fight to the death'. Dr Steiner read this letter out, too, when it was given him, for he knew it had really been so. I always had to fight and I still have to today, only the struggle becomes ever more inward. Thus, too, my first lessons were a struggle, for I faced a completely new world.

I felt that to be a teacher was to transform all fighting into love. I learned to sense the children's souls as messengers from a long past time on earth. I gradually merged into actual history and discovered my own position in the stream of history.

Meanwhile Dr Steiner demonstrated what real history was in his splendid lectures and showed how it could be completed. But he always again and again came into the lessons and brought indescribably beautiful things to the children and the teacher.

I shall tell about some of it at least:

On 9 June 1920 Dr Steiner came into the eighth class just as I was speaking about the Age of Discovery. I demonstrated how the people of that time were looking for Prester John, the son of Parzival's brother Feirehs. Through an alliance with Prester John, who according to the saga ruled in the East, the Portuguese and Spaniards wanted to drive the Moors out of their country. This succeeded, too, in 1492, through the conquest of the last Arab outpost of Granada. I then related how this Prester John was a personality who had great influence. His letters, which he sent to Popes and Princes, had political effects. He was so powerful that the Pope built a church in Rome to Prester John. 'But,' I said, 'the remarkable thing is that this Prester John works on through many centuries.' Dr Steiner said the following to me in private after the lesson: 'Prester John is the leader of a brotherhood which has a special Christian tradition in the East which is much more profound than that of Rome. This brotherhood worked through Scotus Erigena.' To the children, however, he said: 'Before the Age of Discovery man's horizon was restricted to the Mediterranean. Fear prevented people from venturing beyond the Pillars of Hercules. In Dante we meet the opinion, which was prevalent at that time, that westward of the Pillars of Hercules the sea rises up to heaven, and to the east of the Mediterranean it descends into hell. People thought that if one travelled westwards one would plunge from the heights of heaven into the depths of hell. After Columbus had completed his journey westwards this fear was overcome. "Bold sailors" one called these people who sailed across the sea. It really required courage to flout these old terror-inspiring beliefs handed down from the past and to risk the journey'.

After the lesson Dr Steiner said to me personally: 'In this way one must enter into the soul-condition of people of earlier times, that is of the greatest importance for a truly historical approach.' But to the children he said: 'When one sailed out across the ocean in this way, one was not able to venture forth without having something to show one the way. What might that be?' 'The compass,' answered the children. 'Yes, the compass, quite right', said Dr Steiner. 'But, just consider, long before the compass had been invented, people had other means of finding their direction.' 'The stars', called out the children. 'Yes, the stars. Now look,' he continued, 'people saw the morning and the evening star. They did not yet know that it was one and the same star, so they called the two together "The Twins". Taking their bearings from these Twins people of the Orient sailed abroad on the high seas long before the time of Christ.'

In the same lesson I had mentioned the effect of the invention of printing. To that Dr Steiner asked: 'What was the first book that was printed?' The children pondered over it. At last one of them said: 'The Bible.' 'Yes, the Bible,' said Dr Steiner, 'it now became generally known. And that was something of universal importance. For until that time there had not been much said about those parts of the Bible where equality of man is spoken about. The "Nobility" and the "Clergy" emphasised more superiority and inferiority. But now, when people could read, for instance, about Christ washing the feet of the Apostles, they discovered that many things were said which they had not heard before. And so there arose the kind of mood out of which such things as the Peasants' Revolt could result.'

Concerning the Arabs Dr Steiner also said on that occasion: 'The Arabs do not portray plants or animals in their living image but as inanimate objects. This inanimate presentation is called an "arabesque". This tendency towards what is inanimate had very important historical consequences for Europe.' Dr Steiner said to me with regard to this matter: 'One has to show how one cultural stream continues into another, even though this may happen unconsciously.'

Perhaps one can gain an idea of the wealth which flowed out from Dr Steiner when one considers that what I have just described came out of a single visit to the eighth class. And for six years he was with us time and time again. There may perhaps be an opportunity to say more about this. For the present, however, I wish to recount what Dr Steiner was for me, is still and will be for ever.

Even during my first stay in Munich Dr Steiner spoke words to me which became an inner guide to me on my way. This was repeated after longer or shorter intervals and thus his teachings became for me ever more and more filled with life. And so I thank him for the fact that I have become more and more of a human being. When I travelled with him in the train from Munich to Stuttgart after the last lecture he had delivered in the former city, he sat opposite me. He looked at me long and pensively, kindly and affectionately. Then he said to me: 'Do you know what would have become of you if you had never got to know about Anthroposophy?' This question made me suddenly aware of what I was through *myself* alone and what I was through *him*. He told it to me, too, and I stood before an abyss of self-knowledge. Thus he led me in kindness and affection, but also over many an abyss. In the spring of last year I became mortally ill. I faced death in all its reality. My life came to an end. But he rescued me. How can the life he gave me belong other than to him? I owe him everything. The health of my wife and child. My profession. The inner vitalisation. The meaning of my life. Life itself. For such gifts as these can my stammering thanks be anything other than love? Love extending beyond death. Love which is so close and intimate that in sensing its nearness words must fail?

2
Supplementary Indications referring to particular chapters

Note 1 [p 43]
From the lectures of 13 and 30 September 1914:
On 26 July I had spoken to our friends about things which concerned our building and had referred in a few words to the serious state of affairs now confronting us. And I must say, it was only with tears in my eyes that I read the letter that one of our younger friends, present at the time, had written to his mother soon afterwards. He had been called up straight away, had moved to his home in Austria and precisely through the strength from the spiritual world, which he had drawn from our endeavours—he was still a very young member—he had found in the most beautiful, I would like to say in the most holy and purest way, the strength to occupy the post which karma had allotted to him.

And again, there was another person [W.J. Stein], who had been present on 26 July, who wrote to me himself while on his way to the Serbian front. He was full of the aspirations nourished, on the one hand by confidence flowing from a belief in victory and the unconquerability of the spirit, on the other hand by full enthusiasm that he was able to directly participate in the events of our time from the place allotted him.

Truly, my dear friends, one felt in these times that the souls were growing and ripening and it was wonderful, it was touching, to see how the sensations and feelings which they had acquired over the years were proving a fit means of leading them in the right way to their proper place under very difficult circumstances. *Mitteleuropa zwischen Ost und West*, (Middle Europe between East and West), G.A. 174a.

It was only with tears in my eyes that I was able to read the letter to his mother, written by a young Austrian who had been one of those who had listened to the words spoken in Dornach on 26 July. It tells how the outlook and strength given by Anthroposophy lives in his heart and enables him to carry out his duty there where destiny has placed him. And the same feelings and thoughts were expressed in the letter of another young friend [W.J. Stein], who had also attended the meeting in Dornach and had then gone to the front. It is such thoughts and feelings as these which must necessarily live in our souls today; where duty bids us try to bring them to fulfilment, allows our power of judgement to hold sway and be attentive, which demands our love. Then one thing will come to pass in future: when one day the nations of Europe no longer confront one another in battle, then, among all our thoughts, those which we now send forth will be the lasting ones, they will be the strongest, they will represent something eternal. Our present feelings will work beneficially when they are linked with the feeling that *one* victory is inevitable: the victory of the spirit.

Die geistigen Hintergründe des Ersten Weltkrieges (The spiritual background of the First World War), GA 174b

Note II [p 84]
Those who took part in the basic courses:
Marie Steiner, Emil Molt, Bertha Molt; the twelve founder member—Leonie von Mirbach, Johannes Geyer, Hannah Lang, Herta Kögel, Caroline von Heydebrand, Friedrich Oehlschlägel, E.A. Karl Stockmeyer, Walter Johannes Stein, Paul Baumann, Elisabeth Dolfuss-Baumann, Herbert Hahn, Rudolf Treichler; further to these—Alexander Strakosch, Andreas Körner, Luise Kieser, Elfriede Herrmann, Mieta Waller, Ludwig Noll, Rudolf Meyer, Herr Wolfer (cf. Ch. E. Lindenberg, *Rudolf Steiner—Eine Chronik*, Stuttgart, 1988, p. 419).

Note III (p 93]
Stein was accused of using anthroposophical material in his lessons. As proof of this, use was made of a comparison between the heavenly hierarchies and the military ranks which a girl from the ninth class had copied into her book. Stein explained the sequence of the events in his history lesson in a letter to Kolisko: 'I had given an example of secularisation, as is prescribed in the curriculum, and shown that the nine-fold hierarchy has its reflexion in the military orders. I wrote them both down

alongside one another. Frau Steiner read out [in the General assembly]: that I had compared an angel to a lieutenant. One read the thing horizontally instead of vertically'.

He wrote to Hermann Poppelbaum in the same vein and added, to justify himself: 'I used this example many times, among others in the presence of Dr Steiner. There can be no question of the fact that any kind of anthroposophical content was imparted thereby in a wrong way. The names of the hierarchies are known to the children from their history lessons, where they must be introduced during discussions about the Areopagite.'

Stein's letter to Kolisko referred to above (published Lili Kolisko, op. cit.) bears the date 8 April 1932. It reads as follows:

Dear Eugen,   Stuttgart, 8 April 1932
I have just got back from my journey. I held 42 lectures in 42 days. I have made Dr Steiner's teachings known throughout eight countries. On my return I must perforce discover that I have been treated abominably, my lectures and my teaching in the school have been reviled. One has not even shrunk from letting children give up their school books. Without asking me Frau Marie Steiner read from them quite out of context. I had given an example of secularisation, as is prescribed in the curriculum, and shown how the nine-fold hierarchy has its reflexion in the military organistion. I wrote both alongside one another. Frau Steiner read out that I had compared an angel to a lieutenant. People read the thing horizontally instead of vertically.

When I now returned home Herr Molt asked me to give up my lecturing. He had taken it upon himself, along with I know not whom, on the order of Dornach, to cancel my already accepted invitation to lecture at the Whitsuntide Conference. He now demanded that I should take on an extra lesson in order to fill in my free period. I answered: 'You want to gag me. Thanks. I herewith hand in my notice'. Today I have done the same to the Board of Directors.

I am now going with my family to London, where Mr Dunlop and Miss Osmond want to help us to start a new life. I want to continue to give many lectures in Germany and hope for your help in that. I shall be quite independent and will be armed against all attacks . . . I shall now be an itinerant preacher.

With hearty greetings
Yours Walter.

Note IV [pp 24 and 122]
Rudolf Steiner's report of the Vienna Congress 18 June 1922: (a hitherto unpublished extract)

Yes, those are the things which have to be considered if one wishes to get an idea of the importance of this East-West Congress. You see, everything was arranged so that it might build a bridge between East and West. Scientific results, scientific methods, artistic matter, everything possible was looked at in this way.

It is exceptionally difficult for me to find the right form for what I want to say about my impressions; but it seems to me that when I outline them in a few pictures, these pictures will convey something of the impressions one can have.

You see, among our Austrian speakers at the Vienna Congress the Austrian element was not at all lacking. One could even psychoanalyse the speakers. That was possible, and I hope it will not be taken amiss of me, for you to see it is quite well meant and, after all, it is not a bad thing if a general understanding can be brought about between us.

You see, we have our exceptionally efficient Kolisko. But if we wish to understand his individuality, if we wish to get a picture of what he represents, when he now speaks again in Vienna, we would have to say: 'We shall really quite involuntarily be led to ask ourselves: What sort of monk would he have been if he could have chosen his education in the pre-Theresian age? Well, our dear Kolisko would undoubtedly have become a Dominican. Just as surely would Baravalle and Blümel have become Benedictines, Dr Schubert would have become a Piarist and Dr Stein a Cistercian.

So you see, even in so far as such material details are concerned, one can discover, I would like to say, what actually lay at the foundation of such souls. I would say: He who has an ear can still hear today in Baravalle and Blümel what only the Benedictines possessed in the way of delicate spiritual perception within the Austrian culture; in Schubert what was possessed by the Piarists, in Stein what the Cistercians have effected. Likewise, the trained Dialectic and that which seeks expression in sharply contoured thoughts, in the pure striving after what is scientific, this most decidedly reminds one, if one looks at it from this point of view, of what entered Austrian culture via the Dominicans—this can only be done if one institutes a cultural-historical survey, as

Kolisko did now through his important contribution to the
Vienna Congress.

Note V [p 122]
*Elisabeth Vreede enumerates the Goetheanum speakers nomi-
nated by Rudolf Steiner:*

Among the speakers whom Dr Steiner nominated at that time belong
Dr Stein and Dr Kolisko, ('that is by matter of course' said Dr Steiner
to us in the Vorstand), Dr Unger, Dr von Heydebrand, Dr Karl
Schubert, Dr Rittelmeyer, Dr von Baravalle, Dr Poppelbaum, Dr E.
Schwebsch, Herr M. Bartsch, Herr Werbeck. Dr Steiner also nomi-
nated Mr Collison, Mr Dunlop and Mr George Kaufmann [Adams] in
England. Naturally members of the Vorstand were included in the list
of those entitled to speak, in so far as they were lecturers.

*Zur Geschichte der Anthroposophischen Gesellschaft seit der
Weihnachtstagung 1923*, (Contributions to the History of the
Anthroposophical Society since the Christmas Foundation Meet-
ing 1923), privately printed, 1934, p 23. Cf Lili Kolisko, op. cit.,
S462f.

Note VI [p 135]
Rudolf Steiner's written letter reads:

My dear Dr Stein!
In answer to your query regarding the history course:
It would be good to arrange the course so that, to begin with, you
speak more in general about what history would resemble if it were
solely founded on external documents and what history would be like
if it had woven into it the results of spiritual investigation, e.g. the fifth
Cultural Epoch.
Then, after you have described this in general, you can, as it were,
confirm it with examples of older, medium old and more recent
history.
You can offer something in that sphere with which you are *familiar*
through years of historical research.
As opposed to this it would be rather dangerous for you *and* for
your lecture if you were to treat straightway of a subject, such for
instance as the Alexander theme, which you have only recently
approached and which needs to be carried within you for a long time.

That does not, of course, exclude the possibility that a detail, such for instance as in your essay about the founding of Alexandria, might not be a *very good* thing. But to speak 'about Alexander the Great and to link his immediate mission onto the continuous stream of history in general' that would be—after not yet a year has passed since my Alexander expositions at Christmas—rather too much of a good thing. It really is not just a matter of what one says, but of *how* one says it.

But this should not discourage you again, as it did at that time in the Hague, it should rouse you to *activity*. My wish is directed to that end, just as much as are the facts of the situation and your own endeavour.

Goetheanum, 24 November 1924.

Yours most heartily
Rudolf Steiner

Note VII [p 160]
Ita Wegman writes to Stein on 18 April 1930:
'We should work together again quite intensively, also with respect to the Persephone work, because I, too, feel that this should unconditionally take place'.

NOTES

In the case of works and lectures by Rudolf Steiner the 'Collected Edition' number is quoted (abbreviated as GA). [For English titles use has been made of the *Bibliographical Reference List, London, Rudolf Steiner Press, 1977*. Those enclosed by brackets ( ) are titles suggested by the translator where no published translations are available. Those without brackets are from the bibliography]. For sources not otherwise given material from private archives has been used.

1   Undated verse by Rudolf Steiner included in *Wahrspruch-worte, Richtspruchworte, Sprüche und Widmungen*, Dornach, 1953.

2   Herbert Hahn, *Walter Johannes Stein, In Memoriam*, Stuttgart, privately printed, 1959.

3   W.J. Stein *The Ninth Century and the Holy Grail*, London, Temple Lodge Press, 1988.

4   Rudolf Steiner: *Konferenzen mit den Lehrern der Freien Waldorfschule in Stuttgart*, (Conferences with Teachers of the Waldorf School in Stuttgart), with an introduction by Erich Gabert, GA 300a-c.

5   W.J. Stein, *Erziehungsaufgaben und Menschheitsgeschichte*, (Educational Tasks and the History of Mankind), Stuttgart, 1980.

6   W.J. Stein, *Der Tod Merlins*, Dornach 1984; *The Death of Merlin, Arthurian Myth and Alchemy*, Edinburgh, Floris Books, 1989. W.J. Stein/Rudolf Steiner, *Dokumentation eines wegweisenden Zusammenwirkens*, (Documentation of a trail-blazing collaboration), edited by Thomas Meyer.

7   *Das Goetheanum*, No. 39, 1922.

8   *Das Goetheanum*, Nos. 16 and 17, 1925.

9   *The Present Age*, Vol 1, Nos. 8, 9 and 11, July, August, October 1936; also: *The Death of Merlin*, op. cit. pp. 15–68.

9a   cf. *Die Wiener Moderne, Literatur, Kunst and Musik zwischen 1890 und 1910*, Stuttgart, Gotthard Wunberg, 1981.

10   *Zeit und Welt*, Stockholm, 1949.

11   *The Theory of Knowledge implicit in Goethe's World Conception*, New York, Anthroposophic Press, 1978.

12   Unpublished manuscript.

13   cf. Lecture by Rudolf Steiner, 29.12.1923, GA 233. *World History in the Light of Anthroposophy*, London, Rudolf Steiner Press, 1977.

14   cf. Rudolf Steiner, *The Course of My Life*, Anthroposophic Press, New York, 1986. Rudolf Steiner, *An Autobiography*, New York 1970, GA 28; also Karl König, *Geister unter dem Zeitgeist, Biographisches zur Phänomenolgie des 19 Jahrhunderts*, Stuttgart, 1973 (Spirits inspired by the Spirit of the Age, Biographical considerations of the Phenomenology of the 19th Century).

15   Lili Kolisko, *Eugen Kolisko, Ein Lebensbild, zugleich ein Stück Geschichte der Anthroposophischen Gesellschaft* (Eugen Kolisko, a description of his Life, and at the same time of a period of history of the Anthroposophical Society). Printed privately 1961, p. 9 et seq.

16   Rudolf Steiner, Lecture from 27.4.1924, GA 236: *Karmic Relationships Vol. II*, London, Rudolf Steiner Press, 1974, p. 76.

17   Rudolf Steiner, *Occult Science, An Outline*, London, Rudolf Steiner Press, 1979.

18   ibid., preface to 1st edition, p. 21.

19   ibid., preface to 1925 edition. p. 10.

20   Unpublished manuscript.

21   *How I discovered my Guide, Rudolf Steiner* (see appendix).

22   'Über die Mysterienspiele in München und die Ursprünge des Baues', in: E. Beltle, K. Vierl (editors), *Erinnerungen an Rudolf Steiner*, Stuttgart 1979 (concerning the Mystery Plays in Munich and the Building of the Goetheanum: in 'Memories of Rudolf Steiner').

23   Lecture 24.8.1913, GA 147. *Secrets of the Threshold*,

London, New York, Rudolf Steiner Press, Anthroposophic Press, 1987.

24 Letter from 24.8.1913 to Friedrich Kayssler in: *Christian Morgenstern, Briefe*, Munich 1973 (Christian Morgenstern, Letters).

25 Andrej Belyj, *Verwandeln des Lebens, Erinnerungen an Rudolf Steiner*, Basle, 1975 (Transformation of Life, Memories of Rudolf Steiner).

26 Unpublished manuscript, included in part in: W.J. Stein/ Rudolf Steiner, *Dokumentation* . . . , op. cit.

27 cf. Lecture by Rudolf Steiner, 14.4.1914, GA 153. *Inner Nature of Man and the Life between Death and a New Birth*, London, Anthrop. Pub. Co., 1959.

28 Assja Turgenieff in afterword to: *Rudolf Steiner, Der Dornacher Bau*. . . GA 287 (Rudolf Steiner, The Dornach Building. . .).

29 Lecture 26.7.1914, GA 291.

30 Herbert Hahn, *From the Wellsprings of the Soul*, Helios Fountain.

30a Contained in: W.J. Stein/Rudolf Steiner, *Dokumentation* . . . op. cit., p. 75 et seq.

31 *Anthroposophie—ein Fragment aus dem Jahre 1910*, GA 45.

32 Lecture 2.10.1920 in GA 322 *Boundaries of Natural Science*, New York, Anthroposophic Press, 1983.

32a GA 21 *Von Seelenrätseln* Parts published in *The Case for Anthroposophy*, London, Rudolf Steiner Press, 1970.

33 *W.J. Stein/Rudolf Steiner, Dokumentation* . . . op. cit., pp. 75, 137, 167 et seq.

34 Lectures from 4, 5 and 6 April, 1912 in GA 136, *The Spiritual Beings in the Heavenly Bodies and in the Kingdoms of Nature*, N. Vancouver, Steiner Books, 1981.

35 Letter from W.J. Stein to German friends, Easter 1933.

36 cf. William M. Johnston, *Österreichische Kultur- und Geistesgeschichte*, Graz, 1974 (Cultural and Spiritual History of Austria).

37 cf. Rudolf Steiner's allusion to Brentano's death in his book: *Von Seelenrätseln*, GA 21 (Riddles of the Soul).

38 Ludwig Graf Polzer-Hoditz, *Politische Betrachtungen auf der Grundlage der Dreigliederung des sozialen Organis-*

mus, Stuttgart, 1920 (Political Observations in connection with the Threefold Social Organism).

39   Otto Graf Lerchenfeld, Rundbriefe, *Zur Dreigliederung des sozialen Organismus—Was wir vom Nationalökonomischen Kurs Rudolf Steiners wissen sollen*, reproduced privately, 1929-1932 (About the Threefold Social Organism—What we should know about Rudolf Steiner's World Economy Course). cf. Roman Boos, *Rudolf Steiner während des Weltkrieges* Dornach, 1933 (Rudolf Steiner during World War I).

40   Karl Dietrich Bracher, *Geschichte und Gewalt, Zur Politik im 20. Jahrhundert*, Berlin, 1981 (History and the Use of Force, Consideration of the Politics of the 20th Century).

40a *Aufsätze über die Dreigliederung des sozialen Organismus und zur Zeitlage 1915-1921*, GA 24.

41   Friedrich Rittelmeyer, *Rudolf Steiner Enters my Life*, Edinburgh, Floris Books, 1982.

42   Account by Martha Haebler from an Anthroposophical study group in Stuttgart, 13 July 1932 in: *Mitteilungen aus der anthroposophischen Arbeit in Deutschland*, Easter, 1983 (Quarterly News Bulletin of Anthroposophical Work in Germany).

42a Novalis, *Die Christenheit oder Europa*; *Christendom or Europe*, trans. Charles E. Passage, Liberal Arts Press, 1960.

43   Lecture from 12.1.1917. GA 174 *Zeitgeschichtliche Betrachtungen* Vol. V (Contemplation of the History of the Times).

44   *Mitteilungen aus der anthroposophischen Arbeit in Deutschland*, Easter 1983, op. cit.

45   Lecture from 23.12.1921, GA 303. *Die gesunde Entwicklung des Leiblich-Physischen als Grundlage der freien Entfaltung des Seelisch-Geistigen* p. 9 (1949 ed.). Not contained in English translation.

45a GA 24, op. cit.

45b Helmuth von Moltke, *Erinnerungen, Briefe, Dokumente 1877-1916*, Stuttgart, 1922 (Memoirs, Letters, Documents).

46   Emil Molt, *Entwurf meiner Lebensbeschreibung*, Stuttgart, 1972 (A sketch describing my life).

47   GA 328 *Die Soziale Frage* (The Social Question).

48   GA 23, *Towards Social Renewal*, London, Rudolf Steiner
     Press, 1977.

48a See J. Tautz, 'Walter Johannes Stein' in: *Der Lehrerkreis um
     Rudolf Steiner*, (p. 59), Stuttgart, 1977 (The Circle of
     Teachers around Rudolf Steiner).

49   Letter to Willhelm Hübbe-Schleiden, 16.8.1902 in: *Rudolf
     Steiner, Letters, Vol II*, Dornach 1953.

50   Geoffrey Barraclough, *Tendenzen der Geschichte im 20
     Jahrhundert*, Munich, 1967 (Tendencies of History in the
     Twentieth Century).

51   Herbert Hahn, *Der Weg, der mich führte. Lebenserinnerun-
     gen*, Stuttgart, 1969, p. 673 (The Way that led me.
     Memoirs).

52   ibid., p. 655.

53   The belongings he had left behind were brought to him in
     a huge rucksack by his friend Karl Schubert, when he was
     called soon afterwards to the Stuttgart School.

54   Emil Molt (see Note 46), p. 203.

55   Unpublished manuscript by E.A.K. Stockmeyer.

56   See: Christoph Lindenberg, *Rudolf Steiner, Eine Chronik*,
     Stuttgart, 1988, p. 419.

57   Herbert Hahn (see Note 51).

58   Lecture 21.8.1919, GA 293: *Study of Man*, London, Rudolf
     Steiner Press, 1966.

59   J. Tautz, 'Walter Johannes Stein' in: *Der Lehrerkreis um
     Rudolf Steiner* op. cit.

60   Rudolf Steiner, *Briefe an die Mitglieder* in: GA 26 (Letters
     to Members) *Anthroposophical Leading Thoughts*, Lon-
     don, Rudolf Steiner Press, 1973.

61   Oral statement made to the Author by Herbert Hahn.

62   See: *Freie Waldorfschule, Bericht über die zwei ersten
     Schuljahre 1919/1920 und 1920/1921*, Stuttgart, undated.
     (Free Waldorf School, report of the first two school years
     1919/1920 and 1920/1921).

63   Rudolf Grosse, *Erlebte Pedagogik*, Dornach, 1968 p. 71 et
     seq. (Pedagogy as I experienced it).

64   Friedrich Hiebel, *Entscheidungszeit mit Rudolf Steiner*,
     Dornach, 1987, p. 22 (A time of decision with Rudolf
     Steiner).

64a See *Haager Gespräch* (The Hague talks) in: W.J. Stein/
     Rudolf Steiner, *Dokumentation* ... op. cit. p. 293 et seq.
65   *Der Lehrerkreis um Rudolf Steiner* op. cit. p. 150.
65a Esoteric Class Lesson, 24.4.1912.
66   Published in W.J. Stein/Rudolf Steiner, *Dokumentation* op.
     cit., p. 280 et seq.
67   cf. W.J. Stein, *The Ninth Century and the Holy Grail*, op. cit.
     Chap. 5, footnote 4, p. 68, also Illustration No. 7.
68   W.J. Stein *The Principle of Reincarnation*, New York, St
     George Publications, 1986, p. 17.
69   Friedrich Hiebel, (note 64) p. 366 et seq., see also Note
     64a.
70   Rudolf Steiner, lecture 12.8.1924, GA 240: *Karmic Rela-
     tionships Vol. VIII*, London, Rudolf Steiner Press, 1977, pp.
     9, 11.
71   GA13, Rudolf Steiner, *Occult Science*, London, Rudolf
     Steiner Press, 1984.
72   Rudolf Grosse (Note 63) p. 72 et seq.
73   Wolfram von Eschenbach, *Parzival*. Book V, verse 254, 2.
     The Ninth Century and the Holy Grail, op. cit. p.1.
74   Unpublished manuscript.
75   *The Ninth Century* op. cit., see facsimile reproductions
     Nos. 15-18.
76   See lectures 23.7.1922 from GA 214, 'The Mystery of the
     Trinity' and 14.9.24 from GA 238, *Karmic Relationships
     Vol IV*, London, Rudolf Steiner Press, 1983.
77   *The Ninth Century* op. cit., p. 222.
78   ibid., p. 224.
79   Otto Willmann, *Geschichte des Idealismus*, Braunschweig,
     1907, Vol II, p. 111 (History of Idealism).
80   ibid.
81   *The Ninth Century* op. cit., p. 65.
81a Rudolf Steiner, lecture 3.12.1905 in Cologne (not yet
     included in GA).
82   *The Ninth Century* op. cit., p. 152.
83   ibid., pp. 107, 108.
83a Rudolf Steiner, lecture 16.11.1919, Dornach: 'Human
     Responsibility, Universal Responsibility, Human Civilisa-
     tion'. Typescript translation Z 426 of Bibliography.
84   W.J. Stein, *Rudolf Steiner als Philosoph und Theosoph, eine*

Antwort auf die gleichnamige Schrift Dr Friedrich Traubs, Stuttgart, 1920 (Rudolf Steiner as Philosopher and Theosophist, an answer to an article under the same title by Dr Friedrich Traub).

85   cf. Rudolf Steiner, lecture 21.12.1919, 'The Cosmic New Year' p. 32, contained in GA 195.

86   Contained in GA 194 *Die Sendung Michaels*; *The Mysteries of Light, Space and of the Earth*, London, Rudolf Steiner Pub. Co. 1945.

87   *Von Seelenrätseln* (Riddles of the Soul) GA 21.

88   Unpublished manuscript. cf. Thomas Meyer, *D.N. Dunlop, ein Zeit- und Lebensbild*, Dornach, 1987, p. 274. (Biography of D.N. Dunlop).

89   See GA 330 *Neugestaltung des sozialen Organismus* (Reform of the Social Organism); cf. also: Hans Kühn, *Dreigliederungszeit*, Dornach 1978 and Hans Erhard Lauer, *Ein Leben im Frühlicht des Geistes*, Freiburg, 1977, p. 37 et seq.

90   Lecture 23.12.21 in GA 303 (see Note 45).

91   Report by Rudolf Steiner of his Opening Speech 26.9.1920, published in *Waldorf Nachrichten* (Waldorf News) 1921, Nos. 4 and 5.

92   *Aenigmatisches in Kunst und Wissenschaft. Anthroposophische Hochschulkurse der Freien Hochschule für Geisteswissenschaft*, Goetheanum, Dornach, 26 September-16 October 1920, Stuttgart 1922 (Riddles of Art and Science).

93   Rudolf Steiner, *Philosophy of Spiritual Activity* (1922 ed.) Chapter titled 'The Consequences of Monism', p. 259—additional material added by Rudolf Steiner in 1918.

94   *Aenigmatisches* . . . (Note 92) p. 79.

95   Stein wrote to Eliza von Moltke, 21.8.1926: 'It was I who suggested to Dr Steiner the title "East-West" for the Vienna Anthroposophical Conference. It happened quite unknowingly out of the karma of the Ninth Century'.

96   Letter from Ita Wegman to Madeleine van Deventer, 16.12.1935.

97   See bibliography in appendix to *Death of Merlin*, op. cit.

98   Stuttgart 1932. Some, or all, were published in English as pamphlets at about the same time.

99   *Die Drei*, No. 2, May 1925, p. 124.

100   *Dreigliederung des sozialen Organismus*, No. 43, 27.4.1922.

101   Teachers' Conference 16.1.1921.

102   *Der Lehrerkreis* ... (Note 48a) pp. 212, 213.

103   cf. *W.J. Stein/Rudolf Steiner* ..., op. cit., p. 293 et seq.

104   Andrej Belyj (Note 25).

105   ibid., p. 266 et seq.

106   Lecture 11.6.1922 in GA 211. 'Anthroposophy: a striving for a spiritual understanding of nature permeated by Christ', Z 234.

107   Lili Kolisko, (Note 15) p. 45.

108   Lecture 16.2.1923 in *Rudolf Steiner und die Zivilisationsaufgaben der Anthroposophie. Ein Rückblick auf das Jahr 1923*, Dornach, 1943, p. 42 et seq. 'Moral Impulses'.

109   Andreas Körner, *Meine Erinnerungen an Dr Rudolf Steiner* (My memories of Dr Rudolf Steiner), Unpublished manuscript.

110   *Rudolf Steiner und die Zivilisationsaufgaben...* op. cit. p. 104.

111   ibid., p. 48.

112   ibid., p. 69.

113   Lectures from 27 and 28 February 1923 in GA 257. *Awakening to Community*, New York, Anthroposophic Press, 1974.

114   *Studienmaterial aus den Sitzungen des Dreissiger Kreises* (Study material from sessions of the 'Dreissiger Kreis') Stuttgart, 1922-23, distributed by Marie Steiner, private duplication 1947, p. 6.

115   GA 260a, 2nd edition 1987, p. 27. *Die Konstitution der Allgemeinen Anthroposophischen Gesellschaft und der Freien Hochschule für Geisteswissenschaft. Der Wiederaufbau des Goetheanum* (Constitution of the General Anthroposophical Society and the Free High School for Spiritual Science. The rebuilding of the Goetheanum).

116   Rudolf Steiner, 24.12.1923, GA 260. 'Christmas Meeting for the Founding of the General Anthroposophical Society', (opening lecture).

117   23.12.1923, GA 232, 'Mystery Knowledge and Mystery Centres'.

118   Lecture 23.11.1905 in GA 54, 'Die Welträtsel und die

Anthroposophie' (Riddles of the World and of Anthroposophy).

119 Address from 25.12.1923, GA 260 (note 116).

120 Friedrich Hiebel, (note 64) p. 257.

121 GA 233, *World History in the Light of Anthroposophy*, op. cit.

122 GA 126, *Occult History*, London, Rudolf Steiner Press, 1982.

123 GA 233, Lecture 26.12.1923 (note 13).

124 ibid. Lecture 29.12.1923.

125 Rudolf Steiner, *The Course of My Life*, op. cit. Chap. 27.

126 GA 233, Lecture 28.12.1923 (note 13).

127 ibid., Lecture 1.1.1924.

128 ibid.

129 Emil Bock, *Rudolf Steiner, Studien zu seinem Lebensgang und Lebenswerk*, Stuttgart, 1967, p. 259. (Studies in the Life and Work of Rudolf Steiner).

130 GA 26, *Anthroposophical Leading Thoughts*, op. cit.

131 cf. Hans Peter van Manen, *Twin Roads to the New Millenium*, London, Rudolf Steiner Press, 1988.

132 GA 260a, (note 115), p. 690.

133 Contained in *Der Lehrerkreis* ... op. cit., p. 404 et seq.

134 *Anthroposophie*, weekly periodical for free spiritual life, No. 14, 5.4.1925.

135 Report about the Educational Conference 1925 of the Free Waldorf School, *Anthroposophie*, ibid., No. 19, 10.5.1925.

136 Konrad Sandkühler, *Wirken durch Worte und Klänge*, Stuttgart, 1986, p. 202 (Working through words and sounds).

137 Walter Johannes Stein, *Weltgeschichte im Lichte des Heiligen Gral*, [Foreword by Hahn, 1966 edition], p. XXIV.

138 Marie Steiner, *Briefe und Dokumente*, Dornach, 1981, p. 130, (Letters and Documents).

139 The full text of the letter is contained in *Briefe und Dokumente* ibid., p. 141 et seq.

140 From: Rudolf Steiner, *Anthroposophical Leading Thoughts*, op. cit. No. 54, from 22.6.1924.

141 GA 27, Rudolf Steiner/Ita Wegman, *Fundamentals of Therapy*, London, Rudolf Steiner Press, 1983.

142   Nora Stein von Baditz *Aus Michaels Wirken* (A collection of Legends about Michael), Stuttgart, 1959.

143   ibid., p. 10.

144   Margarete Morgenstern, *Michael Bauer, Ein Bürger beider Welten*, Stuttgart, 1965, p. 161 et seq. (Michael Bauer, A Citizen of Both Worlds).

145   The date of Eliza von Moltke's death as noted by one of her daughters, Countess Astrid Bethusy.

146   Lecture 1.2.1904 in GA 52. 'Die Geschichte des Spiritismus' (History of Spiritualism).

147   cf. Helmuth von Moltke, 'Generaloberst' (Chief of General Staff), (note 45b) pp. 8-28.

148   Lecture 20.6.1916 in GA 169, 'Cosmic Being and Egohood'.

149   From his knowledge of the Moltke documents Emil Bock was able to work out the connections between the ninth and twentieth centuries in a historically based account. See Emil Bock, *Rudolf Steiner, Studien* . . . , op. cit.

150   cf. Thomas Meyer: *D.N. Dunlop* . . . , op. cit. p. 317.

151   Emil Leinhas, 'Das Kamp de Stakenberg' in: *Anthroposophie—Wochenschrift für freies Geistesleben*, No. 35, 31.8.1930. (Weekly periodical for free Spiritual Life).

152   Emanuel Zeylmans, *Willem Zeylmans van Emmichoven, Ein Pioneer der Anthroposophie*, Arlesheim, 1979, p. 346 et seq. (A Pioneer of Anthroposophy).

153   Emil Leinhas (note 151).

154   Letter to Eliza von Moltke from 13.8.1930.

155   Emanuel Zeylmans (note 152) p. 171.

156   Lecture 1.10.1911, GA 130, *The Etherisation of the Blood*, London, Rudolf Steiner Press, 1985.

157   Lecture 25.1.1910, GA 118, 'The True Nature of the Second Coming'.

158   *Natura*, 1929-30.

159   cf. Margarethe Kirchner-Bockholt und Erich Kirchner-Bockholt, *Die Menschheitsaufgabe Rudolf Steiners und Ita Wegman* (Rudolf Steiner's Mission and Ita Wegman). Privately printed for members of the Anthroposophical Society, London, Rudolf Steiner Press, 1977.

160   Ita Wegman, 'Die Mysterienstätte Ephesus' in: *Was in der Anthroposophischen Gesellschaft Vorgeht*, 25.10.1925.

(The Mystery Centre Ephesus—news bulletin of the Anthroposophical Society.)

161 Ita Wegman, 'Der Schulungsweg der antiken Mysterien und der Bildungsgang der modernen Menschen', in: *Natura*, No. 6, March 1930 (The course of Instruction in the Ancient Mysteries and the Educational Methods of Modern Mankind).

162 Letter to Nora Stein, 31.7.1930.

163 Lecture 2.12.1923 in GA 232, 'Mystery Knowledge and Mystery Centres'. Lectures from 26 and 27 December 1923 in GA 233, *World History in the Light of Anthroposophy* op. cit. Lecture from 14.8.1924 in GA 243, *True and False Paths in Spiritual Investigation*, London, Rudolf Steiner Press, 1985.

164 Emanuel Zeylmans (note 152), p. 174.

165 Ita Wegman, 'An die Mitglieder', in *Was in der Anthroposophischen Gesellschaft vorgeht*, 13.9.1925 (Members' News Sheet).

166 Letter to Ita Wegman, 14.8.1925.

167 ibid.

168 Letter to Ita Wegman, 19.8.1925.

169 Lectures 26 and 27 December, 1923 in GA 233: *World History in the Light of Anthroposophy*, op. cit.

170 Unpublished manuscript.

171 cf. Rudolf Steiner's lecture 13.8.1924 in GA 243, *True and False Paths in Spiritual Investigation*, op. cit.

172 cf. Mechthild Werner, *Burgenland, Aus dem Lande, in dem Rudolf Steiner seine Kindheit verbrachte*, Dornach, 1961 (Burgenland: From the land in which Rudolf Steiner spent his youth).

173 cf Oskar Schmiedel, *Aus dem Lande, in dem Rudolf Steiner seine Kindheit und Jugend Verbrachte*, Dornach, 1952 (From the land in which Rudolf Steiner spent his childhood and youth).

174 Letter to Nora Stein, 18.2.1931.

175 ibid., 19.2.1931.

176 ibid., 28.2.1931.

177 Friedrich Häusler, *Weltenwille und Menschheitsziele in der Geschichte*, Dornach, 1961 (Universal Will and Human Aims in History), p. 8.

178   cf. Theodor Maurer in: *Die Menschenschule*, No. 5, May 1933 (Organ of Waldorf Pedagogy in Switzerland).

179   W.J. Stein, 'England as the nucleus of the foundation of commercial towns. The Origin of the Lohengrin Saga traced according to English History', *Present Age*, Vol. 1, No. 3, February, 1936.

180   cf. Rudolf Steiner's lecture given in Cologne 3, 12, 1905, see note 81a, (translation Z 212. 'Parsifal und Lohengrin'), or lecture from GA 54, 'Parzival and Lohengrin', Berlin 29.3.1906.

181   See chapter: 'The Mid Point of Life'.

182   Alex Leroi had planned to write a historical survey of Portugal. He was unable to fulfil this task and, shortly before his death in 1968, he handed on the material to Friedrich Häusler, who was given the impulse through that to write his book: (Henry the Navigator. The Portuguese Discoverers and the Social Ideas of the Templars under the sign of a New Universal Consciousness), Stuttgart 1979.

183   cf. W.J. Stein, 'Basil Valentine, the Alchemist' in: *Korrespondenz der anthroposophischen Arbeitsgemeinschaft*, No. 6, Stuttgart, 1935. Ditto: 'Portugal', No. 11, Stuttgart, 1935.

184   Letter to Nora Stein, 7.4.1931.

185   ibid.

186   ibid., 9.4.1931.

187   ibid., 12.4.1931.

188   ibid., 15.2.1932.

188a   ibid., 16.2.1932.

189   ibid., 26.2.1932.

190   W.J. Stein, *Gold in History and in Modern Times, Labour in History and in Modern Times, West-East*. A series of booklets, London, Anthroposophical Pub. Co. 1932.

191   *West-East, A Study in National Relationships*, ibid.

192   Letter to Nora Stein, 17.3.1932.

193   Letter to Eliza von Moltke, 24.3.1932.

194   Letters to Nora Stein, 22.3.1932.

195   ibid., 27.3.1932.

196   ibid., 31.3.1932.

197   ibid., 28.3.1932.

197a   In GA 40 'Es bedarf der Mensch . . .' (Man needs an inner trust . . .).

198 Letter to Nora Stein, 12.12.1932.
199 W.J. Stein: *West-East*, op. cit., p. 36.
200 Letter to Nora Stein, 14.12.1932.
201 ibid., 20.12.1932.
202 ibid. 16.12.1932.
203 ibid., 15 and 17.12.1932.
204 Letter to Ita Wegman, 4.4.1937.
205 *Reiseeindrücke in Italien* (Travel impressions in Italy), unpublished manuscript.
206 Motto to the volume: *Initiations-Erkenntnis*, *Evolution of Consciousness*, London, Rudolf Steiner Press, 1966 [not hitherto included in Engl. translation]
207 Letter to Ita Wegman, 4.4.1937.
208 Unpublished autobiographical sketch.
209 Letter to Ita Wegman, 4.4.1937.
210 Goethe, *Italienische Reise*, Rome, 2.12.1786.
211 Report to friends in Stuttgart, 12.7.1935.
212 Rudolf Steiner, lecture 28.2.1907 in GA 55, 'Die Erkenntnis des Übersinnlichen in unserer Zeit und deren Bedeutung für das heutige Leben', p. 173.
213 Thomas Meyer, *D.N. Dunlop* . . ., op. cit.
214 ibid., p. 246.
215 ibid., p. 278.
216 Letter to German acquaintance, 6.4.1934.
217 Letter to unknown recipient, 16.4.1934.
218 ibid.
219 ibid.
220 Letter to German friends, 24.9.1933.
221 Letter to a Dutch friend, 1.6.1934.
222 cf. *The Present Age*, Vol II, No. 7, June-July, 1937.
223 German draft of first chapter.
224 German draft of last chapter.
225 Published in a slightly shortened version under the title: 'Notizen zu einer Wesenskunde der Engländer', in *Die Kommenden*, Nos. 18-22, Freiburg, 1959. (Also published in England under the title: *The British, their Psychology and Destiny*, new edition in preparation April 1990, Temple Lodge Press.)
226 Thomas Meyer, *D.N. Dunlop*, op. cit., p. 281.
227 *World Survey*, 2.5.1935.

228   'Space and Time in Economics', *Present Age*, Vol I, No. 2, London 1936.

229   D.N. Dunlop (Power, People, Industry) *World Survey*, No. 1 April 1935.

230   Thomas Meyer, *D.N. Dunlop* op. cit., p. 280.

231   ibid., p. 288.

232   *Mitteilungen für die Mitglieder der Anthroposophischen Arbeitsgemeinschaft in Deutschland*, No. 1, July 1935 (News Sheet of Anthroposophical Study Groups in Germany).

233   Private record.

234   Letter to Eugen Kolisko, 9.4.1933 in: Lili Kolisko (note 15) p. 321.

235   *Present Age*, Vol I No. 1. London 1935.

236   *Six Months of the Present Age*, Vol I, No. 7, June 1936.

237   *Die Anthroposophischen Zeitschriften von 1903 bis 1985, Bibliographie und Lebens bilder*, (Anthroposophical periodicals 1903-1985, Bibliography and biographies) Stuttgart, 1987, p. 146.

238   Rudolf Steiner, *Anthroposophical Leading Thoughts*, op. cit. Chapter entitled: 'The Michael-Christ-Experience of Man'.

239   'The Death of Merlin', *Present Age*, Vol I, No. 7, June 1936. Also: *The Death of Merlin* Floris Books, 1989, p. 167 et seq.

240   ibid. pp. 173, 174.

241   'A Suggestion for the Coronation', *Present Age*, Vol I, No. 11, 1936.

242   cf. Eugen Kolisko 'World Congress of Faiths', *Present Age*, Vol I, No. 10, 1936.

243   cf. 'A School for Spiritual Science', *Present Age*, Vol I, No. 10, 1936.

244   'The Present World Situation', *The Present Age*, Vol III, No. 4, 1938.

245   *The Present Age*, Vol II, No. 5.

246   'Reminiscences of Life — an aid to the understanding of our time', *Present Age*, Vol I, Nos. 8, 9, 11, London 1936.

247   'Memories of Rudolf Steiner' by Count Polzer-Hoditz. *The Present Age*, Vol I No. 12; Vol II, Nos. 1, 3, 4, 5, London 1936-7.

248 Ludwig Polzer-Hoditz, 'Erinnerungen an Rudolf Steiner', Dornach 1985 (Memories of Rudolf Steiner).

249 Lili Kolisko (note 15), p. 400.

250 Rudolf Steiner, lecture 18.5.1924 in GA 236: *Karmic Relationships, Vol. II*, op. cit.

251 Herbert Hahn, 'Versuch einer biographischen Skizze'. (Attempt at a biographical sketch) in *Mitteilungen aus der anthroposophischen Arbeit in Deutschland*, Michaelmass 1957 (News Sheet of Anthroposophical work in Germany)).

252 Letter to Emmy Mattes, from 6.7.1947.

253 GA 128, *An Occult Physiology*, London, Rudolf Steiner Press, 1983.

254 Rudolf Steiner, lecture 12.12.1921, GA 209, 'The Relation of Youth to Age'.

255 *The Present Age*, Vol II, Nos. 9 and 10, 1937.

256 Unpublished report.

257 Lecture in Oxford, 20.8.1922, GA 305, 'The Attainment of Spiritual Knowledge'.

258 Verbatim report of the speech reported in *The Times*, London, 18.11.1937.

259 Lecture from 29.8.1920, GA 199. 'The Tapestry of the Senses, the Mirror of Memories and the Regions of the Spiritual World underlying them'.

260 *Gold in History and in Modern Times*, op. cit.

261 cf. Rudolf Steiner, lecture 6.8.1922 GA 340, *World Economy*, London, Rudolf Steiner Press, 1972.

262 cf. D. Ferguson, 'International Monetary Stabilisation', *The Present Age*, Vol III, Nos. 2 and 3, 1938. 'The Gold-Wheat-Standard, Critique and Reply', *The Present Age*, Vol III, No. 9, 1938.

263 Letters from 29.9.1938 and 16.6.1938.

264 Letter from 29.9.1938.

265 'Vierzig Jahre danach, Der Geist von Bretton Woods', *Frankfurter Allgemeine Zeitung*, 27.7.1984 (Forty years later, The Spirit of Bretton Woods).

266 cf. Bernd Martin, 'Friedensinitiativen und Machtpolitik im zweiten Weltkrieg 1939-45' (Peace Initiatives and Power Politics in World War II 1939-45) Düsseldorf, 1974. *Archiv der Gegenwart* 23.8.1939, p. 4181 et seq.

267   Emanuel Zeylmans (note 152), p. 226.
268   Account by the Author.
269   cf. Roger Keyes, *Being the Biography of Admiral of The Fleet Lord Keyes by Cecil Aspinall-Oglander*, London 1951.
270   Letter to Emmy Mattes, 6.7.1947.
271   Lecture from 13.2.1923. *Awakening to Community*, op. cit.
272   See Rudolf Steiner's lecture 14.12.1919 in GA 194, 'The Mysteries of Light, of Space and of the Earth'.
273   Lecture from 27.8.1924. GA 240. *Karmic Relationships Vol. VIII*, London, Rudolf Steiner Press, 1975, p. 93.
274   Letter to the Author from Rudi Lissau, 6.5.1986.
275   Letter to Emil Bock, 4.2.1952.
276   Lecture, 4.7.1924, GA 237. *Karmic Relationships, Vol. III*, London, Rudolf Steiner Press, 1974.
277   Lecture, 23.7.1922, GA 214, 'The Mystery of the Trinity'.
278   Letter from 24.12.1949.
279   W.J. Stein, 'Mythologie' in *Beiträge zu einer Erweiterung der Heilkunst*, Year 4, No. 5-6, 1951. (Contributions towards an extension of the Art of Healing.)
280   Rudolf Steiner, 12.9.1908 in GA 106, *Egyptian Myths and Mysteries*, New York, Anthroposophic Press, 1971.
281   Letter from Rudi Lissau, 14.7.1957.
282   ibid., 4.7.1957.
283   ibid., 15.8.1957.
284   Published verbatim in Lili Kolisko (note 15), p. 132. [Quotation from Mystery Drama: *The Soul's Probation*, Words spoken by Second Master of Ceremonies, Scene 8].

About the Author:
Johannes Tautz, Dr Phil was born in Konstanz 1914. He studied German Philology, History, Philosophy and the Science of Religion. He taught in the Stuttgart Waldorf School and took part in the Teachers' Seminary and in the Vorstand of the Bund der Freien Waldorfschulen. His literary subjects are Education and contemporary history.